4S G-TELP 65점 대비

세무사 / 노무사 / 회계사 / 감정평가사 / 소방간부 후보생용

JN398950

65 Signature
시그니처
실전모의고사

리스닝 모의고사 3회분   독해 모의고사 3회분

G-TELP 65점대가 목표인 수험생들을 위한
리스닝과 독해까지 최단기에 끝낼 수 있는 종합서!

동영상 및 학습문의   www.lovehan.net

PREFACE

리스닝 만렙을 위한
실전모의고사
이 책의 **인사말**

안녕하세요. **4S G-TELP의 한사랑**입니다.

G-TELP 평균 65점을 대비하시는 수강생 분들이 가장 힘들어하시고
시간과 노력을 투자 해야만 점수가 나오는 섹션이 바로 리스닝입니다.
많은 수강생 분들이 '기둥을 세우고 나왔다'라는 표현을 하실 정도로
G-TELP 리스닝 섹션이 만만하지 않다는 것에 공감하실 겁니다.

맞습니다. 리스닝 실력은 오랜 시간과 많은 노력을 요구합니다.
하지만 우리가 원하는 것은 최단기간에 우리의 목표점수를 획득하는 것입니다.
그러기 위해서는 최대한 각각의 리스닝 파트의 스크립트 종류를 파악하고
문제유형을 익히는 것입니다.
또한 타 영어인증시험과는 다르게 G-TELP 리스닝 섹션의 경우
문제가 시험지에 나와 있지 않기 때문에 문제를 듣고 빠르게
dictation (받아쓰기)를 하는 충분한 훈련이 필요합니다.

이 교재는 여러분들이 실제 시험을 치루기전 충분하게 리스닝 섹션의 문제풀이 방식을
훈련할 수 있게끔 구성되어 있으며 실제 시험에서 다루는 스크립트의 주제와
유사한 주제들로만 선별을 하였습니다.
저 4S G-TELP 한사랑이 여러분들이 원하는 점수를
최단기간에 획득하실 수 있도록 해드릴겁니다.

이제 훈련 시작합니다!

2020년 11월

한사랑

CONTENTS

 리스닝 만렙을 위한 실전모의고사

실전모의고사 1회분

Actual Test Part1 ······ 17
Actual Test Part2 ······ 31
Actual Test Part3 ······ 45
Actual Test Part4 ······ 63

실전모의고사 2회분

Actual Test Part1 ······ 77
Actual Test Part2 ······ 91
Actual Test Part3 ······ 105
Actual Test Part4 ······ 119

실전모의고사 3회분

Actual Test Part1 ······ 135
Actual Test Part2 ······ 147
Actual Test Part3 ······ 159
Actual Test Part4 ······ 171

2 독해 만렙을 위한 실전모의고사

실전모의고사 1회분

Actual Test Part1 ········· 192
Actual Test Part2 ········· 200
Actual Test Part3 ········· 208
Actual Test Part4 ········· 218

실전모의고사 2회분

Actual Test Part1 ········· 230
Actual Test Part2 ········· 238
Actual Test Part3 ········· 246
Actual Test Part4 ········· 256

실전모의고사 3회분

Actual Test Part1 ········· 268
Actual Test Part2 ········· 274
Actual Test Part3 ········· 282
Actual Test Part4 ········· 292

1 구성

문제수	소요시간	지문구성
26개	약 30분	총 4개 파트

2 순서

리스닝 섹션을 시작하면서 약 1분 30초간 General direction을 들려준다.
이때 파트 1-4까지 대략적으로 보기들을 보기 쉽게 정리해놓는다.

"Now, listen to the questions.." 이란 멘트가 나오면
바로 딕테이션을 할 준비를 한다.

각 문항의 문제를 받아 적을 때 최대 3단어를 넘어가지 않도록 주의한다.

3 G-TELP와 유사 시험(TOEIC, TOEFL)간의 차이점

(1) 질문의 제시 정도와 순서

시험종류	질문 제시 정도	질문 제시 순서
G-TELP	시험지에 질문이 제시 되지 않음 (음성으로만 2회 제시)	★ 지문 듣기 전, 후에 질문제시 (문제 듣기→지문 듣기→문제 듣기)
TOEIC	Part 1, 2 : 시험지에 제시되지 않음 Part 3, 4 : 시험지에 제시됨	Part 2 : 문제 듣기 → 지문 듣기 Part 3, 4 : 지문 듣기 → 문제 듣기
TOEFL	시험지 (iBT의 경우 화면)에 제시됨	지문 듣기 → 문제 듣기

(2) 파트 1-4까지 6문제 또는 7문제가 출제되어 총 26문제가 출제된다.
(3) 문제가 따로 나와 있지 않아 문제를 듣고 note-taking이 필요함.
   (총 2번 들려줌)
(4) 두 번째로 질문을 들려줄 때는 다음 파트로 넘어가 보기를 보면서
   warm-up을 해야 한다.

4 파트 별 유형

각 파트 별로 스크립트 유형이 정해져 있음
→ 유형을 숙지하고 미리 대비하는 것이 필요!

Part 1 / Informal Talk	**Conversation** 내용: 두 명의 화자가 실생활에서 경험한 다양한 주제를 전달 및 교환하는 형식 ex. 주말에 결혼식을 올리는 Jason이 신혼여행지로 어디가 좋은지 Mindy와 나누는 대화문
Part 2 / Formal Talk	**Speech** 내용: 한 화자(전문가)가 하나의 주제에 대한 정보를 제공하거나 세부 요소 및 과정을 설명 또는 제안하는 형식 ex. 성공적인 비즈니스 창업을 위한 10가지 스텝들
Part 3 / Informal Talk	**Conversation** 내용: 두 화자가 특정 문제에 대하여 서로 정보를 교환하는 형식 (의견 제시 요청이나 이유 및 충고 요청) ex. 현재 본인의 예산을 알맞게 잘 활용하고 있는지 친구에게 조언을 구하는 내용의 대화문
Part 4 / Formal Talk	**Speech** 내용: 한 화자가 특정 주제에 대해서 청중에게 논리적으로 설명하는 형식 (연구결과 발표, 강연 등) ex. 사회적 문제가 되고 있는 무절제한 성형수술에 대한 강연

상대적으로 파트 1,3 (두 사람의 대화형식) 이 파트 2,4 (연설자 혼자 강연형식) 보다 수월하다. 두 사람의 대화이기 때문에 중간 중간에 이해를 하고 넘어갈 수 있는 시간차가 있지만 혼자 하는 강연은 쉬는 타이밍이 없기 때문이다. 최대한 파트 1,3에서 점수를 획득해야한다.

01

4S G-TELP

SIGNATURE

리스닝 만렙을 위한
실전모의고사

리스닝 만렙을 위한 원포인트 레슨

1

리스닝섹션 시작단계의 direction부분 1분30초를 잘 활용하라!

리스닝 섹션을 시작하면서 성우가 direction을 읽어주는 시간이

대략 1분 30초 정도 되며 그동안 파트1-4까지의 보기들을 최대한 읽고

눈에 바로 들어올 수 있도록 주요 키워드를 찾아 놓아야한다.

리스닝을 들으면서 보기까지 해석할 여유가 없기 때문이다.

SIGNATURE

1 회

리스닝 만렙 실전모의고사

PART 1 문제 유형

1 대화의 주제를 묻는다.

두 사람이 대화하고 있는 내용, 즉 주제를 묻는다. 대부분 대화 초반에 언급되고 후에 대화 전반에 주제에 대한 세부적인 내용들이 열거되므로 어렵지 않게 답을 찾을 수 있다.

What is the conversation about?

What is this conversation mainly about?

2 화자에 대한 느낌, 서로 간의 관계 및 직업을 묻는다.

두 사람 간의 대화방식과 서로를 부르는 명칭 및 대화 내용으로 짐작 가능한 내용이 질문으로 나올 수 있다. 또한, 화자가 관심분야에 대한 전문적인 의견을 내놓는 경우, 직업 및 신분을 유추해 볼 수 있다.

Where does A probably work?

What does A do for a living?

Based on the conversation, what can be said about A?

How is A probably related to B?

Which statement is probably true about the speaker A?

3 세부내용을 묻는다.

대화 전체에 대한 세부내용을 이해해야 한다는 부담은 갖지 말자. 문제를 먼저 들려주기 때문에 키워드만 적어둔다면 전략적 듣기가 가장 유용한 문항들이다.

What is said about something?
How did A manage to get something?
With whom did A go to watch something?
Where was B looking for something?
Why doesn't C allow someone in somewhere?
What does C do when~?
According to D, when did E~?
Based on the conversation, what is one reason for something?

4 본문에서 언급되지 않은 내용을 묻는다.

언급되지 않은 내용을 묻는 문제의 경우, 본문에서 언급된 내용과 유사하게 혹은 반대로 보기가 주어진다. 전체적인 내용을 이해했어야만 풀 수 있으므로 난이도가 높은 문항들이다.

Which of the following was not discussed in the conversation?
What was not discussed about something?
Based on the conversation, what did A not mention to B about something?

5 대화자 중 한 명이 대화 이후 무엇을 할까를 묻는다.

주로 대화의 마지막 부분에 언급되며 질문을 하던 사람이 친구로부터 얻는 정보를 실천하겠다는 의지를 보이거나 대화를 마치기 위해 해야 할 일에 대해서 언급한다.

What will A probably do based on her talk with B?
What will A probably do right after this conversation?

LISTENING SECTION

DIRECTIONS:

The Listening Section has four parts. In each part you will hear a spoken passage and a number of questions about the passage. First you will hear the questions. Then you will hear the passage. From the four choices, choose the best answer.
Then blacken in the correct circle on your answer sheet.

Now you will hear an example question. Then you will hear an example passage.

Now listen to the example question.

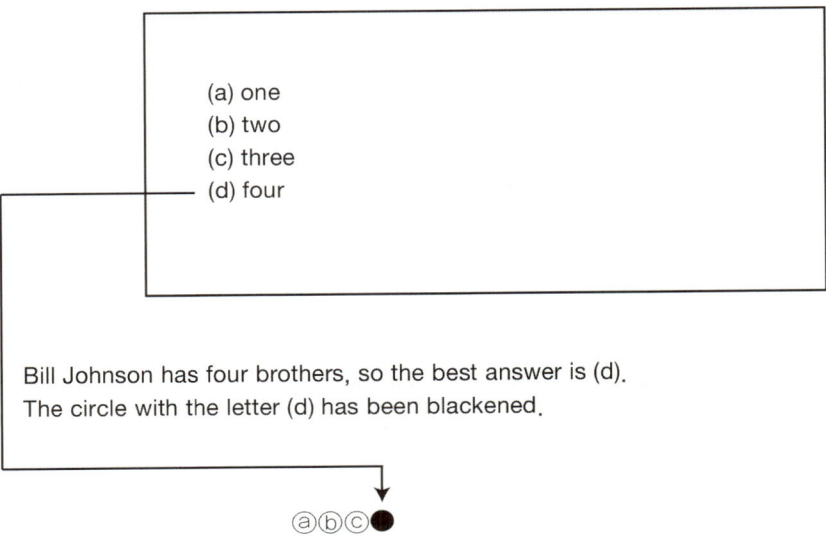

Bill Johnson has four brothers, so the best answer is (d).
The circle with the letter (d) has been blackened.

NOW TURN THE PAGE AND BEGIN

 **문제를 잘 듣고 받아쓰기 연습을 미리 해보세요.**

기억하세요! 3단어가 넘어가면 안 됩니다.

1.

2.

3.

4.

5.

6.

7.

Part 1. You will hear a conversation between two people. First you will hear questions 1 through 7. Then you will hear the conversation. Choose the best answer to each question in the time provided.

01

(a) He is allergic to 32 types of wild flowers, and he might break out in a terrible rash.
(b) He thinks that having flowers might be too costly.
(c) It might be too messy to have extra ornaments for the wedding.
(d) Peter and Sophia have a low budget.

02

(a) to get married at the wedding hall as planned
(b) to get married in Peter's grandparent's backyard
(c) to get married at Peter and Sophia's house
(d) to skip the wedding ceremony

03

(a) She is afraid that the wedding guests will look down on her.
(b) She wants to do the wedding at the wedding hall.
(c) The backyard is really messy and in bad shape.
(d) The backyard is under construction.

04

(a) He thinks the price is reasonable.
(b) He assumes it is expensive.
(c) He considers it is unnecessary.
(d) He claims it is poor because it is located far away from where they are living.

05

(a) an appearance
(b) a function
(c) a price
(d) a brand

06

(a) having catering service "At Your Service" come with a variety of food
(b) having Peter's mother's tuna fish sandwiches to save money for the honeymoon
(c) ordering Oishi Sushi
(d) making spaghetti with Peter

07

(a) to go for snow skiing and snowboarding
(b) to visit Sophia's grandparents' house
(c) to meet up with Sophia and Peter's friends
(d) to call Peter's brother and see if his brother could let them stay at his house

Wedding Plans 결혼식 계획

Sophia Honey! Come see this. Aren't these flowers so beautiful?
Sophia 자기야! 와서 이것 좀 봐봐. 이 꽃들 너무 예쁘지 않아?

Peter Not bad. What are they for?
Peter 나쁘지 않네. 어디에 쓰려고?

Sophia They are for decorating the wedding hall. It's going to be the most incredible one in the world.
Sophia 예식장 장식할 때 쓰려고. 세상에서 제일 멋진 예식장이 될 거야.

Peter Uh, I don't know. I don't think this...
Peter 글쎄. 모르겠네. 나는 이거 별로...

Sophia Oh, come on. It would be great. It's so beautiful, and it's peaceful, and it's really romantic. Come on.
Sophia 오, 제발. 정말 멋질 거야. 정말 아름답고 평화롭고 낭만적이잖아. 제발.

Peter I don't know. You know I'm <u>allergic</u> to 32 types of wild flowers...
Peter 모르겠어. 나 야생화들 32종에 <u>알레르기 있는</u> 거 알잖아...

Sophia You'll be okay. Take an allergy pill before the wedding.
Sophia 괜찮을 거야. 결혼식 전에 알레르기약 먹으면 되지.

Peter And I might <u>break out</u> in a terrible rash.
Peter 그리고 나 심각한 발진이 <u>나타날 수도</u> 있어.

Sophia You'll be okay. Come on. Well, let's ... I'm sure we can <u>come up with</u> something nice. Come on. Let's think about it.
Sophia 괜찮을 거야. 제발. 그래, 우리... 뭔가 좋은 방법을 <u>생각해 낼 수</u> 있을 거라고 생각해. 알았지. 같이 생각해 보자.

Peter Wh ... wh ...We could get married in my grandparent's backyard. Yeah. We just need to move the dogs for a few hours.
Peter 음... 우리 조부모님 댁 뒷마당에서 결혼식 올려도 돼. 그래. 개들만 몇 시간 정도 옮겨두면 돼.

Sophia No! Don't even think about it. Their backyard is really messy. It's in bad shape. And their house is like, right next to the freeway. It's only half a block from the freeway. It's so noisy. Come on. There is a real nice reception hall only a couple miles away. We can do that. You don't have to worry about your allergies.

Sophia 안 돼! 그런 생각은 하지도 마. 당신 조부모님 댁 뒷마당 진짜 엉망이잖아. 상태도 별로고. 게다가 그 집, 고속도로 바로 옆에 있잖아. 고속도로에서 고작 반 블록 떨어져 있어. 엄청 시끄럽잖아. 몇 마일 떨어진 곳에 진짜 멋진 연회장소가 있어. 그렇게 하면 되겠다. 당신 알레르기는 걱정 안 해도 돼.

Peter Ah, that sounds expensive!

Peter 아, 비쌀 것 같아.

Sophia It's not that expensive... just a little. Speaking of it, let's talk about your tuxedo. I thought these two look good on you, and finally I selected the white one. I bet you will like it.

Sophia 거기 그렇게 안 비싸... 그냥 조금? 말이 나와서 말인데, 당신 턱시도 얘기 좀 하자. 이 두 개가 당신한테 잘 어울리겠다고 생각했어. 그리고 최종적으로 나는 이 하얀색 턱시도 골랐어. 당신도 분명 좋아할 거야.

Peter Both of two look the same to me.

Peter 내 눈에는 두 개 다 똑같아 보이는데.

Sophia No way! How come they look the same? The white one is much more expensive than the black one.

Sophia 말도 안 돼! 어떻게 이 두 개가 똑같아? 하얀색이 검은색보다 훨씬 더 비싸.

Peter Much more?

Peter 훨씬 더?

Sophia I mean... just a little. Don't worry, Peter. And the white one fits better on you.

Sophia 내 말은... 그냥 조금. 걱정하지 마, Peter. 그리고 하얀색이 당신한테 훨씬 잘 어울려.

Peter It doesn't matter which one. And you know, I don't need anything expensive. It's OK for me to wear the cheaper one.

Peter 어떤 거든 상관없어. 그리고 알다시피, 난 비싼 건 필요 없어. 나는 저렴한 거 입어도 돼.

Sophia But... I've already paid for the white one. If I cancel the payment, I will have to pay commission. Like half of how much I paid...

Sophia 하지만... 나 이미 하얀 턱시도로 결제했는데. 결제 취소하면, 수수료 내야 해. 거의 내가 지불한 금액의 반 정도...

Peter What? You've never told me that. OK, OK, thank you, Sophia. You just want me to look good, right? OK.

Peter 뭐라고? 당신 나한테 말 한 적도 없잖아. 알았어, 알았어, 고마워, Sophia. 그냥 내가 멋지게 보이길 원하는 거지? 알았어.

Sophia And then, let's move on to the catering service. You know my friend Alice? At her wedding, she had a catering service "At Your Service", which is really popular these days. And she said everything was nice. I mean the food was so tasty, and all the servers were very friendly. That's why Alice recommends it. So, we can have that catering service come, and they're going to serve a variety of food! It sounds perfect, doesn't it? Come on, and then, you know, for our breakfast, our wedding breakfast, we could go to that Japanese restaurant... I can't remember. What's it called?

Sophia 그리고, 출장 연회 음식 서비스 얘기로 넘어가 보자. 당신 내 친구 Alice 알지? Alice 결혼식에서, "At Your Service"라는 출장 연회 음식 서비스 업체 이용했는데, 거기가 요즘 정말 인기래. Alice도 다 마음에 들었다고 했고. 내 말은, 음식도 너무 맛있었고, 직원들도 다 엄청 친절했대. 그래서 Alice가 추천한 거야. 그러니까, 우리 그 **출장 연회 음식 서비스 업체** 부르면 되겠어. 그러면 거기서 다양한 음식들 준비해 줄 거야! 완벽하지? 봐, 그리고 또, 있잖아, 우리 아침은, 우리 결혼식 아침, 그 일본 음식점 가자... 생각이 안 나는데. 이름이 뭐였지?

Peter You mean, Oishi Sushi?

Peter Oishi Sushi 말하는 거야?

Sophia Yeah, Oishi Sushi! When I went there last time, the food was so good. So I think it's going to be a good place for our wedding breakfast. Come on, come on.

Sophia 그래, Oishi Sushi! 우리 지난번에 거기 갔었을 때, 음식 진짜 맛있었어. 그래서 우리 결혼식 날 아침에 가기에 좋을 것 같아. 어때?

Peter That sounds so expensive.

Peter 너무 비쌀 것 같은데.

Sophia But it's okay. It's worth it. Come on, Peter! Come on!

Sophia 그래도 괜찮아. 그럴 만한 가치가 있지. 맞잖아, Peter! 제발!

Peter How about my mother's tuna fish sandwiches instead?

Peter 대신에 우리 어머니가 만드신 참치 샌드위치는 어때?

Sophia Peter. We can spend a little more money than what you keep in that old stupid jar on your desk. Come on.

Sophia Peter. 당신 책상 위에 있는 그 오래되고 형편없는 병에 보관해 둔 돈보다 조금 더 써도 돼. 제발.

Peter Well, I was trying to save money for the honeymoon.

Peter 음, 나는 신혼여행을 위해서 돈을 좀 아끼려고 했었어.

Sophia Well, yeah. Well, okay. Well, I've been thinking about it too. I've been thinking about it for weeks.

Sophia 아, 그랬어? 그럼, 좋아. 그래, 나도 그 생각은 하고 있었어. 나도 몇 주 동안 그 생각 했어.

Peter Me too. Now look, look at this Website. We could go to Lake Louise, Canada.
Peter 나도. 자, 이 웹사이트 좀 봐. 우리는 Canada의 Lake Louise 갈 수 있어.

Sophia That would be so cool! I heard that it is a place where you must visit before you die! And it is well known for its ski resort. It has the best snowboarding and skiing, and their snow. It is the best snow. This time of year would be perfect. Oh, Peter, we're going to love that. That would be wonderful. You know how much I love snowboarding and skiing.
Sophia 진짜 멋지겠다! 거기 죽기 전에 꼭 가 봐야 하는 데라고 들었어! 그리고 스키장으로도 유명하잖아. 스노보드, 스키, 눈이 최고래. 최고의 눈. 이맘때쯤이면 완벽하겠다. 오, Peter, 너무 좋을 것 같아. 정말 멋질거야. 당신도 내가 스노보드랑 스키 타는 거 얼마나 좋아하는지 알잖아.

Peter I... I... I was thinking about visiting some local art and natural history museums instead. Snow skiing just isn't my thing.
Peter 나...나... 나는 대신에 지역 미술관과 자연사 박물관에 가볼까 생각하고 있었는데. 스노스키는 내 취향이 아냐.

Sophia Oh, Peter. Come on.
Sophia 오, Peter. 제발.

Peter You... you know. I don't do well in the cold.
Peter 당신... 당신도 알잖아. 나 추위에 약해.

Sophia Well... What should we do then?
Sophia 음... 그럼 우리 어떻게 해야 해?

Peter Oh, yeah! I have a good idea. Let me call my brother.
Peter 오, 그래! 나한테 좋은 생각이 있어. 나 형한테 전화 좀 할게.

Sophia Wait, why do you call your brother? For what?
Sophia 잠깐만, 당신 형한테 왜 전화해? 뭐 때문에?

Peter He lives there, and he probably could let us stay at his house.
Peter 형 거기에 살잖아. 그리고 아마 형도 우리가 형 집에서 지낼 수 있게 해 줄 거야.

Sophia For our honeymoon?
Sophia 우리 신혼여행인데?

Peter Oh, yeah! Wait, wait! Where are you going? Come back. Did I say anything wrong?
Peter 그래! 기다려봐, 잠깐만! 어디가? 돌아와. 내가 뭐 잘못 말한 거 있어?

Vocabulary and Sample Sentences

어휘 그리고 예제 문장들

단어	의 미
peaceful (adjective) quiet, calm	평화로운 (형용사) 조용한, 차분한 **예문** The family played very peaceful music during the wedding ceremony and reception. 그 가족은 결혼식과 피로연 동안 매우 평화로운 곡을 연주했다.
allergic (adjective) having a medical condition that makes you sick after you touch, eat, or breathe something	알레르기가 있는 (형용사) 무언가를 만지거나, 먹거나, 호흡한 후 아프게 되는 건강 상태 **예문** The bride is very allergic to milk products, so they didn't serve ice cream during the reception. 그 신부는 유제품에 매우 알레르기가 있어서 그들은 피로연 동안 아이스크림을 제공하지 않았다. Some guests might be allergic to peanuts, so let's not serve any during the reception. 손님 중 일부는 땅콩에 알레르기가 있을지도 모르니, 피로연 동안 땅콩은 제공하지 말자.
break out (verb) to suddenly begin to have a rash on your skin	발생하다, 벗어나다 (동사) 피부에 갑자기 발진이 시작되는 것. **예문** Emily's son broke out in a very bad rash after he was stung by a bee in the backyard. Emily의 아들은 뒷마당에서 벌에게 쏘인 후에 아주 심한 발진이 발생했다.

단어	의미
come up with (verb) to think of, create, or present an idea	생각해내다, 떠오르다 (동사) 어떤 생각을 생각해 내거나, 창조하거나 제시하는 것 **예문** My friends were going to have a wedding reception outside, but because the weather was going to be bad, they came up with the idea of having a friend's house nearby. 내 친구들은 야외에서 결혼식 피로연을 하려고 했지만, 날씨가 나쁠 것 같아서 근처에 있는 친구의 집에서 피로연을 하는 방법을 생각해냈다.

단어	의미
messy (adjective) in poor condition, dirty	엉망인 (형용사) 형편없는 상태인, 더러운 **예문** Unfortunately, they lived for a short time in a real messy apartment until they could afford something better. 불행히도 그들은 더 나은 곳을 살 여유가 있을 때까지, 엉망진창인 아파트에서 잠시 살았다.

단어	의미
catering service (noun) a company that prepares and serves food for parties, weddings, and other activities	출장 연회 음식 서비스 (명사) 파티, 결혼식 그리고 다른 활동들을 위해 음식을 제공하고 준비해주는 회사 **예문** My parents hired a catering service to prepare the food for the wedding. 부모님은 결혼식 음식을 준비하기 위해서 출장 연회 음식 서비스 업체를 이용했다.

정답 01. (a)　02. (b)　03. (c)　04. (b)　05. (c)　06. (a)　07. (d)

01 영어문제 | 문제 한글 해석

According to Peter, why does he think that having flowers for the wedding hall would not be great?

(a) He is allergic to 32 types of wild flowers, and he might break out in a terrible rash.
(b) He thinks that having flowers might be too costly.
(c) It might be too messy to have extra ornaments for the wedding.
(d) Peter and Sophia have a low budget.

Peter에 의하면 그는 왜 결혼식장에 꽃을 두는 것이 좋은 생각이 아니라고 생각하는가?

(a) 그는 야생화 32종에 알레르기가 있어 심한 발진이 날 수도 있다.
(b) 그는 꽃을 사는 것이 돈이 많이 들 거로 생각한다.
(c) 추가로 장식품들을 두는 것은 지저분해 보일 수도 있다.
(d) Peter와 Sophia는 자금이 충분하지 않다.

문제해설

Peter가 32가지 종류 야생화들에 알레르기가 있어서 발진이 날 수 있다는 것을 알 수 있다.

> I don't know. You know I'm allergic to 32 types of wild flowers, and I might break out in a terrible rash.

02 영어문제 | 문제 한글 해석

What option did Peter provide as an alternative for the wedding hall?

(a) to get married at the wedding hall as planned
(b) to get married in Peter's grandparent's backyard
(c) to get married at Peter and Sophia's house
(d) to skip the wedding ceremony

Peter가 결혼식장에 대한 대안으로 무슨 선택권을 주었는가?

(a) 예정대로 결혼식장에서 결혼하는 것
(b) Peter의 조부모님 댁 뒷마당에서 결혼하는 것
(c) Peter와 Sophia의 집에서 결혼하는 것
(d) 결혼식은 생략하는 것

문제해설

Peter가 조부모님 댁 뒷마당에서 결혼할 수도 있다고 말하고 있다.

> We could get married in my grandparent's backyard. Yeah. We just need to move the dogs for a few hours.

03 영어문제 | 문제 한글 해석

Why does Sophia think that having a wedding at Peter's grandparent's backyard would not be great?

(a) She is afraid that the wedding guests will look down on her.
(b) She wants to do the wedding at the wedding hall.
(c) The backyard is really messy and in bad shape.
(d) The backyard is under construction.

Sophia는 왜 Peter 조부모님 댁 뒷마당에서 결혼식을 하는 것이 좋지 않다고 생각하는가?

(a) 그녀는 결혼식 하객들이 그녀를 무시할까 봐 두렵다.
(b) 그녀는 결혼식장에서 결혼하고 싶어 한다.
(c) 뒷마당은 너무 지저분하고 상태도 별로다.
(d) 뒷마당은 공사 중이다.

문제해설

Sophia가 뒷마당은 너무 엉망이고 상태도 별로라고 말한다. 또한 Peter 조부모님의 집은 고속도로에서 반 블록 떨어져 있기 때문에 엄청 시끄럽다고 생각한다며 몇 마일 떨어진 곳에 있는 연회 장소에서 결혼하자고 말하고 있다.

> No! Don't even think about it. Their backyard is really messy. It's in bad shape. And their house is like, right next to the freeway. It's only half a block from the freeway. It's so noisy. Come on. There is a real nice reception hall only a couple miles away. We can do that. You don't have to worry about your allergies.

04 영어문제 | 문제 한글 해석

What does Peter think about the reception hall?

(a) He thinks the price is reasonable.
(b) He assumes it is expensive.
(c) He considers it is unnecessary.
(d) He claims it is poor because it is located far away from where they are living.

Peter는 피로연장에 대해 어떻게 생각하는가?

(a) 가격이 합리적이라고 생각한다.
(b) 비쌀 것 같다고 생각한다.
(c) 불필요하다고 생각한다.
(d) 그들이 거주하는 곳에서 멀리 떨어져있음으로 별로라고 주장한다.

문제해설

Sophia가 피로연장에 대해 말한 뒤 Peter는 그 연회 장소에서 결혼하는 것은 비쌀 것 같다고 답한다.

> Once Peter suggests having the wedding at his grandparent's backyard, Sophia says, "Come on. There is a real nice reception hall only a couple miles away. We can do that. You don't have to worry about your allergies." Peter replies, "Ah, that sounds expensive!"

05 영어문제 | 문제 한글 해석

What does Peter consider as the highest priority when choosing a tuxedo?

(a) an appearance
(b) a function
(c) a price
(d) a brand

Peter가 턱시도를 고를 때 어떤 것을 가장 우선순위로 생각하는가?

(a) 외관
(b) 기능
(c) 가격
(d) 브랜드

문제해설

Sophia가 두 개의 턱시도 사진들을 보여줬을 때 Peter는 두 개 다 똑같아 보인다고 대답한다. Peter는 비싼 거 필요 없고 저렴한 턱시도를 입어도 된다고 말한다.

> Both of two look same to me. It doesn't matter which one. And you know, I don't need anything expensive. It's OK for me to wear the cheaper one.

06 영어문제 | 문제 한글 해석

Based on the conversation, what does Sophia suggest for the catering service?

(a) having catering service "At Your Service" come with a variety of food
(b) having Peter's mother's tuna fish sandwiches to save money for the honeymoon
(c) ordering Oishi Sushi
(d) making spaghetti with Peter

대화를 바탕으로 Sophia가 출장 음식 서비스에 대해 무엇을 제안하는가?

(a) 다양한 종류의 음식을 제공하는 출장연회 서비스 At your Service를 이용하는 것
(b) 신혼여행을 위해 돈을 아끼고자 Peter의 어머니가 만드신 참치 샌드위치로 대접하는 것
(c) 오이시 초밥을 주문하는 것
(d) Peter와 함께 스파게티를 만드는 것

문제해설

Sophia의 친구가 결혼할 때 이용했던 출장연회 서비스에 대해 말하고 있다는 것을 알 수 있다. 그녀는 음식이 매우 맛있었고 다양하며 웨이터들이 친절했다고 말하며 친구 Alice가 추천했다고 말하고 있다. 따라서 Sophia는 Peter에게 출장연회 서비스를 받자고 제안한다.

> And then, let's move on to the catering service. You know my friend Alice? At her wedding, she had a catering service "At Your Service", which is really popular these days. And she said everything was nice. I mean the food was so tasty, and all of the servers were very friendly. That's why Alice recommends it. So, we can have that catering service come, and they're going to serve a variety of food! It sounds perfect, doesn't it?

07 영어문제 | 문제 한글 해석

What does Peter suggest for the honeymoon at the end?

(a) to go for snow skiing and snowboarding
(b) to visit Sophia's grandparents' house
(c) to meet up with Sophia and Peter's friends
(d) to call Peter's brother and see if his brother could let them stay at his house

마지막에 Peter는 신혼여행에 대해서 무엇을 제안하는가?

(a) 스키와 스노보드 타러 가기
(b) Sophia의 조부모님 댁 방문하기
(c) Sophia와 Peter의 친구들과 만나기
(d) Peter의 형에게 연락해서 그의 집에서 지내도 되는지 묻기

문제해설

Peter의 형이 그곳에서 살고 있다는 것을 알 수 있다. Peter는 형에게 전화해보겠다고 한다. Peter는 형이 Peter와 Sophia가 형 집에서 머물 수 있도록 해줄 것으로 생각한다.

> Oh, yeah! That's a good idea. Let me call my brother. He lives there, and he probably could let us stay at his house. Oh, yeah! Wait, wait! Where are you going? Come back. Did I say anything wrong?

PART 2 문제 유형

1 발표의 주제를 묻는다.

발표 초반에 발표를 듣는 청중 대상을 알 수 있는 내용과 더불어 주제가 제시된다.

What is the purpose of the talk?
What is the purpose of the presentation?

2 발표를 듣는 대상을 묻는다.

강연 초반에 주제와 함께 직접적으로 청중이 언급되거나 주제가 언급된 내용에서 유추할 수 있도록 제시된다. 강연 마지막 부분에서 청중이 다시 언급되기도 한다.

To whom is the talk most likely being given?
What kind of audience is the speaker addressing?
To whom are the instructions most likely being given?

3 강연의 한 부분으로 언급한 특정 내용에 대해 묻는다.

강연 주제에 대해서 여러 단계 혹은 과정을 나열해서 설명하기도 하고 장단점을 설명하기도 한다. 부분 혹은 각 과정에 대한 세부내용을 묻는 문제다.

According to the speaker, how ~?
What should someone expect while doing ~?
What is the use of something?

4 주제에 관련된 제작/생산 순서를 묻는다.

주제와 관련된 대상의 제작 및 생산순서는 first, next(second), …, last 등의 signpost를 사용해 열거되기 마련이다. 이러한 유형의 문항은 질문 청취가 관건이다.

Based on the presentation, what step follows ~?

What is the first step in making ~?

5 강연자의 태도에 대해 묻는다.

강연 전체 내용에 대한 강연자의 태도 및 주제와 관련되어 강연자가 선호하는 특정 대상에 대한 질문이 주어지기도 한다.

How does the speaker feel about something?

What is the general tone of the speaker?

What best describes the speaker's attitude towards something?

 **문제를 잘 듣고 받아쓰기 연습을 미리 해보세요.**

기억하세요! 3단어가 넘어가면 안 됩니다.

1.
2.
3.
4.
5.
6.

Part 2. You will hear a lecture. First you will hear questions 1 through 6.
Then you will hear the talk. Choose the best answer to each question in the time provided.

01
(a) It is good for sleep, weight loss, and metabolism.
(b) It contains a large quantity of minerals, vitamins, carbohydrates, and proteins.
(c) Eating it cleans blood and generates blood tissues.
(d) It is cheaper compared to other fruits and makes you feel full easily.

02
(a) regions where there are only little trees planted
(b) places where there are lots of worms that help with germination
(c) USDA plant hardiness zones 4 to 7
(d) areas where plants can absorb large amounts of sunlight

03
(a) to compared to sweet cherries, sour cherries are cheaper
(b) to compared to sweet cherries, sour cherries contain a higher vitamin
(c) to grow in zones 5 to 7 where temperatures are mild and humidity is low
(d) to grow in zones 4 to 6 where the climate is cool

04
(a) the quality of soil
(b) the weather
(c) the seeds
(d) the speed of wind

05
(a) to buy some cherry seeds and find a spot where enough sunlight can be absorbed
(b) after eating some cherries, put the pits in a bowl of warm water, and dry the pits
(c) to chew some cherries, put the pits in a bowl of cold water, and dry the pits
(d) to collect cherry seeds from the cherry trees, and soak the seed with hot water

06
(a) remove the pits, leave in room temperature, and put into a small container
(b) plant the cherry tree seeds right away once the ten weeks passed
(c) remove the pits and put the pits into a flower pot with moistened soil
(d) take out the pits, and dry them in room temperature

 스크립트 해석

Tips For Planting Cherry Seeds 체리 씨앗을 심을 때 조언들

Cherries are amazing fruit. That's because there are a lot of good things about eating cherries. First, eating cherries can improve your sleep quality. So when you suffer from insomnia, just pick and eat cherries. Second, it's helpful for losing weight. If you are planning to lose some weight, add cherries to your diet.

체리는 놀라운 과일입니다. 이는 체리를 섭취하면 많은 장점이 있기 때문입니다.
첫 번째로, 체리를 섭취하면 수면의 질이 향상됩니다. 그래서 당신이 불면증에 시달릴 때는, 일단 체리를 집어 드세요.
두 번째로, 체리는 체중을 줄이는 데 도움을 줍니다. 만일 당신이 체중을 줄일 계획이 있다면 당신의 식단에 체리를 추가하세요.

As you know, cherries are low in calories. Moreover, they are full of vitamins that strengthen your metabolism. So you don't need to worry about your health when you are on a diet with cherries. Finally, they go well with many foods. You can add cherries to pies, yogurts, salads, smoothies and so on. They are versatile and incredibly delicious.

알다시피, 체리는 저열량 식품입니다. 게다가, 체리는 신진대사를 강화해주는 비타민이 풍부합니다. 그래서 식단에 체리를 포함 시킨다면 체중 감량 시에도 건강에 대해 걱정할 필요가 없습니다. 마지막으로, 체리는 많은 음식과 잘 어울립니다. 당신은 체리를 파이, 요거트, 샐러드, 스무디 등에 넣을 수 있습니다. 체리는 다용도 식품이고 놀라울 정도로 맛있습니다.

And I can say that many people love cherries for those reasons. If you're a cherry lover, you've probably spit your share of cherry pits, or maybe it's just me. At any rate, have you ever wondered, "Can you grow a cherry tree pit?"
If so, how do you grow cherry trees from pits? Let's find out.

많은 사람들이 이러한 이유로 체리를 사랑합니다. 체리 애호가라면, 아마 체리 씨의 일부분을 뱉은 적이 있을 것입니다. 아니면 아마 저만 그런가요. 어쨌든, 여러분은 "체리 씨앗으로 체리 나무를 키울 수 있을까?"라고 궁금해한 적이 있으신가요?
그렇다면, 어떻게 체리 씨로 체리 나무를 기를 수 있을까요? 함께 알아봅시다.

Can You Grow a Cherry Tree Pit? Yes, indeed. Growing cherry trees from seed is not only an inexpensive way to grow a cherry tree, but it's so much fun and delicious! First off, you should check if you can grow a cherry tree in your region. Cherry varieties are rated through USDA plant hardiness zones 4 to 7.

씨앗으로 체리 나무를 키울 수 있을까요? 네, 확실합니다. 씨앗으로 체리 나무를 기르는 것은 비싸지 않은 방법일 뿐 아니라 재미있고 맛도 좋습니다. 우선, 지역에서 체리 나무를 키울 수 있는지 확인해야 합니다. 체리의 품종들은 USDA 식물 내한성(안전) 구역 4에서 7내에서 등급이 매겨집니다.

A hardiness zone is a geographic area defined to encompass a certain range of climatic conditions relevant to plant growth and survival.
내한성(안전) 구역은 식물의 성장과 생존에 관련된 것으로 특정 범위의 기후적 조건을 아우르기 위해 정의된 지리적 영역입니다.

And depending on the types of cherries, the number of hardiness zones varies. Cherries have two types - sweet cherries and sour ones.
그리고 체리의 품종에 따라서, 내한성 구역 숫자는 다양합니다. 체리에는 두 종류가 있습니다 — 달콤한 체리와 신맛이 나는 체리.

The cherries you can easily find in markets must be sweet ones. They grow in hardiness zones 5 to 7. It means that they are best suited for areas with mild temperatures and low humidity.
시장에서 쉽게 찾을 수 있는 체리들은 달콤한 체리일 것입니다. 이 체리들은 내한성 구역 5에서 7에서 자랍니다. 온화한 기온과 낮은 습도를 가진 지역에 가장 적합하다는 의미입니다.

On the other hand, sour cherries grow in zones 4 to 6. It means that they grow in cooler climates and need some winter temperatures. The weather is a key factor in fruiting.
반면에, 신맛이 나는 체리들은 내한성 구역 4에서 6에서 자랍니다. 이는 신맛이 나는 체리들은 더 시원한 기후에서 자라고 겨울 기온이 필요하다는 것을 의미합니다. 날씨는 열매 맺기에 핵심 요소입니다.

And there should be a number of chilling hours in the winter for cherry trees to stimulate flower and produce fruit. So before you plant cherry seeds, you should check how the weather is like in your place and what kind of cherry trees you want to have.
그리고 체리 나무의 개화를 촉진하고 열매를 맺게 하기 위해서는 겨울에 여러 차례 쌀쌀한 기간이 있어야 합니다. 그래서 체리 씨앗을 심기 전에, 사는 지역에 날씨가 어떠한지, 어떤 체리 나무를 키우기를 원하는지 확인해야 합니다.

Now comes the hard part. Eat some cherries. That's a tough one, huh? Use cherries from either a tree growing in the area or purchase at a farmers market. Cherries from the grocers are stored in such a way, refrigerated, that starting seeds from them is unreliable.
이제 어려운 부분이 나옵니다. 체리를 먹어 보세요. 힘든 일이지요? 그 지역에서 자라는 나무의 체리를 사용하거나 농산물 시장에서 구매하세요. 식료품점에 있는 체리들은 냉장 보관되기 때문에 이 체리들로 씨앗을 심는 것은 신뢰할 수 없습니다.

Save the pits from the cherries you've just devoured and put them in a bowl of warm water. Let the pits soak for five minutes or so and then lightly scrub them free of any clinging fruit. Spread the clean pits out on a paper towel in a warm area and let them dry for three to five days. Then, transfer the dry pits to a plastic container, labeled and fitted with a tight lid.
방금 **먹어 치운** 체리의 씨앗을 남겨 두었다가 따뜻한 물이 담긴 그릇에 담으세요. 씨앗들을 5분 정도 물에 담가 두었다가 달라붙는 과일이 없도록 가볍게 문지르세요. 깨끗한 씨앗들을 종이 수건에 펼친 후에 따뜻한 장소에서 3일에서 5일 정도 건조 시키세요. 그리고 딱 맞고 이름표가 붙여진 뚜껑이 있는 플라스틱 용기로 건조된 씨앗을 옮기세요.

Store the pits in the refrigerator for 10 weeks. Why are you doing this? Cherries need to go through a cold stratification period that occurs naturally during the winter, prior to germination in the spring. Refrigerating the pits is artificially mimicking this process. Okay, seed planting of cherry trees is now ready to commence.

그 씨앗들은 10주 동안 냉장고에 보관하세요. 왜 이걸 할까요? 체리들은 추운 **성층화** 거쳐야 하는데 이 과정은 봄에 **발아** 기간 전 겨울 동안에 자연스럽게 나타납니다. 씨앗을 냉장 보관하는 것은 이 과정을 **인공적으로 모방하는** 것입니다. 좋습니다. 이제 체리 나무의 씨앗을 심기 시작할 준비가 되었습니다.

Once the ten weeks has passed, remove the pits and allow them to come to room temperature. You are now ready for planting the cherry seeds. Put two to three pits into a small container filled with planting medium and water the seeds in.

일단 10주가 지나면, 씨앗을 치우고 상온으로 옮기세요. 이제, 여러분은 체리 씨를 심을 준비가 되었습니다. 두세 개 정도의 씨앗을 식물 배양액으로 차 있는 작은 용기에 담고 씨앗에 물을 주세요.

Vocabulary and Sample Sentences

어휘 그리고 예제 문장들

단어	의 미
spit (verb) to force a small amount of saliva out of your mouth	뱉다, 침을 뱉다 (동사) 입에서 소량의 침을 억지로 빼다 **예문** His son ate a huge amount of spaghetti at once and suddenly spit it out. 그의 아들은 한 번에 어마어마한 양의 스파게티를 먹고 갑자기 뱉어 버렸다.
region (noun) a particular area or part of the world, or any of the large official areas into which a country is divided	지역, 지방 (명사) 세상의 특정한 지역이나 부분, 혹은 한 국가가 나누어지는 큰 공식적인 영역 **예문** These days, people don't go to that region because many crimes have happened in the region. 요즘, 그 지역에서 많은 범죄가 발생했기 때문에, 사람들은 그 지역에 가지 않는다.
pit (noun) the single large hard seed in some fruits	씨, 핵 (명사) 어떤 과일에 있는 하나의 크고 딱딱한 씨앗 **예문** Parents must be careful so that their children don't swallow the pit of peach when they eat it. 부모님들은 자녀가 복숭아를 먹을 때, 복숭아의 씨를 삼키지 않도록 주의해야 한다.

단어	의 미
hardiness (noun) the ability of a plant to live through the winter without protection from the weather	인내력, 내한성, 억셈 (명사) 날씨로부터 보호 없이 겨울 동안 살아낼 수 있는 식물의 능력 **예문** Cactus has the hardiness to endure the dry climate of the desert. Due to its hardiness, many people find it easy to grow cactus. 선인장은 사막의 건조한 기후를 견뎌낼 수 있는 내한성을 가지고 있다. 선인장의 내한성 때문에, 많은 사람들이 선인장 기르기가 쉽다고 여긴다.
devour (verb) to eat something quickly because you are very hungry	걸신들린 듯이 먹다, 집어삼키다 (동사) 매우 배고파서 빠르게 어떤 것을 먹어 치우다. **예문** Jane has not eaten anything for 24 hours. So, she devoured everything that she can see. Jane은 24시간 동안 아무것도 먹지 않았다. 그래서 그녀는 눈에 보이는 모든 것을 먹어 치웠다.
stratification (noun) the fact that the different parts of something exist in or have been arranged into separate groups	성층, 계층화 (명사) 어떤 것의 다른 부분들이 존재하거나 분리된 집단들로 배열되어 있다는 사실 **예문** The problem of stratification in modern society is very serious, so many experts try to solve it. 현대 사회의 계층화의 문제는 매우 심각해서, 많은 전문가는 이를 해결하려고 노력한다.
germination (noun) The process of a seed starting to grow, or the act of causing a seed to start growing	발아, 성장 (명사) 씨앗이 자라기 시작하는 과정, 혹은 씨앗이 자라기 시작하도록 하는 행위 **예문** The important experiment for science class this semester is to observe the germination of the plants and write the report about it. 이번 학기 과학 수업의 중요한 실험은 식물들의 발아를 관찰하고 이에 대한 보고서를 쓰는 것이다.

단어	의미
artificially (adverb) in a way that uses an industrial process or substance, rather than being natural	인공적으로, 인위적으로 (부사) 자연적인 방법이라기보다는, 공업적인 과정이나 물질을 사용한 방법으로 This lake is artificially made, rather than naturally made. Many town people prefer to have natural lake rather than the artificially-made lake. 이 호수는 자연적으로 만들어졌다기보다는 인공적으로 만들어졌다. 많은 마을 사람들은 인공적으로 만들어진 호수보다는 자연적인 호수를 선호한다.

단어	의미
mimic (verb) to copy the way in which a particular person usually speaks and moves	흉내를 내다, 모방하다 (동사) 어떤 특정한 사람이 말하고 행동하는 방법을 따라 한다. When babies start to speak, they tend to mimic their parents whom they spend most of the time with. 아기들이 말을 하기 시작하면 대부분의 시간을 함께 보내는 부모를 모방하는 경향이 있다.

| 정답 | 01. (a) | 02. (c) | 03. (d) | 04. (b) | 05. (b) | 06. (a) |

01 영어문제

What are the benefits of eating cherries?

(a) It is good for sleep, weight loss and metabolism.
(b) It contains a large quantity of minerals, vitamins, carbohydrates, and proteins.
(c) Eating it cleans blood and generates blood tissues.
(d) It is cheaper compared to other fruits and makes you feel full easily.

문제 한글 해석

체리를 먹는 것에 대한 장점은 무엇인가?

(a) 수면의 질을 향상하고, 체중을 줄이는 데에 도움을 주고, 신진대사를 강화해준다.
(b) 체리는 미네랄, 비타민, 탄수화물, 단백질이 대량 함유되어 있다.
(c) 체리를 먹는 것은 피를 맑게 하고, 혈액 조직을 생성한다.
(d) 다른 과일에 비하면 가격이 저렴하고 쉽게 포만감을 느끼게 만든다.

문제해설

지문에 따르면 체리를 먹는 것은 수면의 질을 향상시켜주며 체중을 줄이는데 도움을 준다. 게다가, 체리는 신진대사를 강화해주는 비타민이 풍부하고 마지막으로, 체리는 많은 음식과 잘 어울린다.

> Cherries are amazing fruit. That's because there are a lot of good things about eating cherries. First, eating cherries can improve your sleep quality. So when you suffer from insomnia, just pick and eat cherries. Second, it's helpful for losing weight. If you are planning to lose some weight, add cherries to your diet. As you know, cherries are low in calories. Moreover, they are full of vitamins that strengthen your metabolism. So you don't need to worry about your health when you are on a diet with cherries. Finally, they go well with many foods. You can add cherries to pies, yoghurts, salads, smoothies and so on.

02 영어문제

What is the regional characteristic that cherry trees can grow?

(a) regions where there are only little trees planted
(b) places where there are lots of worms that help with germination
(c) USDA plant hardiness zones 4 to 7
(d) areas where plants can absorb large amounts of sunlight

문제 한글 해석

화자에 따르면 체리 나무들이 자랄 수 있는 지역적 특징은 무엇인가?

(a) 나무가 조금만 심겨 있는 지역
(b) 발아에 도움이 되는 많은 지렁이가 있는 장소
(c) USDA 식물 내한성 구역 4에서 7 정도
(d) 식물들이 다량의 햇빛을 흡수할 수 있는 지역

문제해설

내한성(안전) 구역은 식물의 성장과 생존에 관련된 특정 범위의 기후적 조건을 아우르기 위해 정의된 지리적 영역으로 체리가 강건하게 자랄 수 있는 범위를 4-7로 설명하고 있다.

> Cherry varieties are rated through USDA plant hardiness zones 4 to 7. A hardiness zone is a geographic area defined to encompass a certain range of climatic conditions relevant to plant growth and survival.

03 영어문제 | 문제 한글 해석

According to the speaker, which is true about sour cherries?

(a) to compared to sweet cherries, sour cherries are cheaper
(b) to compared to sweet cherries, sour cherries contain a higher vitamin
(c) to grow in zones 5 to 7 where temperatures are mild and humidity is low
(d) to grow in zones 4 to 6 where the climate is cool

화자에 따르면 신 체리에 대한 내용 중 사실인 것은?

(a) 단 체리와 비교했을 때 신 체리가 더 저렴하다.
(b) 신맛이 나는 체리는 더 많은 비타민을 함유한다.
(c) 기온이 온화하고 습도가 낮은 내한성 구역 5에서 7에서 자란다.
(d) 기후가 시원한 내한성 구역 4에서 6에서 자란다.

문제해설

신맛이 나는 체리들은 4에서 6 구역 사이에서 자란다는 것을 지문 내의 설명을 통해 알 수 있다. 이는 신맛이 나는 체리들은 더 시원한 기후에서 자라고 겨울 기온이 필요하다는 것을 의미한다.

On the other hand, sour cherries grow in zones 4 to 6. It means that they grow in cooler climates and need some winter temperatures.

04 영어문제 | 문제 한글 해석

Based on the presentation, what is the essential element for fruiting?

(a) the quality of soil
(b) the weather
(c) the seeds
(d) the speed of wind

발표에 의하면 열매맺기에 핵심요소는 무엇인가?

(a) 토양의 질
(b) 날씨
(c) 씨앗
(d) 풍속

문제해설

기후와 습도등 날씨가 열매 맺기에 핵심요소라고 직접적으로 설명하고 있다.

On the other hand, sour cherries grow in zones 4 to 6. It means that they grow in cooler climates and need some winter temperatures. The weather is a key factor in fruiting.

05 영어문제 | 문제 한글 해석

What do you have to prepare before planting the cherry trees?

(a) to buy some cherry seeds and find a spot where enough sunlight can be absorbed
(b) after eating some cherries, put the pits in a bowl of warm water, and dry the pits
(c) to chew some cherries, put the pits in a bowl of cold water, and dry the pits
(d) to collect cherry seeds from the cherry trees, and soak the seed with hot water

체리 나무를 심기 전에 무엇을 준비해야 하는가?

(a) 체리 씨앗 몇 개를 구매하고 체리 나무가 충분히 햇빛을 흡수할 수 있는 장소를 찾는 것
(b) 체리를 먹은 후 씨앗을 따뜻한 물이 담긴 그릇에 넣어둔 뒤 건조하는 것
(c) 체리 몇 개를 씹은 뒤, 씨앗을 차가운 물에 넣어둔 뒤 건조하는 것
(d) 체리 나무로부터 체리 씨앗들을 채집하고, 뜨거운 물에 씨앗을 담그는 것

문제해설

해석에 따르면 일단 약간의 체리들을 먹은 다음에 그 씨앗을 따뜻한 물에 넣어 불린 후 5일 정도 건조하라고 나와 있다.

Eat some cherries. That's a tough one, huh? Use cherries from either a tree growing in the area or purchase at a farmers market. Cherries from the grocers are stored in such a way, refrigerated, that starting seeds from them is unreliable. Save the pits from the cherries you've just devoured and put them in a bowl of warm water. Let the pits soak for five minutes or so and then lightly scrub them free of any clinging fruit. Spread the clean pits out on a paper towel in a warm area and let them dry for three to five days. Then, transfer the dry pits to a plastic container, labeled and fitted with a tight lid. Store the pits in the refrigerator for 10 weeks.

06 영어문제 | 문제 한글 해석

What should you do after ten weeks passed?

(a) remove the pits, leave in room temperature, and put into a small container
(b) plant the cherry tree seeds right away once the ten weeks passed
(c) remove the pits and put the pits into a flower pot with moistened soil
(d) take out the pits, and dry them in room temperature

10주가 지난 뒤에 당신을 무엇을 해야 하는가?

(a) 씨앗들을 제거하고 제거한 씨앗들을 상온에 두고, 작은 용기에 넣는다.
(b) 10주가 지난 뒤 바로 체리 나무 씨앗을 심는다.
(c) 씨앗들을 제거하고 씨앗들을 촉촉한 흙이 있는 화분에 넣는다.
(d) 씨앗들을 꺼내 상온에서 건조한다.

문제해설

10주가 지난 뒤, 씨앗들을 제거해 실온에 둔 후 씨앗들을 작은 용기에 넣어 물을 주라고 나와 있다.

Once the ten weeks has passed, remove the pits and allow them to come to room temperature. You are now ready for planting the cherry seeds. Put two to three pits into a small container filled with planting medium and water the seeds in.

PART 3 문제 유형

1 조언을 구하는 대상 및 조언의 내용을 묻는다.

한 사람이 전문가이거나 경험이 많은 다른 한 사람에게 주제에 대한 조언을 구하는 대화 내용이므로, 조언을 구하는 대상 및 전체적인 조언이나 어느 세부적인 조언 내용을 묻는 문항들이 출제된다.

What challenge is A facing?
What is A most concerned about?
What advice did A ask B for?
What kind of advice is A seeking from B?
Why does A recommend buying something?
What advice did A give to B about something?
What is A's advice to B?

2 세부내용을 묻는다.

when 언제, where 어디서, what 무엇을, why 왜, how 어떻게 등에 해당하는 문항들이며 Part 3에서 출제되는 문항의 대부분이 이 유형에 속한다. Part 1과 유사한 문항 형태들이 많다.

Why wasn't A able to go back to college to finish his degree?
What made A think of going back to school?
What is the first thing to consider when buying stocks?
What guarantee is given that stock brokers will not run off with the money?
Where is the condominium located?
As expressed by A, what are two of her major considerations?

3 조언을 받은 대화자의 반응을 묻는다.

전문지식 혹은 경험을 가진 대화자의 조언에 반응을 묻는 문제다. 긍정적으로 받아들이는지, 부정적으로 받아들이는지, 혹은 자신 없어 하거나 두려워하는지 등 태도나 감정 상태에 대한 질문들이다.

How did A react to B's suggestion about ~?

How did the woman feel after the conversation?

4 대화자 중 한 명이 대화 이후 무엇을 할까를 묻는다.

주로 대화의 마지막 부분에 언급되며 질문을 하던 사람이 상대방으로부터 얻는 정보를 실천하겠다는 의지를 보이거나 대화를 마치기 위해 해야 할 일에 대해서 언급한다.

What will A do after his talk with B?

 **문제를 잘 듣고 받아쓰기 연습을 미리 해보세요.**

기억하세요! 3단어가 넘어가면 안 됩니다.

1.
2.
3.
4.
5.
6.
7.

Part 3. You will hear a conversation between two people. First you will hear questions 1 through 7. Then you will hear the conversation. Choose the best answer to each question in the time provided.

01

(a) some supplies for the 72-hour kits for any possible emergency
(b) some canned goods since they are easy to carry with
(c) some rocks to open some canned goods
(d) some branches to make a shelter

02

(a) basic water filter or water purification tablets, and food
(b) basic tools like screwdriver
(c) at least three pairs of shoes
(d) extra phones to carry

03

(a) because it's too expensive to purchase
(b) because it's too heavy and annoying to carry
(c) because a tent might not enough space to hold all the family members
(d) because you might have to carry many things other than the tent

04

(a) by spotting a safe place and dig a hole to build a shelter
(b) by using resources that you can spot around you like trash bags
(c) by calling an expert in advance to build a shelter for you
(d) by using used clothes to build a shelter

05

(a) to use a mobile phone to call your family members
(b) to call 911 to ask to find your family members
(c) to stay at your original spot because moving around may cause confusion
(d) to use two-way radios because you shouldn't depend on cell phones

06

(a) a magnifying glass, a high-quality lighter, and waterproof matches
(b) some paper, a high-quality lighter, and a few pieces of wood
(c) some clothes, a high-quality lighter, and waterproof matches
(d) a magnifying glass, a few pieces of wood, and some clothes

07

(a) by bringing a children's book to read for them
(b) by packing small card games or jigsaw puzzles
(c) by preparing a radio to play music for them
(d) by packing some cookies or snacks to share with

스크립트 해석

72-Hour Emergency Kit 72시간 응급 상자

Emma Hey, Henry. So, are you doing some last-minute shopping before the weekend?
Emma 저기, Henry. 그래서 주말 전에 마지막 쇼핑 좀 할 거야?

Henry Well, actually, I'm looking for supplies to put together 72-hour kits for each member of my family.
Henry 그게, 사실은, 나 우리 가족 모두를 위한 72시간짜리 응급 상자를 준비하려고 비축품들 좀 찾고 있거든.

Emma 72-hour kit? What's that?
Emma 72시간 응급 상자? 그게 뭔데?

Henry Basically, a 72-hour kit contains emergency supplies you would need to sustain yourself for three days in case of an emergency, like a hurricane.
Henry 기본적으로, 72시간 응급 상자는 허리케인 같은 응급 상황에서 3일 동안 견디기 위해 필요한 비상용품이 들어 있어.

Emma A hurricane?! We haven't had a hurricane in years.
Emma 허리케인이라고? 몇 년 동안 허리케인 온 적 없었잖아.

Henry Well, you never know; you have to be prepared. Hey, if hurricanes don't get you, it could be a flood, drought, hurricane, snowstorm, power outage, fire or an alien attack. Well, you never know. Think of any situation in which you might find yourself without the basic necessities of life, including shelter, food, and water, for over a period of time.
Henry 뭐, 그거야 절대 모르지; 준비해 둬야 해. 야, 만약에 허리케인이 안 와 닿는다면, 홍수, 가뭄, 허리케인, 눈보라, 정전, 화재 또는 외계인 침략 같은 걸 수도 있어. 뭐, 모르는 거지. 피난처, 음식, 그리고 물을 포함한 기본적인 생활필수품들 없이 얼마 동안 살아야 할지도 모르는 상황들을 생각해봐.

Emma Hum. So, what do you keep in a 42-hour, um... I mean 72-hour kit?
Emma 음, 그래서 너는 42시간, 아니, 음... 그 72시간 응급 상자에 뭘 넣는데?

Henry Well, you should have enough food and water to last you three days, and you might want to pack a basic water filter or water purification tablets in case your only water source turns out to be a murky pool of bug-infested water. Sometimes you don't have a choice, and as for food, you should keep it simple: food that requires no preparation and that doesn't spoil. And no canned goods because they are often too heavy and bulky. And unless you have a can opener or the can has a pull-tab lid, you'll have to use a rock or something to open them. Yeah, and oh, emergency food can be energy bars, beef jerky, and a mix of nuts, cookies and chocolate.

Henry 뭐, 3일 동안 버틸 수 있는 충분한 물이랑 음식이 있어야 해. 그리고 유일한 수원이 벌레에 감염된 **탁한** 물일지도 모르는 상황에 대비해서 기본적인 정수기나 물 **정화** 약도 **챙겨야** 할 수도 있어. 때로는 선택의 여지가 없는 거야. 그리고 음식에 관해 말하자면, 음식도 간단하게 해야 해: 준비도 필요하지 않고 **상하지** 않는 음식. 그리고 통조림 제품은 너무 무겁고 **부피가 커서** 안 돼. 그리고 만약에 통조림 따개가 없거나, 통조림이 잡아당겨서 따는 뚜껑이 아니면, 너는 그거 열려고 바위 같은 걸 써야 할 거야. 그래, 그리고, 아, 비상식량은 에너지바, 소고기 육포, 견과류, 쿠키, 그리고 초콜렛 같은 거면 돼.

Emma Huh, the food might be nasty, but I guess you could survive... barely.

Emma 허, 음식은 **형편없겠지만**, 너 생존은... 가까스로 할 수 있겠다.

Henry Well, the food doesn't have to taste nasty; just select things that are easy to prepare, and you might want to include some basic comfort foods like a couple of candy bars. Then, you have to decide on the type of shelter you might need.

Henry 뭐, 음식이 형편없을 필요는 없지; 그냥 준비하기 쉬운 것들로 골라, 그리고 캔디바 같이 기본적인 편안한 음식도 포함해야 될 거야. 그러고 나서, 너는 네가 필요로 할 수 있는 피난처가 어떤 종류일지 결정해야해.

Emma A hotel sounds nice.

Emma 호텔 좋겠다.

Henry Yeah, but that's really not an option. In reality, you might have to evacuate to a shelter, possibly with hundreds or thousands of other people.

Henry 그래, 근데 그건 선택지에 없어. 실제로, 너는 아마도 수백, 수천 명의 사람들이랑 피난처로 **대피해야** 할지도 몰라.

Emma That doesn't sound very fun... everyone packed together like sardines in a can. Unsanitary conditions. Disease.

Emma 그건 별로다... 모두가 통조림 안에 **정어리들처럼 꽉 채워져 있다니**, 비위생적인 상태네. 질병도 그렇고.

Henry Ah, now you're sounding paranoid, but if a shelter isn't available, you might be completely on your own. Then where would you sleep? On the street? In the park? You should prepare your own shelter in this case. Of course, you can bring a tent, but you know, a tent can be too heavy and annoying to carry especially when disasters break out. Surprisingly, something can replace it! It can be found around us. Look at there! What can you see? Yes! A couple of trash bags, combined with a rope, and then they can make an incredibly effective one-man tent. If you don't have a rope, then you can just use a branch. And it'll become an amazing temporary shelter! As you know, it's not easy to set up a real tent in the wild. With trash bags, you can save time and energy at the same time. Also, we can use them to keep us warm as sleeping bags and blankets, too. What's important here is that they must be super thick!

Henry 아, 이제는 결벽증 같은 소리를 하네. 근데, 만약에 피난처를 못 구하면, 너는 온전히 혼자 있어야 할 거야. 그러면 너는 어디서 잘건데? 길거리에서? 공원에서? 너는 이 상황에서는 너만의 피난처를 준비해야 해. 물론, 텐트를 가지고 올 수도 있지, 근데 너 그거 알지, 텐트는 너무 무겁고 특히나 재해가 발생했을 때는 들고 다니기 성가실 거야. 놀랍게도, 그걸 대체할 수 있는게 있어! 우리 주변에서 찾아질 수 있어. 저기를 봐! 뭐가 보여? 그래! 쓰레기 봉지 몇 개를 밧줄로 연결하면 놀랍도록 효율적인 일인용 텐트를 만들 수 있어. 만약에 밧줄이 없으면, 그냥 나뭇가지를 쓰면 돼. 그러면 훌륭한 임시 피난처가 될 거야! 너도 알다시피, 허허벌판에서 진짜 텐트를 친다는 게 쉬운 게 아니야. 쓰레기 봉지를 사용하면 시간과 에너지를 동시에 절약할 수 있어. 그리고, 쓰레기 봉지를 침낭이나 담요로 써서 따뜻하게 할 수도 있어. 여기서 중요한 건, 쓰레기 봉지가 두툼해야 한다는 거야.

Emma Oh, I see. I've never thought a trash bag could save me. That's good to know.

Emma 아, 알았어. 쓰레기 봉지가 내 목숨을 살릴 거라곤 생각도 못 했네. 알게 돼서 다행이네.

Henry When survival experts were asked "What would you bring with you if you can take just one item to the wild?", most of them chose a trash bag. That means it's really useful and essential. You got it? That's why I always pack trash bags in the event that I have to survive on the street or in a park.

Henry 생존 전문들이 "한 가지만 야생에 가져갈 수 있다면 무엇을 가져가실 건가요?"라는 질문에 대부분이 쓰레기 봉지를 선택했대. 그만큼 정말로 유용하고 필수적이란 거야. 알았니? 그게 내가 길거리나 공원에서 생존해야 할 상황에서 쓰레기 봉지들을 항상 챙기는 이유야.

Emma Wow

Emma 와우

Henry And among other things, you should pack a flashlight, local map, portable radio, extra batteries, a small first-aid kit, personal items like a toothbrush or toothpaste or extra clothes, socks, shoes, underwear... Having a change of clothing is also important.

Henry 그리고 무엇보다도 손전등, 현지지도, 휴대용 라디오, 여분의 배터리들, 소형 구급상자, 칫솔이나 치약 같은 개인용품이나 여벌의 옷, 양말, 신발, 속옷 등을 챙겨야해. 갈아입을 옷이 있는 것도 중요해.

Emma What about money? I have a credit card.

Emma 돈은 어때? 나 신용카드 있는데.

Henry Right. Like that's going to help when the power is out. You'd better be prepared with coins and cash, and having small bills is a must.

Henry 맞아. 전기가 나갔을 때 그게 참도 도움이 되겠다. 동전이랑 현금을 좀 준비하는 게 좋겠고 잔돈 좀 갖고 있는 건 필수지.

Emma So, what do you do to communicate with other family members in case you get separated?

Emma 그래서, 다른 가족들이랑 떨어졌을 경우엔 어떻게 연락할 건데?

Henry Oh, in that case? I always pack two-way radios to communicate with the group. You can never depend on cell phones. Plus, you should decide on a meeting point in case your family gets separated.

Henry 아, 그런 상황에선 나는 무리랑 의사소통하려고 항상 송수신 겸용 라디오를 챙겨 다녀. 너 절대 핸드폰에 의존하면 안 된다. 또, 너는 가족들이랑 떨어졌을 때를 대비해서, 만남의 장소를 정해야 해.

Emma	Well, that sounds like a detailed plan, definitely.
Emma	음, 확실히 구체적인 계획처럼 들린다.
Henry	Oh, that's not all. You never know what weather conditions you might encounter, so packing a rain poncho, a jacket, and something to start a fire with could be very useful.
Henry	아, 그게 다가 아니야. 어떤 기상 상황을 마주할지 절대 모르기 때문에 **우비**, 자켓, 그리고 불을 피울 수 있는 뭔가를 챙기는 건 매우 유용할 수 있겠지.
Emma	Like Matches?
Emma	성냥 같은 거?
Henry	Matches? If you drop those in a puddle of water, you're toast. You need to pack at least three forms of fire starter: a magnifying glass, a high-quality lighter, and waterproof matches.
Henry	성냥? 만약에 네가 성냥을 물웅덩이에 떨어뜨려 봐. 그러면 너는 **끝장이야**. 너는 적어도 부싯돌 역할을 할 수 있는 세 가지, 즉 돋보기, 고성능 라이터, 그리고 방수 성냥을 챙겨야 해.
Emma	Wow. I never thought about those either. So, what do you do if you have small kids? They'd probably go stir-crazy under such conditions.
Emma	와. 그건 또 생각 못 했네. 그래서 만약 어린 애들이 있으면 어떻게 할 거야? 그런 상황이면 애들이 **미쳐 버릴** 텐데.
Henry	You're exactly right, so a little extra preparation for them is needed. If you have to evacuate to a shelter to wait out a disaster, kids soon will be bored out of their minds, so you have to pack small card games or jigsaw puzzles or paper and something like pencils or crayons to draw with.
Henry	너 아주 정확했어. 그래서 애들을 위한 약간의 추가준비도 필요해. 재난이 **끝나기를 기다리기** 위해서 피난처로 대피해야 하면, 아이들은 곧 **미치도록 지루해 할 테니까**, 작은 카드 게임이나 조각 퍼즐 그리고 그림 그릴 종이랑 색연필이나 크레용 같은 것들 좀 챙겨야 해.
Emma	You know, preparing a 72-hour kit makes perfect sense...
Emma	그거 알아? 72시간 응급 상자, 완전 일리 있다...
Henry	Yeah, but most people think about it after it is too late.
Henry	그래, 근데 사람들 대부분이 너무 늦은 후에 생각한다니깐.

Vocabulary and Sample Sentences

어휘 그리고 예제 문장들

단어	의미
sustain (verb) keep yourself alive	견디다, 지속시키다 (동사) 당신이 살아있게 해준다. **예문** You need a lot of water to sustain yourself in the hot desert sun. 뜨거운 사막의 태양에서 자신을 견딜 수 있게 해주는 많은 물이 필요하다.
flood (noun) a large amount of water that covers an area that is generally dry	홍수 (명사) 일반적으로 건조한 지역을 덮치는 많은 양의 물 **예문** We lost a lot of our possessions in last week's flood. 우리는 지난주 홍수로 많은 재산을 잃었다.
power outage (noun) a period of time when you do not have electrical power	정전 (명사) 전력이 없는 기간 **예문** The power outage lasted over 10 hours, and we had to use flashlights and candles to see in the dark. 정전은 10시간 계속되었고 우리는 어둠 속에서 보기 위해 손전등과 양초를 사용해야 했다.
shelter (noun) a structure used for protection from weather or danger	피난처 (명사) 날씨나 위험으로부터 보호하기 위해 사용되는 구조물 **예문** After the hurricane, many residents fled to shelters because their homes had been destroyed by wind and water. 허리케인이 지나간 후, 많은 주민들의 집이 바람과 물로 파손되었기 때문에 그들은 피난처로 피신했다.

단어	의미
pack (verb) fill or put things into a container like a suitcase or box	싸다, 챙기다 (동사) 여행용 가방이나 상자와 같은 용기에 물건들을 넣거나 채우다. 예문 Hurry and pack your suitcase. We need to leave in 15 minutes. 서둘러 여행 가방을 챙겨. 15분 후에 출발해야 해.
purification (noun) the process of removing dirty parts from something (also a verb purify)	정화 (명사) 어떤 것으로부터 더러운 부분들을 제거하는 과정 (동사로는, 정화하다) 예문 You really need to purify the water from the stream because it probably contains bacteria. 시냇물은 아마도 박테리아를 포함하고 있기 때문에, 시냇물을 정화할 필요가 있다.
murky (adjective) dark and dirty that is difficult to see through	탁한 (형용사) 어둡고 지저분하여 육안으로 보기 어려운 예문 The water that comes out of the kitchen faucet is really murky due to the fact that the city is working on some of the water lines in this area. 시 당국이 이 지역의 일부 수로를 정비하고 있어서 주방 수도꼭지에서 나오는 물은 정말로 탁하다.
spoil (verb) go bad or decay so you cannot eat or drink something any longer	상하다 (동사) 상하거나 썩어서 더 이상 먹거나 마실 수 없다. 예문 The food in the refrigerator started to spoil after the power had been off for two days. 냉장고 안에 음식들이 2일 동안 전기가 나간 후로 상하기 시작했다.

단어	의미
bulky (adjective) something difficult to carry because of its size	부피가 큰 (형용사) 크기 때문에 휴대하기 어려운 **예문** Your backpack is too bulky to carry easily in case of an emergency; you should remove some of the items and then repack it. 배낭의 부피가 너무 커서 긴급한 경우 쉽게 휴대할 수 없으니 물건들을 좀 빼고 다시 싸야 해.

단어	의미
nasty (adjective) having a bad smell, taste, or appearance	형편없는, 끔찍한, 지저분한 (형용사) 냄새나, 맛이나, 모양이 나쁜 **예문** The food looked so nasty that I couldn't bring myself to try it. 그 음식은 너무 형편없어 보여서 나는 직접 먹어 볼 수가 없었다.

단어	의미
evacuate (verb) move from an unsafe place to safety	대피하다 (동사) 안전하지 못한 곳에서 안전한 곳으로 이동하다. **예문** In case of fire, the school will evacuate all of its students to a safer location. 화재 시에, 학교는 모든 학생들을 안전한 장소로 대피시킬 것이다.

단어	의미
be packed together like sardines (idiom) be crowded together in a small place	꽉 채워졌다, 빈틈없이 차있다 (숙어) 좁은 곳에 함께 붐비다. **예문** The emergency shelter was only designed to accommodate 100 evacuees, but because all other shelters were overcrowded, this shelter accepted everyone who came, and the people were packed together like sardines for two days. 비상대피소는 100명의 피난민들만 수용하도록 만들어졌지만 모든 대피소들이 붐비기 때문에 이 대피소는 온 사람들을 모두 수용했고 사람들은 이틀 동안 빈틈없이 붙어 있었다.

단어	의미
unsanitary (adjective) very dirty and unhealthy	비위생적인 (형용사) 매우 더럽고 건강하지 못한 **예문** The unsanitary conditions at the refugee camp were terrible, and nothing could be done until additional aid arrived. 난민촌에서의 비위생적인 상태는 끔찍했으며, 추가적인 지원이 도착할 때까지 아무것도 할 수 없었다.

단어	의미
poncho (noun) a light coat made a one piece of material to protect you from wind and rain	판초 (명사) 비바람을 막기 위해 한 벌로 된 가벼운 외투 **예문** I always carry a poncho in my backpack when I hike in case it starts to rain suddenly. 갑자기 비가 내리기 시작할 때를 대비해서 등산할 때, 나는 항상 배낭 속에 판초/우비를 넣고 다닌다.

단어	의미
be toast (noun, slang) be in a desperate or very difficult situation	끝장나기/죽기 십상이다 (명사, 속어) 절망적이거나 매우 어려운 상황에 있다 **예문** If you don't have supplies during a severe emergency, you're toast, and no one will there to help you. 만약에 심각한 긴급 상황 동안 비축품이 없다면, 너는 끝장나기 십상이고 아무도 너를 도울 수 없을 것이다.

단어	의미
stir-crazy (adjective) very nervous or anxious	미쳐버리는, 돌아버리는 (형용사) 매우 긴장되거나 불안해하는 **예문** Many of the people at the shelter have been there for a week, and they are beginning to feel stir-crazy because they have nothing to do, and they don't know their futures. 피난처에 많은 사람이 일주일 동안 그곳에 있었고, 할 일이 없고 그들의 미래에 대해 알 수 없어서 흥분하기 시작했다.

단어	의미
wait out (phrasal verb) wait until something unpleasant finishes or passes	**끝나기를 기다리다** (구동사) 불편한 것이 끝나거나 지날 때까지 기다린다. **예문** We should just wait out the storm before we attempt to cross the river. 우리는 강을 건너기 전에 폭풍우가 끝나기를 기다려야 한다.

단어	의미
be bored out of your mind (idiom) very bored	**미치도록 지루한** (숙어) 매우 지루한 **예문** The students were bored out of their minds during the lecture on ancient religious practices. 그 학생들은 고대 종교 관례에 대한 강의 중에 미치도록 지루해했다.

| 정답 | 01. (a) | 02. (a) | 03. (b) | 04. (b) | 05. (d) | 06. (a) | 07. (b) |

01

영어문제

According to the talk, what is Henry looking for and why?

(a) some supplies for the 72-hour kits for any possible emergency
(b) some canned goods since they are easy to carry with
(c) some rocks to open some canned goods
(d) some branches to make a shelter

문제 한글 해석

대화에 따르면, Henry는 무엇을 왜 찾고 있는가?

(a) 가능한 비상사태 대비를 위한 72시간 키트를 위한 저장품들
(b) 휴대하기 쉽기 때문에 통조림 제품들
(c) 일부 통조림 제품을 열기위한 바위들
(d) 대피소를 만들기 위한 몇 개의 나뭇가지들

문제해설

Henry가 가족 각자를 위해 72시간 키트에 넣을 저장품을 찾는다고 말한다.

> Well, actually, I'm looking for supplies to put together 72-hour kits for each member of my family. Basically, a 72-hour kit contains emergency supplies you would need to sustain yourself for three days in case of an emergency, like a hurricane.

02

영어문제

What does Henry keep in the 72-Hour Emergency Kit?

(a) basic water filter or water purification tablets, and food
(b) basic tools like screwdriver
(c) at least three pairs of shoes
(d) extra phones to carry

문제 한글 해석

Henry는 72시간 응급 키트에 무엇을 보관하는가?

(a) 기초 정수필터나 정수용정제와 음식
(b) 나사돌리개와 같은 기본 공구
(c) 최소 3켤레의 신발들
(d) 가지고 다닐 여분의 핸드폰

문제해설

Henry는 3일을 버티기 위해 충분한 음식과 물이 있어야 한다고 말하며 단 하나뿐인 수원이 벌레가 들끓는 탁한 웅덩이로 변할 수 있는 상황을 대비하기 위해 기초 물 필터나 정수용정제를 준비하고 싶을 수 있다고 말한다.

> Well, you should have enough food and water to last you three days, and you might want to pack a basic water filter or water purification tablets in case your only water source turns out to be a murky pool of bug-infested water. [Ugh!] Hey, sometimes you don't have a choice, and as for food, you should keep it simple: food that requires no preparation and that doesn't spoil.

03 영어문제 | 문제 한글 해석

Why would it be the case that the tent is not an ideal option?

(a) because it's too expensive to purchase
(b) because it's too heavy and annoying to carry
(c) because a tent might not has enough space to hold all the family members
(d) because you might have to carry many things other than the tent

왜 텐트가 이상적인 선택이 아닐 수 있는가?
(a) 구매하기에 너무 비싸기 때문에
(b) 너무 무겁고 들고 다니기 귀찮기 때문에
(c) 텐트가 가족들을 다 수용할 만큼 공간이 충분하지 않을 수도 있기 때문에
(d) 텐트 이외에 많은 것을 가지고 다녀야 할 수도 있기 때문에

문제해설

텐트를 가져와도 되지만 텐트가 너무 무겁고 만약 재난이 일어나면 들고 다니기 귀찮을 수도 있다고 한다.

> You should prepare your own shelter in this case. Of course, you can bring a tent, but you know, a tent can be too heavy and annoying to carry especially when disasters break out.

04 영어문제 | 문제 한글 해석

Based on the talk, how can you build a shelter if you don't have access to a tent?

(a) by spotting a safe place and dig a hole to build a shelter
(b) by using resources that you can spot around you like trash bags
(c) by calling an expert in advance to build a shelter for you
(d) by using used clothes to build a shelter

대화에 의하면, 텐트가 없을 때 어떻게 대피처를 만들 수 있는가?
(a) 대피처를 짓기 위해 안전한 장소를 찾아서 땅을 판다.
(b) 주변에 구할 수 있는 쓰레기봉투들과 같은 자원들을 이용한다.
(c) 전문가에게 미리 연락해 대피처를 만들어달라고 한다.
(d) 대피처를 만들기 위해 헌 옷을 사용한다.

문제해설

Henry는 밧줄과 엮은 쓰레기봉투 몇 개로 무척 효율적인 일인용 텐트를 만들 수 있다고 말한다.

> Surprisingly, something can replace it! It can be found around us. Look at there! What can you see? Yes! A couple of trash bags, combined with a rope, and then they can make an incredibly effective one-man tent. If you don't have a rope, then you can just use a branch. And it'll become an amazing temporary shelter!

05

영어문제

How can you communicate with your family members in case you get separated?

(a) to use a mobile phone to call your family members
(b) to call 911 to ask to find your family members
(c) to stay at your original spot because moving around may cause confusion
(d) to use two-way radios because you shouldn't depend on cell phones

문제 한글 해석

만약 가족들과 동떨어진다면 어떻게 연락을 할 수 있는가?

(a) 휴대전화로 가족들에게 연락한다.
(b) 가족들을 찾기 위해 911에 전화한다.
(c) 움직이는 것은 혼란스러울 수도 있기 때문에 원래 장소에 있는다.
(d) 핸드폰에 의지하면 안 되므로 송수신 겸용 라디오를 사용한다.

문제해설

Henry는 그룹과 소통하기 위해 항상 송수신 겸용 라디오를 싼다고 말한다. 그는 핸드폰에 절대 의지할 수 없다고 말한다.

> Oh, in that case? I always pack two-way radios to communicate with the group. You can never depend on cell phones. [Okay.] Plus, you should decide on a meeting point in case your family gets separated.

06

영어문제

What are the three forms of fire starter?

(a) a magnifying glass, a high-quality lighter, and waterproof matches
(b) some paper, a high-quality lighter, and a few pieces of wood
(c) some clothes, a high-quality lighter, and waterproof matches
(d) a magnifying glass, a few pieces of wood, and some clothes

문제 한글 해석

세 형태의 부싯돌은 무엇인가?

(a) 확대경, 고품질 라이터, 방수 성냥
(b) 종이 몇 장, 고품질 라이터, 나무 몇 조각
(c) 옷가지, 고품질 라이터, 방수 성냥
(d) 확대경, 나무 몇 조각, 옷가지

문제해설

Henry는 최소 세 형태의 부싯돌을 싸놓아야 한다고 말하며 이 부싯돌들은 확대경, 고품질의 라이터, 방수 성냥이다.

> Matches? If you drop those in a puddle of water, you're toast. You need to pack at least three forms of fire starter: a magnifying glass, a high-quality lighter, and waterproof matches.

07 영어문제 | 문제 한글 해석

How will you get prepared in case your children get bored?
(a) by bringing a children's book to read for them
(b) by packing small card games or jigsaw puzzles
(c) by preparing a radio to play music for them
(d) by packing some cookies or snacks to share with

아이들이 지루해할 것을 어떻게 대비하는가?
(a) 그들에게 읽어주기 위해 동화책을 가지고 옴으로서
(b) 작은 카드 게임이나 조각 그림 퍼즐등을 챙김으로서
(c) 그들에게 노래를 틀어주기 위해 라디오를 준비하므로서
(d) 같이 나눠먹을수 있는 쿠키나 간식을 챙김으로서

문제해설

Henry는 아이들을 위해 조금 더 추가적인 준비가 필요하다고 말한다. 재난으로 인해 피신처로 대피할 때 아이들은 금방 지루해하기 때문에 작은 카드 게임이나 조각 그림 퍼즐 또는 종이와 그릴 수 있는 연필이나 크레용을 준비해야 한다고 말한다.

You're exactly right, so a little extra preparation for them is needed. If you have to evacuate to a shelter to wait out a disaster, kids soon will be bored out of their minds, so you have to pack small card games or jigsaw puzzles or paper and something like pencils or crayons to draw with.

MEMO

PART 4 문제 유형

1 프레젠테이션의 주제 혹은 목적을 묻는다.

프레젠테이션의 주제 혹은 목적이 청중 대상과 함께 초반에 제시된다. 대부분 목적이 뚜렷하게 제시되는 경우가 많다.

What is he presenting to ~?

What is the speech mainly about?

What is the main purpose of the talk?

2 프레젠테이션을 듣는 청중 대상을 묻는다.

프레젠테이션 초반에 주제와 함께 직접적으로 청중이 언급되거나 주제가 언급된 맥락에서 유추할 수 있도록 제시된다. 프레젠테이션 마지막 부분에서 청중이 다시 언급되기도 한다.

To whom is the talk being given?

What kind of audience is the speaker addressing?

3 세부내용: 이름, 숫자 등 단편적인 것을 묻는다.

전체적인 이해력과는 상관없이 언급된 사물의 이름이나 대표적인 문구, 언급된 숫자 등을 묻는 질문이 출제된다. 문제를 먼저 들려주므로 받아 적어 놓으면 쉽게 답할 수 있는 문제들이다.

What is the name of X?

What is the magazine's "X"?

What award did A receive during ~?

4 세부내용: 해야 할 것과 하지 말아야 할 것

프레젠테이션 형식의 특성상 해야 하는 것과 하지 말아야 할 것을 강조해서 설명한다. 조언 형태로 서술되며 강조하고 있는 내용에 대한 세부질문이다.

What did the speaker say must be avoided when ~?
What did the speaker not recommend to ~?

5 화자가 프레젠테이션 이후 무엇을 할지를 묻는다.

프레젠테이션 이후 화자가 무엇을 할지에 관해서 묻는 문제가 마지막 부분에 언급된다. 카탈로그를 배포한다든지, 질문을 받는다든지 등이 답이 될 수 있다.

What did the speaker intend to do after the talk?

 **문제를 잘 듣고 받아쓰기 연습을 미리 해보세요.**

기억하세요! 3단어가 넘어가면 안 됩니다.

1.

2.

3.

4.

5.

6.

Part 4. You will hear a lecturer talking to a group of people. First you will hear questions 1 through 6. Then you will hear the talk. Choose the best answer to each question in the time provided.

01

(a) a procedure / surgery that impacts the lives of people who suffer from congenital defects, accidents, or animal bites
(b) a non-medical form of operating skin regeneration
(c) a form of cosmetic surgery that is for people who wish to have a better appearance
(d) a procedure that alters people's appearances to look younger

02

(a) The developing countries get financial support to do it.
(b) They can't afford reconstructive surgery.
(c) Worldwide organizations with volunteers make regular visits.
(d) Developing countries train their own doctors and nurses.

03

(a) They provide child-care.
(b) They help with anything that people need.
(c) They provide other surgical activities to developing nations.
(d) They provide training to health care workers.

04

(a) The patients can now feel a greater understanding.
(b) The patients now can live with some normalcy and hope for the future.
(c) The patients can be more self-confident than before.
(d) They can have better jobs.

05

(a) They can feel better with themselves.
(b) They can feel self-esteem as they bring positive changes to the world.
(c) They feel compassion for those who suffer from such defects.
(d) They can be more financially fulfilled.

06

(a) by donating time, money, and supplies to volunteering organizations
(b) by visiting developing countries and provide services
(c) by organizing other volunteer groups to provide greater support
(d) by buying products from volunteering organizations to show support

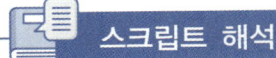 스크립트 해석

Plastic Surgery 성형 수술

Hello everyone! Thank you for inviting me to this class. Have you ever heard about plastic surgery? I'm quite sure that many of you've heard about it. Today I'm going to talk about plastic surgery.
여러분 안녕하세요! 이 강좌에 저를 초대해 주셔서 감사합니다. 여러분은 성형 수술에 관해서 들어본 적이 있나요? 여기 계신 많은 분이 들어봤을 거라고 생각되는데요. 저는 오늘 성형 수술에 대해서 얘기해 보려고 합니다.

Plastic surgery is a surgical specialty involving the restoration, reconstruction, or alteration of the human body. It can be performed for cosmetic reasons or reconstructive ones. We call the surgery for cosmetic aims the cosmetic surgery. And we call the surgery for reconstructive reasons the reconstructive surgery. Sometimes, they are interchangeable.
성형 수술은 인체의 복원, 재구조 혹은 변형을 포함하는 외과 전문 분야입니다. 성형 수술은 미용이나 회복을 목적으로 행해질 수 있습니다. 우리는 미용을 목적으로 하는 수술은 미용 성형 수술이라고 칭합니다. 그리고 복원을 목표로 하는 수술은 재건 성형 수술이라고 부릅니다. 때로는, 호환되어 사용될 수 있습니다.

They are similar in that they **alter** the appearance of an individual, but they are different in many ways. Cosmetic surgery often **evokes** images of famous personalities that want to alter their appearances through elective surgical procedures.
두 수술은 개인의 외모를 **변하게** 한다는 점에서는 유사하지만 많은 면에서 다릅니다. 미용 성형 수술은 선택에 의한 수술 과정을 통해 외모를 바꾸고자 하는 유명 인사들의 모습을 **떠올리게** 합니다.

It is done to improve overall one's appearance by reshaping and adjusting normal anatomy in order to make it visually more attractive. However, reconstructive surgery is a procedure that makes a similar, but different impact on the lives of many around the world, and many of these patients suffer from either **congenital** defects like a cleft palate or injuries sustained in accidents or animal bites.
미용 성형 수술은 원래의 몸을 시각상 더 매력적으로 만들기 위해서 조절하고 재형성하여 전반적인 외모를 개선하기 위해 행해집니다. 하지만, 재건 수술은 전 세계의 많은 이들의 삶에 유사하지만 다른 영향을 주는 수술이며, 이들 환자들 중 상당수는 구개 파열과 같은 **선천적인** 결함이나 사고로 인한 지속적 상처, 혹은 동물에게 물려서 생긴 상처로 고통 받습니다.

Some **disfigurements** can also be due to the effects of disease or infection. And it is performed to restore function and normal appearance, and correct deformities. Yet, the individual with such defects often bares more than just outward physical marks: loss of hope and self-worth is commonplace.
일부 **외모적인 손상**은 질병이나 감염의 영향으로 나타나기도 합니다. 그리고 재건 수술은 기능과 정상적인 외모를 회복하고 기형을 교정하기 위해서 시행됩니다. 하지만, 그러한 결함을 가진 사람은 종종 외형상의 신체적 결점 이상의 것을 드러냅니다: 희망과 자존감의 상실은 흔히 있는 일입니다.

It is considered medically necessary whereas the cosmetic surgery is not. Cosmetic surgery is focused on the appearances while the reconstructive aims to improve the body functions.
재건 성형 수술은 의학적으로 필요하다고 여겨지는 반면 미용 성형 수술은 그렇지 않습니다. 미용 성형 수술은 외모에 초점을 맞추고 있고 재건을 목적으로 한 수술은 신체 기능을 개선하는 것을 목표로 합니다.

Many people think plastic surgery is a relatively new specialty. Surprisingly, plastic surgery has been in existence for many years. You can find the origin of plastic surgery dating back more than 4,000 years ago. Sushruta was the first physician in the world, and he had contributed a lot to the field of plastic surgery.
많은 사람들은 성형 수술이 상대적으로 새로운 전공 분야라고 생각합니다. 놀랍게도, 성형 수술은 수년 동안 존재해 왔습니다. 성형 수술의 기원은 4,000여 년 전으로 거슬러 올라갑니다. Sushruta는 세계 최초의 내과 의사였고, 성형 수술 분야에 많은 공헌을 했습니다.

He was the first one to perform skin grafts. That's why he is described as "Father of Surgery" and "Father of Plastic Surgery". However, it wasn't common to have plastic surgeries at that time.
Sushruta는 피부 이식 수술을 진행한 첫 번째 의사였습니다. 이 때문에, 그는 "수술의 아버지" 그리고 "성형 수술의 아버지"라고 묘사됩니다. 하지만 그 당시에는 성형 수술을 하는 것은 흔한 일이 아니었습니다.

Then, when did the plastic surgery start to spread worldwide? It was after World War I. Around the time, many of the reconstructive procedures were created because of war injuries.
그렇다면 언제부터 성형 수술이 세계적으로 확산하기 시작했을까요? 바로 세계 1차 대전 이후입니다. 그 무렵 전쟁으로 인한 부상으로 인해 많은 재건 수술이 행해졌습니다.

Since then, plastic surgeries were gradually performed in some developed countries. In the past, such plastic procedures were only available in developed countries where the medical expertise and financial resources could afford such operations.
이후 일부 선진국에서 점차 성형 수술이 행해졌습니다. 과거에는 그러한 성형수술을 **감당할 수** 있는 의료 전문가와 자원을 가진 선진국에서만 그러한 수술이 가능했습니다.

On the other hand, developing countries could not afford such things. When someone needed treatment or surgeries, it was difficult for them to have any proper treatment or surgeries. But now, a number of worldwide organizations made up of volunteers make regular visits to developing countries to provide reconstructive surgery to those who could not otherwise receive such care.
반면 개발도상국들은 이를 감당할 형편이 안 되었습니다. 누군가 치료나 수술이 필요할 때, 그들은 적절한 치료나 수술을 받는 것이 어려웠습니다. 하지만 지금은, 자원봉사자들로 구성된 많은 세계적 단체들이 개발도상국에 정기적으로 방문하여 다른 방법으로 그러한 치료를 받을 수 없었던 사람들에게 재건 수술을 제공해줍니다.

In addition to the care they provide, these volunteer specialists also provide training to health care workers in these procedures so that local hospitals, nurses, and doctors can become self-sufficient.
그들이 제공하는 원조 이외에도, 이 자원봉사 전문가들은 이러한 수술 과정에서 의료계 종사자들에게 교육을 제공하여 지역의 병원, 간호사 그리고 의사들이 **자립할 수** 있도록 합니다.

The end results of such efforts have transformed lives: the patient now can live with some normalcy and hope for the future with less fear of being ostracized by neighbors and family, and the health care worker who performs the procedure perhaps feels a greater understanding and compassion for those who suffer from such defects.
그러한 노력의 최종적인 결과는 삶을 변화시킵니다. 이제 환자는 이웃이나 가족에 의해 **외면 받는** 두려움 없이 미래에 대한 희망을 품고 정상적으로 살아갈 수 있습니다. 그리고 수술을 진행한 의료계 종사자는 아마도 그러한 결점으로 고통받는 사람들에 대한 더 큰 이해와 연민을 가질 것입니다.

There are many ways for people to assist in supporting these volunteer efforts. Although most people do not have the medical expertise to perform reconstructive surgery, they can still donate time, money, and supplies to such organizations. So don't hesitate. There are many things you can do to volunteer. A quick search on the Internet can get you started.
사람들이 이러한 자원봉사의 노력을 지원하는 데 도움을 주는 많은 방법이 있습니다. 비록 사람들 대부분이 재건 수술을 수행할 의학적인 전문 기술을 가지고 있지는 않지만, 여전히 관련 단체에 시간, 돈 그리고 보급품을 기부할 수 있습니다. 그러니, 망설이지 마세요. 여러분이 자원봉사를 하기 위해 할 수 있는 일은 많습니다. 인터넷으로 빠르게 찾아보는 것으로 시작할 수 있습니다.

Vocabulary and Sample Sentences

어휘 그리고 예제 문장들

단어	의미
evoke (verb) bring up, call to mind	자아내다, 환기시키다 (동사) 불러일으키다, 상기하다 **예문** Seeing children in need of reconstructive surgery often evokes feelings of sympathy and concern. 재건 수술이 필요한 아이들을 보면 종종 연민과 우려의 감정을 자아냅니다.
alter (verb) change	바꾸다, 고치다 (동사) 바꾸다 **예문** The woman thought she could alter her looks and personality by undergoing plastic surgery. 그 여자는 성형 수술을 해서 그녀의 외모와 성격을 바꿀 수 있다고 생각했다.
congenital (adjective) present at birth	선천적인, 타고난 (형용사) 태어날 때 있는 **예문** Some congenital defects can be corrected with reconstructive surgery. 일부 선천적인 결함들은 재건 수술을 통해 교정할 수 있다.
disfigurements (noun, also a verb, "disfigure") a part of the body that has been damaged	외관 손상, 결함, 상처 (명사, 또는 동사 "외관을 손상시키다") 손상된 신체의 일부분 **예문** The fire in the crash left her face and hands disfigured, and now she is seeking cosmetic surgery to repair the damage and give her more mobility to her fingers. 사고로 인한 화재는 그녀의 얼굴과 손을 망가뜨렸고, 그녀는 손가락에 유동성을 높이고 손상을 복구하기 위해서 성형 수술을 찾아보고 있다.

단어	의 미
afford (verb) have the financial means to do something	**여유/형편이 되다** (동사) 어떤 것을 할 재정적인 수단을 가지다. **예문** A great number of people around the world are in need of reconstructive surgery to improve their lives, but they can't afford the expense of such procedures. 전 세계의 많은 사람들은 그들의 삶을 개선하기 위해 재건 수술을 필요로 하고 있지만, 그들은 수술비용을 감당할 형편이 안된다.

단어	의 미
self-sufficient (adjective) able to provide for your own needs	**자립하는, 자급자족의** (형용사) 당신의 필요를 제공할 수 있는 **예문** Many health care workers in developing countries are still learning to become self-sufficient in terms of handling the medical needs of their people. 개발도상국의 많은 의료계 종사자들은 여전히 국민들의 의료적 요구를 감당하는 데 있어서 자립하기 위해서 배우고 있다.

단어	의 미
ostracize (verb) expel or cast out from a group	**추방하다, 배척하다** (동사) 집단에서 추방하거나 쫓아내다. **예문** The local community ostracized the young boy and his family because of his medical condition. 그 지역 사회는 그의 건강 상태 때문에 어린 소년과 그의 가족을 쫓아냈다.

정답 01. (a) 02. (c) 03. (d) 04. (b) 05. (c) 06. (a)

01

영어문제

According to the presenter, what is reconstructive surgery?

(a) a procedure / surgery that impacts the lives of people who suffer from congenital defects, accidents, or animal bites
(b) a non-medical form of operating skin regeneration
(c) a form of cosmetic surgery that is for people who wish to have a better appearance
(d) a procedure that alters people's appearances to look younger

문제 한글 해석

화자에 따르면, 재건 수술은 무엇인가?

(a) 선천적인 결함이나 사고, 혹은 동물에게 물려서 생긴 상처를 받은 사람들의 인생에 영향을 주는 과정/수술
(b) 비의료적 형식의 피부 재생 수술
(c) 더 나은 외모를 갖고 싶어 하는 사람들을 위한 성형의 한 형식
(d) 수술을 통해 사람들의 외모를 더 젊게 바꾸는 과정

문제해설

재건 수술은 전 세계의 많은 이들의 삶에 유사하지만 다른 영향을 주는 수술이다. 많은 환자가 구개 파열과 같은 선천적인 결함이나 사고로 인한 지속적 상처, 혹은 동물에게 물려서 생긴 상처로 고통 받고 있다고 나와 있다.

> However, reconstructive surgery is a procedure that makes a similar, but different impact on the lives of many around the world, and many of these patients suffer from either congenital defects like a cleft palate or injuries sustained in accidents or animal bites.

02

영어문제

How can developing countries have reconstructive surgery?

(a) The developing countries get financial support to do it.
(b) They can't afford reconstructive surgery.
(c) Worldwide organizations with volunteers make regular visits.
(d) Developing countries train their own doctors and nurses.

문제 한글 해석

개발도상국들은 어떻게 재건 수술을 할 수 있는가?

(a) 개발도상국들은 그것을 하기 위하여 재정적 원조를 받는다.
(b) 재건 수술비를 감당할 수 없다.
(c) 자원봉사자들로 이루어진 세계적인 단체들이 정기적으로 방문한다.
(d) 개발도상국들은 자체적으로 의사와 간호사들을 교육한다.

문제해설

자원봉사자들로 구성된 많은 세계적 단체들이 개발도상국에 정기적으로 방문하여 그러한 치료를 받을 수 없었던 사람들에게 재건 수술을 제공해준다.

> But now, a number of worldwide organizations made up of volunteers make regular visits to developing countries to provide reconstructive surgery to those who could not otherwise receive such care.

03 영어문제 | 문제 한글 해석

Apart from providing the reconstructive surgery, what else do the volunteer specialists provide?
(a) They provide child-care.
(b) They help with anything that people need.
(c) They provide other surgical activities to developing nations.
(d) They provide training to health care workers.

재건 수술을 하는 것 외에, 전문 자원봉사자들은 무엇을 제공하는가?
(a) 그들은 보육 서비스를 제공한다.
(b) 사람들이 필요로 하는 모든 것을 돕는다.
(c) 그들은 개발도상국에 다른 외과수술들을 제공한다.
(d) 의료 종사자를 대상으로 교육을 실시한다.

문제해설

자원봉사 전문가들은 이러한 수술 과정에서 의료계 종사자들에게 교육을 제공하여 지역의 병원, 간호사 그리고 의사들이 자립할 수 있도록 해준다.

In addition to the care they provide, these volunteer specialists also provide training to health care workers in these procedures so that local hospitals, nurses, and doctors can become self-sufficient.

04 영어문제 | 문제 한글 해석

What are the outcomes of reconstructive surgery for the patients?
(a) The patients can now feel a greater understanding.
(b) The patients now can live with some normalcy and hope for the future.
(c) The patients can be more self-confident than before.
(d) They can have better jobs.

환자들을 위한 재건 수술의 결과는 어떠한가?
(a) 환자들은 이제 더 많은 이해를 할 수 있다.
(b) 환자는 이제 어느 정도 정상적인 생활을 할 수 있고 미래에 대한 희망을 품을 수 있다.
(c) 환자들은 전보다 더 자신감을 가질 수 있다.
(d) 그들은 더 나은 직업을 구할 수 있다.

문제해설

재건 수술은 그들의 삶을 변화시킨다: 이제 환자는 이웃이나 가족에 의해 외면 받는 두려움 없이 미래에 대한 희망을 갖고 정상적으로 살아갈 수 있다.

The end results of such efforts have transformed lives: the patient now can live with some normalcy and hope for the future with less fear of being ostracized by neighbors and family, and the health care worker who performs the procedure perhaps feels a greater understanding and compassion for those who suffer from such defects.

05 영어문제

What possible changes did reconstructive surgery bring to the health care workers?

(a) They can feel better with themselves.
(b) They can feel self-esteem as they bring positive changes to the world.
(c) They feel compassion for those who suffer from such defects.
(d) They can be more financially fulfilled.

문제 한글 해석

재건 수술이 의료 종사자들에게 어떤 변화를 가져왔는가?
(a) 그들 스스로 기분이 나아질 수 있다.
(b) 그들이 세상에 좋은 변화를 불러왔기 때문에 자부심을 느낄 수 있다.
(c) 그러한 결함으로 고통받는 사람들에게 연민을 느낄 수 있다.
(d) 그들은 좀 더 경제적으로 풍요로워질 수 있다.

문제해설

재건 수술을 진행한 의료계 종사자는 아마도 그러한 결점으로 고통 받은 사람들에 대한 더 큰 이해와 연민을 가질 것이라는 것을 알 수 있다.

> The end results of such efforts have transformed lives: the patient now can live with some normalcy and hope for the future with less fear of being ostracized by neighbors and family, and the health care worker who performs the procedure perhaps feels a greater understanding and compassion for those who suffer from such defects.

06 영어문제

Based on the speech, how can we assist in supporting volunteer efforts?

(a) by donating time, money, and supplies to volunteering organizations
(b) by visiting developing countries and provide services
(c) by organizing other volunteer groups to provide greater support
(d) by buying products from volunteering organizations to show support

문제 한글 해석

연설을 바탕으로, 우리는 자원봉사 활동에 어떻게 도움이 될 수 있는가?
(a) 시간, 돈, 보급품들을 자원봉사 단체에 기부함으로써
(b) 개발도상국들을 방문하고 봉사함으로서
(c) 다른 봉사 단체를 조직해서 더 많은 후원을 제공함으로써
(d) 자원봉사 단체에서 물건들을 사서 지지함으로써

문제해설

사람들은 관련 단체에 시간, 돈 그리고 보급품을 기부할 수 있다.

> There are many ways for people to assist in supporting these volunteer efforts. Although most people do not have the medical expertise to perform reconstructive surgery, they can still donate time, money, and supplies to such organizations.

필수 단어, 표현, 숙어 암기노트

단어, 표현, 숙어	의미

필수 단어, 표현, 숙어 암기노트

단어, 표현, 숙어	의미

리스닝 만렙을 위한 원포인트 레슨

질문 받아 적기(딕테이션) 훈련이 점수를 가늠한다.

3단어 이상을 넘지 마라!
본인만이 알아볼 수 있는 모든 문자, 기호, 부호, 이미지를 활용하라.
하지만 모든 걸 다 받아 적으려는 욕심을 부리는 순간 타이밍을 놓치고 만다.
우리에게는 질문을 받아 적을 수 있는 시간이 최대 약 4초 정도밖에 없다.

SIGNATURE

2 회

 문제를 잘 듣고 받아쓰기 연습을 미리 해보세요.

기억하세요! 3단어가 넘어가면 안 됩니다.

1.
2.
3.
4.
5.
6.
7.

Part 1. You will hear a conversation between two people. First you will hear questions 1 through 7. Then you will hear the conversation. Choose the best answer to each question in the time provided.

01

(a) He found out about the Zero Diet from his junk mail.
(b) His friends told him about the Zero Diet.
(c) He visited the hospital and a doctor prescribed him the Zero Diet.
(d) His girl friend told him about the Zero Diet.

02

(a) It costs half of Matthew's salary.
(b) It requires $650.
(c) Zero Diet doesn't cost any money.
(d) It costs $750.

03

(a) One Meal A Day diet
(b) One Meal At Dinner diet
(c) One Morning A Day diet
(d) One Mango At Dinner

04

(a) She believes he can be succeeded.
(b) She tells him that the OMAD diet is dangerous.
(c) She thinks he can't manage it.
(d) She shows no reaction to it.

05

(a) to eat smaller portions and good, well-balanced breakfast
(b) to not get stressed and consume food as much as he wants
(c) to eat as usual
(d) to eat smaller portions of breakfast only

06

(a) to get a bigger plate
(b) to eat a lot of fresh fruits and vegetables
(c) to consume lots of sugary food
(d) to drink lots of milk

07

(a) because drinking water gives energy
(b) because water breaks down calories
(c) because water helps to digest food
(d) because drinking water makes the body healthy

 스크립트 해석

Diet Plans 식이요법 계획들

Mathew's Sister   Hey, Mathew! Ma...? Mathew. Mathew.
Mathew 누나   Mathew! Ma...? Mathew. Mathew.

Mathew   What? What's going on?
Mathew   뭐? 왜 그래?

Mathew's Sister   What happened to YOU?
Mathew 누나   너한테 대체 무슨 일이 있던 거야?

Mathew   You mean my hair? How do you like it? I had my hair dyed yesterday.
Mathew   내 머리 말하는 거야 누나? 어때? 나 어제 머리 염색했어.

Mathew's Sister   Uh, I think you know what I mean, Mathew.
Mathew 누나   어, 너 내가 무슨 말 하는지 알지. Mathew.

Mathew   I don't know what you're talking about.
Mathew   누나 무슨 말 하는지 모르겠는데.

Mathew's Sister   Do you want me to be honest? Okay. Mathew. You've put on, like, a ton of weight since I saw you at Christmas time. What on earth happened to you?
Mathew 누나   솔직하게 말했으면 좋겠어? 그래. Mathew. 우리 크리스마스 때 본 이후로 너 살이 많이 쪘어. 대체 무슨 일이야?

Mathew   Why are you always so **blunt**?
Mathew   누나는 왜 항상 그렇게 **직설적이야?**

Mathew's Sister   Well, I'm your big sister. I'm... what am I? Five years older than you, and I can be blunt if I want. Besides, you used to say stuff like that to me all the time. You used to call me **fatso** all the time when I was little.
Mathew 누나   음... 난 네 누나야. 내가... 내가 너보다 5살이나 많아. 그러니까, 필요하면 직설적일 수도 있지. 게다가, 너야말로 항상 직설적으로 얘기해 왔잖아. 어렸을 때 너 맨날 나한테 **뚱뚱보**라고 불렀잖아.

Mathew   Oh, yeah, well, to be honest, uh... , I started changing my life... yesterday. I'm on the Zero Diet.
Mathew   그래, 뭐, 사실은, 음... 나 어제부터 생활을 좀 바꿔보기 시작했어... 나 Zero 다이어트 중이야.

Mathew's Sister What? I've never even heard of the Zero Diet. What is that?
Mathew 누나 뭐? Zero 다이어트라는 건 들어본 적도 없다. 그게 뭔데?

Mathew Ah, it's too difficult to explain. I found information about it in my junk mail the other day...
Mathew 아, 설명하기엔 너무 어려운데. 저번에 스팸메일 함에서 이 다이어트에 대한 정보를 찾았거든.

Mathew's Sister What? You read your junk mail? No one reads their junk mail.
Mathew 누나 뭐? 너 스팸메일도 읽어? 아무도 스팸메일은 안 읽는다.

Mathew And I signed up for it, and it only cost $650.
Mathew 그리고 나 그거 등록도 했어. 650 달러 밖에 안 들었어.

Mathew's Sister You must be kidding me.
Mathew 누나 너 장난치는 거지.

Mathew No...
Mathew 아닌데..

Mathew's Sister You're serious? Six hundred and fifty bucks? Like every month or every week or...?
Mathew 누나 진심이야? 육백오십 달러라고? 그러니까, 매달? 아니면 매주? 아니면..?

Mathew I didn't check that... ah, but... I think...
Mathew 그건 확인을 안 했는데... 아, 근데, 내 생각에...

Mathew's Sister Listen. I think you're getting scammed, and it sounds really stupid. Just forget about the Zero something and listen to me from now on. I'm not fat anymore, so trust me. I... if you want to lose weight, you need to do it the right way.
Mathew 누나 들어봐. 내 생각에, 너 **사기** 당하고 있는 거 같아. 그리고 진짜 바보 같아. Zero 다이어트인지 뭔지는 그냥 잊고 지금부터 내 말 잘 들어. 나는 더 이상 뚱뚱하지 않으니까 날 믿어. 내가... 네가 살을 빼고 싶으면, 올바른 방법으로 해야 해.

Mathew Well, like what?
Mathew 그러니까, 어떻게?

Mathew's Sister Well, okay.
Mathew 누나 자, 좋아.

Mathew Okay, uh, well, look. Look at my running shoes over there.
Mathew 그래, 자, 봐. 저기에 내 운동화 봐봐.

Mathew's Sister		Mathew. They're still in the box. Never used. Besides exercise, yeah, exercise is wonderful. But eating habits are also really important.
Mathew 누나		Mathew. 아직 박스 안에 있어. 신지도 않았네. 운동 말고도, 그래, 운동도 좋지. 근데, 식습관도 정말 중요해.
Mathew		Oh, I was also thinking about the OMAD diet!
Mathew		어, 나 OMAD 다이어트에 대해서도 생각하고 있었어.
Mathew's Sister		What is the OMAD diet?
Mathew 누나		OMAD 다이어트가 뭔데?
Mathew		It means one meal a day diet. So I can eat just once a day.
Mathew		하루에 한 끼만 먹는 거야. 그래서 나 하루에 한 번만 먹을 수 있어.
Mathew's Sister		Are you sure you can make it? I don't think...
Mathew 누나		네가 할 수 있겠어? 아닐 것 같은데...
Mathew		Instead, I can eat whatever I want just for one meal. It doesn't sound that bad, right?
Mathew		대신에, 한 끼는 내가 먹고 싶은 건 뭐든지 먹을 수 있어. 나쁘지 않지, 그렇지?
Mathew's Sister		Umm... I've known you for about 18 years, and I'm sure you can't manage it. Eating just once a day? You? No way. But, don't be disappointed. Here are many things you can do. For example, you need to eat smaller <u>portions</u>. And, and you can't <u>load up</u> your plate with seconds and thirds like you always used to do at the family parties.
Mathew 누나		음... 내가 너를 18년 동안 알아 왔잖아. 너 절대 성공 못 해. 하루에 한 번 먹는다고? 네가? 절대 안 돼. 하지만, 실망하지는 마. 네가 할 수 있는 많은 것들이 있어. 예를 들어서, 적은 **양**을 먹어야 해. 그리고 가족 행사에서 항상 그래왔던 것처럼 2접시 3접시를 **가득 쌓아서** 먹으면 안 돼.
Mathew		Well, okay. I'll just get a bigger plate!
Mathew		그래, 좋아. 그럼 나 더 큰 접시 써야겠다!
Mathew's Sister		Mathew! That won't help. Next Oh yeah. So, first of all, smaller portions Then, you need to make sure you eat a good, well-balanced breakfast first thing in the morning and then you follow that up with smaller meals throughout the day, cause, you know what? If you skip breakfast, then throughout the day, you feel like you need to make up for it by overeating at lunch and dinner and lots of snacks.
Mathew 누나		Mathew! 그러면 도움이 안 될 거야. 다음으로 어, 그래. 우선 첫 번째로, 더 적은 양. 그 다음엔, 아침부터 제대로 균형 잡힌 식사를 확실하게 해야 해. 그리고 나서, 하루 동안은 양을 적게 먹는 거야. 왜냐면, 그거 알아? 아침을 건너뛰면, 그 다음엔 그걸 보충하려고 하루 종일, 점심이랑 저녁에 과식하고 군것질도 많이 하게 돼.

Mathew		Oh, you sound like a professional.
Mathew		오, 누나 전문가 같아.
Mathew's Sister		Anyway, um, oh yeah. Don't eat late at night. Well, you know a lot of people... they want a... they want a late night snack and stuff like that, but a lot of times, that's really, really high-calorie stuff like cake, cookies, and things, and your body's not active to burn it off, so you just store all those calories as fat. You have to throw away... Oh my gosh! That's all you have in your fridge! You've only got cake and chocolate cookies in there! You're going to have to throw that all away?
Mathew 누나		어쨌든, 음, 그래. 밤늦게 먹지마. 어, 알다시피, 많은 사람들이... 사람들이 야식 같은 걸 먹고 싶어 하지만, 대부분, 케이크, 쿠키같이 고열량 음식들이야. 그리고 네 몸은 활발하게 그걸 태우지 않아서 너는 지방으로 그 열량들을 축적하는 거야. 너, 다 갖다 버려야 해... 이게 뭐야! 냉장고에 있는 거라곤 군것질거리들 뿐이잖아. 거기에 케이크랑 초코릿 쿠키밖에 없잖아! 다 갖다 버릴 거지?
Mathew		It's low-calorie things.
Mathew		저열량 식품들이야.
Mathew's Sister		Low cal. No, it's not low-cal. Look right here. Mathew! All the food you've got in here are cake and chocolate ice cream with a lot of sugar.
Mathew 누나		저열량. 아니, 저열량이 아니야. 여기 좀 봐. Mathew! 여기 네가 가진 음식이라곤 설탕이 엄청나게 들어간 케이크랑 초콜릿 아이스크림뿐이야.
Mathew		Well, what else, what else?
Mathew		그래, 또 뭐, 또 뭐가 있는데?
Mathew's Sister		Also, what else are you eating? I mean, seriously. All you eat is ice cream? Oh, oh, oh. Look in your trash. You go to Burger King every day. Every day you're eating fast food? Okay, you got to <u>cut out</u> the fast food. When you know the manger of Burger King by name, and he's your best <u>buddy</u> on Facebook, you know that you're going to Burger King or any fast food place too much.
Mathew 누나		또 뭐 먹고 있어? 진심으로. 너 아이스크림만 먹어? 오, 오, 오. 쓰레기 통 안에 좀 봐. 너 Burger King 매일 가는구나. 너 매일 패스트푸드 먹어? 알겠어, 너 패스트푸드 <u>차단해야</u> 해... 너 Burger King 매니저 이름까지 알고, 그 사람이 Facebook에서도 <u>친구</u>면, 네가 Burger King이나 다른 패스트푸드점에 얼마나 많이 가겠어.
Mathew		Uh, this is going to be <u>tough</u>.
Mathew		어, 그건 <u>힘들</u> 것 같은데.
Mathew's Sister		Yeah. It probably will be. But you also need to eat a lot of fresh fruits and vegetables, <u>cut way back</u> on sugar. No more sugary drinks like those five gallons

Mathew 누나	of Coke you drink every day. 그래. 아마 그럴 거야. 하지만 신선한 과일이랑 채소들도 많이 먹어야 해 그리고 설탕 섭취를 **대폭 줄여.** 더 이상, 네가 매일 마시는 5갤런 콜라처럼 설탕 많이 든 음료수는 그만 마셔.
Mathew Mathew	I don't drink five gallons. 나 5갤런씩 마시진 않아.
Mathew's Sister	Close enough. Look at the size of those cups! How many times do you refill them? You even drink Coke when you get up in the morning. Normally, people drink water.
Mathew 누나	거의 그렇지. 저 컵들 크기 좀 봐! 몇 번이나 저걸 리필하니? 심지어 아침에 일어나서도 콜라 마시지. 보통 사람들은 물을 마셔.
Mathew Mathew	You mean I should drink water instead of Coke? 콜라 대신에 물을 마셔야 한단 얘기야?
Mathew's Sister	Yes! Drinking water every day is so important. Not only does it make your body healthy, but also it helps your skin stop from drying. I mean it's good for both your body and your skin. You're worried about the pimples on your cheeks. Just drink water! Then who knows the pimples will be gone away?
Mathew 누나	그래! 매일 물 마시는 거 진짜 중요해. 몸을 건강하게 해줄 뿐 아니라, 피부가 건조해지는 것도 막아줘. 몸에도 피부에도 좋다는 뜻이야. 너 볼에 여드름 난 거 걱정하지. 일단 물을 마셔! 여드름이 다 없어질지 누가 알아?
Mathew Mathew	Oh, it sounds interesting. 오, 그건 흥미로운데?
Mathew's Sister	Sure thing! But I bet it will be a lot more effective to lose weight than the Zero Diet.
Mathew 누나	당연하지! 근데, Zero 다이어트보다 살 빼는데 훨씬 더 효과적일 거라고 확신해.

Vocabulary and Sample Sentences

어휘 그리고 예제 문장들

단어	의 미
blunt (adjective) direct	직설적인 (형용사) 직접적인 **예문** Ashley is always very blunt about her feelings towards other people. Ashley는 항상 다른 사람들에게 그녀의 감정에 대해서 직설적이다.
fatso (noun) fat or heavy (not polite)	뚱뚱보 (명사) 뚱뚱하거나 육중한 (정중하지 않은) **예문** Kids at school always used to call me fatso. It was a hard time in my life. 학교에 아이들은 항상 나를 뚱뚱보라고 부르곤 했다. 내 인생에서 힘든 시간이었다.
scam (verb; also noun) to cheat or deceive someone	사기 (동사; 또는 명사) 다른 사람을 속이거나 사기 치는 것 **예문** A few dishonest companies scam people into buying things they don't need. 부정직한 몇 회사들은 사람들에게 필요하지 않은 물건들을 팔아서 사기 친다.
portion (noun) amount of food, serving	양 (명사) 음식의 양, 인분 **예문** I sometimes overeat at this restaurant because their portions are very generous. 이 식당의 양이 후해서, 나는 여기서 가끔 과식한다.

단어	의미
load up (verb) fill	가득 싣다, 가득 쌓다 (동사) 채우다 **예문** I know this is an all-you-can-eat restaurant, but you don't have to load up on all those fatty foods. 나는 여기가 양껏 먹을 수 있는 식당이라는 것을 안다. 하지만 너는 저 모든 지방이 많은 음식으로 가득 쌓을 필요는 없다.〉 그 기름진 음식들을 많이 먹을 필요가 없다.

단어	의미
cut out (verb) stop or remove	차단하다 (동사) 중단하거나 제거하다 **예문** If you want to really lose weight, you need to cut out the cakes and cookies after every meal. 만일 네가 정말 체중을 감량하고 싶다면, 매 식사 후에 쿠키와 케이크 먹는 것을 중단할 필요가 있다.

단어	의미
buddy (noun) close friend	친구 (명사) 가까운 친구 **예문** You and your buddy drink way too much soda with your meals. 너와 너의 친구는 식사 때마다 탄산음료를 너무 많이 마신다.

단어	의미
tough (adjective) difficult	힘든 (형용사) 어려운 **예문** It's sometimes tough not to overeat during the holidays. 명절 동안 과식을 하지 않는 것이 어려울 때도 있다.

단어	의미
cut back on something (idiom) reduce the amount of something	어떤 것을 줄이다 (숙어) 어떤 것의 양을 줄이다 **예문** You should cut back on soda and drink water instead. 음료수를 줄이고 대신에 물을 마셔야 해.

정답 01. (a)   02. (b)   03. (a)   04. (c)   05. (a)   06. (b)   07. (d)

01

영어문제

According to the conversation, where did Mathew find information about the Zero Diet?

(a) He found out about the Zero Diet from his junk mail.
(b) His friends told him about the Zero Diet.
(c) He visited the hospital and a doctor prescribed him the Zero Diet.
(d) His girl friend told him about the Zero Diet.

문제 한글 해석

대화에 의하면, Mathew는 어디에서 Zero Diet에 관련된 정보를 얻었는가?

(a) 그의 스팸 메일에서 Zero Diet에 관련된 정보를 찾았다.
(b) 그의 친구들이 Zero Diet에 대해서 알려주었다.
(c) 그가 병원에 방문했을 때 의사가 Zero Diet을 처방해주었다.
(d) 그의 여자친구가 Zero Diet에 대해 말해주었다.

문제해설

Peter가 Zero Diet을 하고 있고 이 다이어트에 대한 정보를 스팸 메일함에서 찾았다는 것을 알 수 있다.

> Oh, yeah, well, to be honest, uh... I started changing my life...yesterday. I'm on the Zero Diet. I found information about it in my junk mail the other day...

02

영어문제

How much does the Zero Diet cost?

(a) It costs half of Matthew's salary.
(b) It requires $650.
(c) Zero Diet doesn't cost any money.
(d) It costs $750.

문제 한글 해석

Zero Diet를 하는 데 얼마나 드는가?

(a) Matthew 월급의 절반이다.
(b) 650불이 든다.
(c) 돈이 들지 않는다.
(d) 750불이 든다.

문제해설

Peter가 누나에게 Zero Diet을 하고 있고 그것이 650달러 밖에 들지 않는다고 말한다는 것을 알 수 있다.

> You're serious? Six hundred and fifty bucks? Like every month or every week or..?

03 영어문제 | 문제 한글 해석

What does the OMAD diet stand for?

(a) One Meal A Day diet
(b) One Meal At Dinner diet
(c) One Morning A Day diet
(d) One Mango At Dinner

OMAD 다이어트는 무엇의 약자인가?

(a) 하루 한 끼 다이어트
(b) 저녁 한 끼 식사 다이어트
(c) 하루아침 한 끼 다이어트
(d) 저녁 식사때 망고 하나

문제해설

Matthew가 누나에게 OMAD 다이어트가 하루에 한 끼만 먹는 다이어트라고 말한다.

> Oh, I was also thinking about the OMAD diet! It means one meal a day diet. So I can eat just once a day.

04 영어문제 | 문제 한글 해석

What is Mathew's sister's reaction to the OMAD diet?

(a) She believes he can be succeeded.
(b) She tells him that the OMAD diet is dangerous.
(c) She thinks he can't manage it.
(d) She shows no reaction to it.

OMAD diet에 대한 Matthew 누나의 반응은 어떠한가?

(a) 그녀는 그가 성공하리라 생각한다.
(b) 그녀는 그에게 OMAD diet는 위험한 것이라고 말한다.
(c) 그녀는 그가 해내지 못하리라 생각한다.
(d) 그녀는 반응을 보이지 않는다.

문제해설

Matthew의 누나가 Matthew에게 하루에 한 끼만 먹을 수 있는지 물어본다. 누나는 Matthew가 OMAD 다이어트 성공을 할 수 없으리라 생각한다.

> Umm… I've known you for about 18 years, and I'm sure you can't manage it. Eating just once a day? You?

05 영어문제 | 문제 한글 해석

What does Mathew's sister suggest as an alternative for the OMAD diet?

(a) to eat smaller portions and good, well-balanced breakfast
(b) to not get stressed and consume food as much as Matthew wants
(c) to eat as usual
(d) to eat smaller portions of breakfast only

Matthew의 누나는 OMAD diet 대신 무엇을 제안했는가?

(a) 소량의 음식 섭취, 균형이 잘 잡힌 아침 식사를 하는 것
(b) Matthew가 스트레스받지 않고 Matthew가 원하는 만큼 먹는 것
(c) 원래 식사하던 대로 먹는 것
(d) 소량의 아침 식사만 하는 것

문제해설

Matthew의 누나가 Matthew에게 식이요법을 제안한다. Matthew의 누나가 음식을 소량만 먹고, 영양분이 균형에 잡힌 아침 식사를 해야 한다고 말하고 있다는 것을 알 수 있다. 그리고 하루 종일 더 적은 식사를 하라고 말한다. Matthew의 누나는 아침을 건너뛰면 점심과 저녁 식사 때 과식을 하고 군것질도 많이 해서 보충하겠다고 느끼게 될 것이라고 말한다.

> Mathew! That won't help. Next Oh yeah. So, first of all, smaller portions Then, you need to make sure you eat a good, well-balanced breakfast first thing in the morning and then you follow that up with smaller meals throughout the day, cause, you know what? If you skip breakfast, then throughout the day, you feel like you need to make up for it by overeating at lunch and dinner and lots of snacks.

06 영어문제 | 문제 한글 해석

Apart from the suggestion above, what does Mathew's sister suggest as dietary habits?

(a) to get a bigger plate
(b) to eat a lot of fresh fruits and vegetables
(c) to consume lots of sugary food
(d) to drink lots of milk

위의 내용 이외에 Matthew의 누나는 식습관으로 무엇을 제안했는가?

(a) 더 큰 접시를 얻는 것
(b) 다량의 신선한 과일과 채소를 섭취하기
(c) 설탕이 든 식품 많이 섭취하기
(d) 우유를 많이 마시기

문제해설

Matthew의 누나가 Matthew에게 신선한 과일과 채소들을 많이 섭취하고 설탕 섭취를 대폭 줄이라고 말한다는 것을 알 수 있다.

> But you also need to eat a lot of fresh fruits and vegetables, cut way back on sugar. No more sugary drinks like those five gallons of Coke you drink every day.

07 영어문제 | 문제 한글 해석

What did Matthew's sister mention as an importance of drinking water?

(a) because drinking water gives energy
(b) because water breaks down calories
(c) because water helps to digest food
(d) because drinking water makes the body healthy

Matthew의 누나가 식수의 중요성으로 언급한 것은?

(a) 물 마시는 것은 몸에 에너지를 주기 때문에
(b) 물이 칼로리를 분해하기 때문에
(c) 물이 소화 시키는 데에 도움이 되기 때문에
(d) 물 섭취는 몸을 건강하게 해주기 때문에

문제해설

Matthew의 누나가 Matthew에게 물을 마시는 것은 몸을 건강하게 해줄 뿐만 아니라 피부가 건조해지는 것을 방지하는 데 도움이 될 것이라고 말을 해주고 있다. 볼에 난 여드름이 사라질 수도 있다고 말한다.

> Yes! Drinking water every day is so important. Not only does it make your body healthy, but also it helps your skin stop from drying. I mean it's good for both your body and you skin. You're worried about the pimples on your cheeks. Just drink water! Then who knows the pimples will be gone away?

 문제를 잘 듣고 받아쓰기 연습을 미리 해보세요.

기억하세요! 3단어가 넘어가면 안 됩니다.

1.

2.

3.

4.

5.

6.

Part 2. You will hear a speech. First you will hear questions 1 through 6. Then you will hear the talk. Choose the best answer to each question in the time provided.

01

(a) It provides a chance for children to be able to observe and appreciate nature.
(b) It improves their social skills.
(c) It is good for children's motor development, brain development, and emotional development.
(d) It is an easy access to a natural playground without time or budget constraint

02

(a) by reducing blood pressure, heart rate, and muscle tension
(b) by increasing heart rate, which helps with blood circulation
(c) by providing fresh air so you would feel easy to breathe
(d) by increasing blood pressure, heart rate, and muscle tension

03

(a) Families can save money for food.
(b) The culinary garden provides a chance for families to spend time together.
(c) Children can see the fruits of labor.
(d) Children will learn how to make some foods themselves.

04

(a) a sense of responsibility and propriety
(b) a sense of guiltiness
(c) a sense of amazement
(d) a sense of happiness

05

(a) a few friends to build a natural playground together
(b) good weather for creating a natural playground
(c) a space like a sandbox and a corner of your garden plot
(d) time to build a natural playground

06

(a) to find a space to create a natural playground
(b) to gather friends to build a natural playground together
(c) to organize timetable to efficiently create a natural playground
(d) to provide activities and tools like children sized garden implements

스크립트 해석

Creating a natural playground 자연 놀이터 만들기

Children love to play outside. According to some studies, spending time in nature is good for children. That's why there are more and more natural playgrounds around you like at parks, school, and more.
아이들은 밖에서 노는 것을 좋아합니다. 몇몇 연구에 따르면, 자연 속에서 시간을 보내는 것은 아이들에게 좋습니다. 그래서 공원, 학교 등 주변에 자연 놀이터가 점점 많아지는 것입니다.

And there are more benefits when children play in a natural playground. Let's say there is the maze in a natural playground. Children have to collaborate with each other to go through the maze. It improves their social skills. And in the middle of the maze, they can get lost or face some obstacles.
그리고 아이들이 자연 놀이터에서 노는 데에는 더 많은 장점이 있습니다. 자연 놀이터에 미로가 있다고 생각해봅시다. 아이들은 미로를 빠져나가기 위해서 서로 협력해야 합니다. 이는 아이들의 사회성을 향상시킵니다. 그리고 미로의 중간에서 아이들은 길을 잃기도 하고 장애물을 마주하기도 합니다.

In those circumstances, they should gather together and struggle to solve the problems. It makes them learn problem-solving skills. In the end, they can feel a sense of accomplishment.
그러한 상황들에서 아이들은 서로 모여 문제들을 해결하기 위해 애써야 합니다. 이것이 문제 해결 기술을 배우도록 합니다. 결국에 그들은 성취감을 느낄 수 있지요.

And, do you know that being in nature can reduce blood pressure, heart rate, muscle tension, too? It even relieves stress and increases pleasant feelings. Exposure to nature makes you feel better not only emotionally but also physically.
그리고 자연에 있는 것이 혈압과 심장 박동 수를 낮추고 근육의 긴장을 풀어준다는 사실을 알고 있나요? 심지어는 스트레스를 완화 시키고 즐거운 감정을 높여줍니다. 자연에 노출되면 정서적으로뿐만 아니라 육체적으로도 기분이 좋아집니다.

You can create your own natural playground. Creating a natural playground is a wonderful way to expose your child to the fascinating world of dirt, plants, bugs and other living and natural things.
여러분은 자신만의 자연 놀이터를 창조해낼 수 있습니다. 자연 놀이터를 만드는 것은 자녀들이 흙, 식물, 벌레 그리고 다른 생물과 자연적인 것들의 매력적인 세계를 **접하게 하는** 훌륭한 방법입니다.

A garden playground for kids will also provide an endlessly entertaining and versatile play area that keeps kids outside in fresh air and active.
정원 놀이터는 아이들이 야외에서 상쾌한 공기를 마시면서 활동성을 유지할 수 있도록 끝없이 재미있고 **다재다능한** 놀이 공간을 마련해줍니다.

Encouraging nature play starts by involving children in outdoor activities and fostering their natural curiosity. A garden playground for kids hits all the marks and is an activity zone that they can enjoy on a daily basis. Kids like to do projects like planting seeds, building forts and mazes, or helping to create habitat for both wild and domestic animals.
자연에서 노는 것을 장려하는 것은 아이들을 야외활동에 참여시키고 그들의 자연스러운 호기심을 **기르는** 것에서 시작됩니다. 아이들을 위한 정원 놀이터는 모든 목표를 달성하고 아이들이 매일 즐길 수 있는 활동 구역입니다. 아이들은 씨앗 심기, **요새**나 미로 짓기나, 야생이나 가축 동물들을 위한 서식지를 만드는 것을 돕는 과제를 좋아합니다.

Their endless curiosity about everything around them encompasses the wild spaces that are not manipulated and are completely natural. Children get maximum sensory experiences when exposed to nature and their wide-eyed take on the outdoors is always individual and unique.
주변의 모든 것에 대한 그들의 끝없는 호기심은 인위적이지 않고 완전히 자연적인 야생 공간까지 **아우릅니다**. 아이들은 자연을 접할 때 최대한의 감각 경험을 하며, 야외 활동에 대한 그들의 순수한 견해는 항상 개성 있고 독특합니다.

Learning how to build a garden playground can help impart a love of this planet along with a sense of ownership and responsibility. It can be something as simple as a small space in the backyard that is turned over to the child to develop in whatever way suits him or her or as a planned space with set activities that utilize the child's skills and asks them to cultivate the area within a curriculum.
정원 놀이터 짓기를 배우는 것은 소유감과 책임감과 함께 지구에 대한 사랑을 **전하도록** 도울 수 있습니다. 정원 놀이터는 아이에게 맞는 어떤 방법으로든 발전시키기 위해 주어진 정원의 작은 공간처럼 간단한 것이 될 수도 있고, 아이들의 능력을 **활용하고** 교육과정 내에서의 특정 분야를 함양시키도록 요구하는 정해진 활동으로 계획된 공간처럼 간단할 수도 있습니다.

Public parks have great programs from which you can draw that emphasize learning and nature in a hands-on manner. "how to build a garden playground" is so much more than monkey bars and a slide, although these can be incorporated into the design.
공원에는 **직접적인** 방식으로 자연과 학습을 강조하는 훌륭한 프로그램이 있답니다. 아무리 놀이터의 놀이기구들이 디자인적으로 만들어졌어도, "정원 놀이터 짓기"는 정글짐이나 미끄럼틀보다 더 의미가 있습니다.

A child's outdoor space is also a classroom and should provide stimuli in the forms of sight, sound, touch, and even taste. A culinary garden planted and tended by a child allows him or her to see the fruits of their labor and develop an appreciation for where their food comes from and how it is grown.
아이에게 야외 공간도 교실이므로 시각, 청각, 촉각 그리고 심지어는 미각의 형태로 **자극**을 주어야 합니다. 아이가 심고 가꾸는 **요리** 정원은 아이들이 노력의 결실을 보고 식자재가 어디서 오고 어떻게 자라는지에 대한 고마움을 키워줍니다.

Paths, mazes and special forts open the space to such imaginary places as a pirate's den or even a princess' tower. Water features, such as ponds, can hold fish which give the child a sense of responsibility and propriety as they tend to their aquatic friends.
길, 미로, 그리고 특별한 **요새**들은 해적 **소굴**이나 심지어는 공주가 사는 탑과 같은 가상의 공간들에 대한 여지를 열어줍니다. 연못과 같은 물놀이 시설은 아이들에게 책임감을 줄 수 있는 물고기의 어항이 될 수 있고 아이들은 물속 친구를 돌보면서 예절을 키웁니다.

Creating a natural playground can encompass all or just a few of these types of spaces. The key is to allow the child to mold the space into something he or she can enjoy and appreciate. Providing some tools will enhance a garden playground for kids and involve them in garden activities.
자연 놀이터를 만드는 것은 이러한 공간들을 아우를 수 있습니다. 핵심은 아이들이 그 공간을 자신이 즐기고 감상할 수 있는 공간으로 **만들도록** 하는 것입니다. 몇 가지 도구를 제공하는 것은 정원 놀이터를 개선하고 아이들을 야외활동에 참여시킵니다.

The first thing you will need is a space. It may be the sand box, a corner of your garden plot, a secret garden in the landscape, or any other outdoor area that can capture the imagination.
가장 먼저 필요한 것은 공간입니다. 이 공간은 모래 상자, 정원 터의 귀퉁이, 풍경 속의 비밀 정원 혹은 상상력을 사로잡을 수 있는 어떤 야외 장소도 될 수 있습니다.

Next, provide activities and tools. These may be child sized garden implements, a bug catching kit, sketch pads and other art supplies, standard outdoor toys, boxes and crates, and anything that can have a function if applied to the imagination.
다음으로는 활동과 도구를 제공하세요. 이는 아이들 크기에 맞는 정원 **도구**, 벌레 잡기 세트, 스케치북 및 미술용품이나 일반적인 야외용 장난감과 상자 그리고 상상력을 발휘하는데 기능할 수 있는 어떤 것이든지 좋습니다.

Ideally, the space should have plenty of seasonal change or the ability to adapt to its user's wishes. Including vegetation and perhaps animals only enhances the space and amps up the interest level of the space.
이상적으로, 그 공간은 계절적 변화나 사용자의 요구에 **적응할** 수 있는 능력이 충분해야 합니다. **식물** 그리고 아마 동물을 포함하는 것이 장소의 **가치를 높여주고** 공간에 대한 흥미를 증가 시켜 줍니다.

One of the simpler but more magical ways to create a garden playground is by planting sunflowers. Children can help plant, care for and watch these monstrous plants as they grow. The area then becomes a maze of color and the possibilities for play are endless.
정원 놀이터를 만드는 더 단순하나 마법과 같은 방법 중 하나는 해바라기를 심는 것입니다. 아이들은 그 **거대한** 식물들을 심는 것을 돕고, 돌보고 그것이 자람에 따라 자라나는 걸 볼 수 있습니다. 그 공간은 색의 미로가 되고 놀이를 위한 가능성은 무궁무진해집니다.

Vocabulary and Sample Sentences

어휘 그리고 예제 문장들

단어	의미
expose (verb) to show something that is usually covered or hidden	노출 시키다, 드러내다 (동사) 보통 덮여 있거나 감춰진 것을 보여 주다 **예문** He has been careful not to <u>expose</u> his own weaknesses to the public for 10 years. 그는 10년 동안 대중에게 자신의 약점을 <u>드러내지</u> 않기 위해 조심해왔다.
versatile (adjective) having many different uses	다재다능한, 다용도의, 다목적의 (형용사) 많은 다양한 용도를 갖는 **예문** Eggs are healthy to eat as it contains a lot of protein and it is <u>versatile</u> as well in that it can be used in many different foods. 달걀은 많은 단백질을 함유하고 있어서 먹기에 건강하고 많은 다양한 음식에 사용될 수 있다는 점에서 <u>다용도</u> 식품이다.
foster (verb) to help a skill, feeling, idea etc develop over a period of time	증진하다, 기르다, 발전시키다 (동사) 일정 기간 동안 기술, 의견, 생각 등이 발달 되도록 도와주다 **예문** The union's aim is to <u>foster</u> better relationship between the members and achieve their annual goal. 이 조합의 목표는 구성원들 간의 더 나은 관계를 <u>증진 시키고</u> 그들의 연간 목표 달성을 목표로 한다.

단어	의 미
fort (noun) a strong building or group of buildings used by soldiers or an army for defending an important place	요새, 보루 (명사) 중요한 장소를 방어하기 위해서 군대나 부대에서 사용되는 튼튼한 건물이나 건물들의 집단 **예문** This region was used as an important fort 100 years ago. So, many people visit the fort as a sightseeing spot 이 지역은 100년 전에 중요한 요새로 사용되었다. 그래서 많은 사람이 관광 장소로 이 요새를 방문한다.
encompass (verb) 1. to include a wide range of ideas, subjects, etc 2. to completely cover or surround something	망라하다, 아우르다 (동사) 1. 넓은 범위의 생각이나 주제를 포함한다. 2. 어떤 것을 에워싸거나 완전히 덮다. **예문** Mia got a new job, which asks her to encompass many responsibilities. Mia는 많은 책임감을 아우르도록 요구하는 새로운 직장이 생겼다.
impart (verb) to give a particular quality to something	전하다, 주다 (동사) 어떤 것에 특정한 자질(격)을 주다 **예문** I want to meet you today as I have many things to impart to you about the events that have happened recently. 최근에 발생했던 사건들에 대해 전해드릴 것이 많아 오늘 만나고 싶습니다.
utilize (verb) to use something for a particular purpose	이용하다, 활용하다 (동사) 특정한 목적을 위해서 어떤 것을 사용한다. **예문** More people started to utilize solar radiation to protect the environment and live the sustainable life. 더 많은 사람이 환경을 보호하고 지속 가능한 삶을 살기 위해서 태양열을 이용하기 시작했다.

단어	의미
hands-on (adjective) doing something yourself rather than just talking about it or telling other people to do it	직접 해 보는, 실천하는, 직접적인 (형용사) 다른 사람이 하도록 하거나 어떤 것에 대해 말만 하기보다는 당신 스스로 직접 해 보는 **예문** Julie is still in the third year of college, but she applied for the internship program so that she can have more hands-on experience. Julie는 아직 대학교 3학년에 재학 중이지만 더 직접적인 경험을 할 수 있도록 인턴십 프로그램에 지원했다.

단어	의미
stimuli (noun) a plural form of stimulus; something that helps a process to develop more quickly or more strongly	자극, 자극제 (명사) stimulus의 복수 형태; 어떤 과정이 더 빠르고 강력하게 진전되도록 도와주는 것 **예문** Reading a book can provide children with creative ideas and stimuli for play. 책을 읽는 것은 아이들에게 창의적인 사고를 제공하고 놀이를 위한 자극을 줄 수 있다.

단어	의미
culinary (adjective) relating to cooking	요리의, 음식의 (형용사) 요리와 관련된 **예문** The restaurant CEO hires Ellen as a top chef as she has a high culinary skills and knowledge. 그 레스토랑의 최고 경영자는 Ellen이 요리 실력과 지식이 뛰어나 수석 요리사로 고용했다.

단어	의미
den (noun) a place where secret or illegal activities take place	소굴, 굴 (명사) 비밀이나 비합법적인 활동들이 발생하는 장소 **예문** This desolate building seems to be used as the den for the thieves 이 황량한 건물은 도둑들을 위한 소굴로 사용되는 것 같다.

단어	의미
mold (verb) to shape a soft substance by pressing or rolling it or by putting it into a mould	**형성하다, ~을 틀에 넣어 만들다** (동사) 누르거나 굴리거나 주형에 무언가를 넣음으로써 부드러운 모양을 형성하다 **예문** For her art project, Jin molds clay into animal shape. As it is highly demanding work, her father helps her mold the clay. Jin은 미술 과제를 위해서, 점토를 주형틀에 넣어서 동물 모양을 만들었다. 고강도의 작업이었기 때문에, 그녀의 아빠는 그녀가 점토를 주형틀에 넣는 데 도움을 주었다.
implement (noun) a tool, especially one used for outdoor physical work	**도구** (명사) 도구, 특히 야외 육체노동을 위해 사용되는 것 **예문** Some children find it difficult to hold their writing implements. 몇몇 아이들은 필기도구를 잡는 것을 어려워한다.
adapt to (verb) to gradually change your behaviour and attitudes in order to be successful in a new situation	**~에 적응하다** (동사) 새로운 환경에서 성공하기 위해서 태도와 행동을 점진적으로 바꾸다 **예문** Jenny moved to USA when she was young because of her father's work. It took many years for her to adapt to new environment and culture. Jenny는 아빠의 직장 때문에 어렸을 때 미국으로 이주했다. 그녀가 새로운 환경과 문화에 적응하는 데 많은 시간이 걸렸다.
vegetation (noun) plants in general	**초목, 식물** (명사) 전반적인 식물들 **예문** Jake's job is to study about vegetation, so he spends most of the time in the laboratory or green house Jake의 직업은 식물을 연구하는 것이어서, 대부분의 시간을 연구실이나 온실에서 보낸다.

단어	의미
enhance (verb) to improve something	**높이다, 향상시키다** (동사) 어떤 것을 향상시키다. **예문** To <u>enhance</u> the quality and taste of the food, the restaurant CEO decided to hire many more top chefs. 음식의 맛과 질을 <u>향상시키기</u> 위해서, 그 레스토랑의 최고 경영자는 더 많은 수석 요리사들을 고용하기로 했다.

단어	의미
monstrous (adjective) very wrong, immoral, or unfair	**거대한, 가공할, 도저히 말도 안 되는, 부조리한** (형용사) 매우 잘못된, 비도덕적인, 혹은 불공정한 **예문** Jim committed a <u>monstrous</u> crime, so he was arrested by the police after he ran away for a while. Jim은 <u>부조리한</u> 범죄를 저질렀기 때문에 잠시 도망친 뒤 경찰에 체포됐다.

정답 01. (b)　02. (a)　03. (c)　04. (a)　05. (c)　06. (d)

01

영어문제

What are the benefits of children playing in a natural playground?

(a) It provides a chance for children to be able to observe and appreciate nature.
(b) It improves their social skills.
(c) It is good for children's motor development, brain development, and emotional development.
(d) It is an easy access to a natural playground without time or budget constraint

문제 한글 해석

아이들이 자연 놀이터에서 노는 것의 장점은 무엇인가?
(a) 아이들에게 자연을 관찰하고 감상할 기회를 준다.
(b) 그들의 사회성을 향상시킨다.
(c) 아이들의 기능 발달, 두뇌 발달, 정서적 발달에 좋다.
(d) 시간이나 돈에 제약되지 않고 쉽게 자연 놀이터에 접근할 수 있다.

문제해설

아이들은 미로를 빠져나가기 위해서 서로 협력해야 하고 이는 아이들의 사회성을 향상시킨다. 그리고 미로의 중간에서 아이들은 길을 잃기도 하고 장애물을 마주하기도 하는데 그러한 상황들에서 아이들은 서로 모여서 문제들을 해결하기 위해 애쓴다는 것을 알 수 있다.

> Children have to collaborate with each other to go through the maze. It improves their social skills. And in the middle of the maze, they can get lost or face some obstacles. In those circumstances, they should gather together and struggle to solve the problems.

02

영어문제

Based on the talk, how can exposure to nature make you feel better physically?

(a) by reducing blood pressure, heart rate, and muscle tension
(b) by increasing heart rate, which helps with blood circulation
(c) by providing fresh air so you would feel easy to breathe
(d) by increasing blood pressure, heart rate, and muscle tension

문제 한글 해석

대화에 의하면, 자연에 노출되면 어떻게 육체적으로 기분을 낫게 해주는가?
(a) 혈압과 심장 박동 수를 낮추고 근육의 긴장을 풀어줌으로써
(b) 혈액순환에 도움이 되도록 심장 박동 수를 올림으로써
(c) 숨쉬기 쉽도록 신선한 공기를 공급함으로써
(d) 혈압과 심장 박동 수를 올리고 근육의 긴장을 증가시킴으로써

문제해설

자연 안에 있는 것이 혈압과 심장 박동 수를 낮추고 근육의 긴장을 풀어준다는 사실을 알고 있는지 묻는다. 자연 안에 있는 것이 심지어는 스트레스를 완화 시키고 즐거운 감정을 높여준다고 한다. 자연에의 노출은 정서적으로뿐 아니라 육체적으로도 당신의 기분을 더 낫게 해준다고 한다.

> And, do you know that being in nature can reduce blood pressure, heart rate, muscle tension, too? It even relieves stress and increases pleasant feelings. Exposure to nature makes you feel better not only emotionally but also physically.

03 영어문제

According to the speaker, what is good about the culinary garden?

(a) Families can save money for food.
(b) The culinary garden provides a chance for families to spend time together.
(c) Children can see the fruits of labor.
(d) Children will learn how to make some foods themselves.

문제 한글 해석

화자에 따르면, 요리 정원은 무엇이 좋은가?

(a) 가족들은 식비를 절약할 수 있다.
(b) 요리 정원은 가족들이 함께 시간을 보내는 기회를 제공한다.
(c) 아이들이 그들의 노동에 대한 결실을 볼 수 있다.
(d) 아이들은 몇가지 음식들을 스스로 만드는 법을 배울 것이다.

문제해설

아이에 의해 만들어지고 보살펴지는 요리 정원은 아이들이 그들의 노동에 대한 결실을 보고 식자재가 어디서 오고 어떻게 자라는지에 대한 고마움을 키워준다.

A child's outdoor space is also a classroom and should provide stimuli in the forms of sight, sound, touch, and even taste. A culinary garden planted and tended by a child allows him or her to see the fruits of their labor and develop an appreciation for where their food comes from and how it is grown.

04 영어문제

What sense of feeling do water features, such as ponds, bring?

(a) a sense of responsibility and propriety
(b) a sense of guiltiness
(c) a sense of amazement
(d) a sense of happiness.

문제 한글 해석

연못과 같은 인공 폭포는 어떤 감정을 불러오는가?

(a) 책임감과 예절
(b) 죄책감
(c) 놀라움
(d) 행복감

문제해설

연못과 같은 인공 폭포는 아이들에게 책임감을 줄 수 있는 물고기의 어항이 될 수 있고 아이들은 물속 친구를 돌보면서 예절을 키운다.

Paths, mazes and special forts open the space to such imaginary places as a pirate's den or even a princess' tower. Water features, such as ponds, can hold fish which give the child a sense of responsibility and propriety as they tend to their aquatic friends.

05 영어문제

What is the first thing you need for creating a natural playground?
(a) a few friends to build a natural playground together
(b) good weather for creating a natural playground
(c) a space like a sandbox and a corner of your garden plot
(d) time to build a natural playground

문제 한글 해석

자연 놀이터를 만들기 위해 가장 먼저 필요한 것은 무엇인가?
(a) 함께 자연 놀이터를 만들 친구 몇 명
(b) 자연 놀이터를 만들 좋은 날씨
(c) 모래 상자와 정원 터의 귀퉁이와 같은 공간
(d) 자연 놀이터를 지을 시간

문제해설

가장 먼저 필요한 것은 공간이다. 이 공간은 모래 상자, 정원 터의 귀퉁이, 주변의 비밀 정원 혹은 상상력을 사로잡을 수 있는 어떤 야외 장소도 될 수 있다.

> The first thing you will need is a space. It may be the sand box, a corner of your garden plot, a secret garden in the landscape, or any other outdoor area that can capture the imagination.

06 영어문제

What is the next thing you need for creating a natural playground?
(a) to find a space to create a natural playground
(b) to gather friends to build a natural playground together
(c) to organize timetable to efficiently create a natural playground
(d) to provide activities and tools like children sized garden implements

문제 한글 해석

자연 놀이터를 만들기 위해 그 다음으로 필요한 것은 무엇인가?
(a) 자연 놀이터를 짓기 위한 장소를 찾기
(b) 함께 자연 놀이터를 지을 친구 몇 명을 모으기
(c) 자연 놀이터를 효율적으로 조성하기 위한 시간표 구성
(d) 아이들 크기에 맞는 정원 도구와 같은 활동 및 도구를 제공하는 것

문제해설

활동과 도구를 제공하라고 나와 있다. 아이들 크기만 한 정원 도구, 벌레 잡기 세트, 스케치북, 그리고 다른 미술용품이나 일반적인 야외용 장난감과 상자 그리고 상상력을 발휘하는데 기능할 수 있는 어떤 것이든 괜찮다는 것을 알 수 있다.

> Next, provide activities and tools. These may be child sized garden implements, a bug catching kit, sketch pads and other art supplies, standard outdoor toys, boxes and crates, and anything that could have a function if applied to the imagination.

 **문제를 잘 듣고 받아쓰기 연습을 미리 해보세요.**

기억하세요! 3단어가 넘어가면 안 됩니다.

1.
2.
3.
4.
5.
6.
7.

Part 3. You will hear a conversation between two people. First you will hear questions 1 through 7. Then you will hear the conversation. Choose the best answer to each question in the time provided.

01

(a) to pay him back his money
(b) to borrow a few bucks because he has no money available
(c) to give assistance for moving house
(d) to check if his budget plan is efficient

02

(a) because of his parents
(b) because of his colleagues
(c) because of his occupation
(d) because of competitions

03

(a) understandable because having a nice view at home is pleasing
(b) not understandable because Gary could find a cheaper place outside the downtown
(c) She thinks he is saving much money by living his apartment.
(d) She believes the amount of money that Gary spends is reasonable.

04

(a) He usually goes out to eat.
(b) He likes cooking, and he invites his friends home to dine together.
(c) He is lazy to cook, so he buys some microwaveable meals.
(d) He seldom eats.

05

(a) He spends too much money on drinks.
(b) He spends a little money for cooking class.
(c) He spends a lot of money on baseball, basketball, and soccer tickets.
(d) Instead of spending money on entertainment, he saves money for the future.

06

(a) on foot
(b) by his sports car
(c) by public bus
(d) by subway

07

(a) to buy her expensive things
(b) to request Gary to buy a house
(c) to save money for his future
(d) to buy himself a nice suit

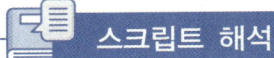

Budget Planner 예산 계획표

Gary Uh, could I borrow a few bucks until payday? I'm a little strapped for cash.
Gary 저기, 월급날까지 몇 달러만 빌릴 수 있을까? 나 약간 돈에 쪼들려서.

Julie Uh, yeah, I guess, but I'm pinching pennies myself, and you still owe me $30 from last week. And mom and your friend Tom said you borrowed money from them this past week. How are things going anyway?
Julie 아, 그래, 아마도. 근데 나 요새 절약하고 있거든. 그리고 너 지난주에 30달러 빌린 것도 아직 안 갚았어. 그리고 엄마랑 네 친구 Tom이 근래 몇 주에 네가 돈 빌렸다고 그러던데. 어쨌든, 요새 어때?

Gary Well, not very well. To be honest, I'm really in the hole, and I can't seem to make ends meet these days.
Gary 뭐, 좋진 않아. 솔직히 말해서, 나 완전히 적자야. 요새는 입에 겨우 풀칠이나 하는 것 같아.

Julie What do you mean? I thought you landed a great job recently, so you must be loaded.
Julie 무슨 소리야? 너 최근에 괜찮은 직장 구해서, 돈 많을 거로 생각했는데.

Gary Well, I do have a job, but I need to buy a lot of things like suits, shoes, ties, and bags for my work. As I'm a sales person, it's important how I look. And it helps me gain trust from my clients. So, I've used my credit cards to pay off those things recently, but now, I can't seem to pay the money off.
Gary 그래, 직업은 있지. 근데 일 때문에 정장, 신발, 넥타이, 그리고 가방 같은 거 다 사야 해. 내가 판매원이라서, 어떻게 보이는지가 중요해. 고객들한테 신뢰를 얻는 데 도움이 된다고. 그래서 최근에 그거 다 갚느라고 신용카드 썼어. 근데 이제는 감당이 안 될 것 같아.

Julie Uh, I understand, but don't you have a budget? I mean, how do you keep track of your income and expenses?
Julie 그래, 이해는 하지만 예산이 없어? 수입이랑 지출을 어떻게 기록하니?

Gary Well, when my money runs out, I come to you. Of course. No, but I guess I should have some financial plan.
Gary 뭐, 돈이 다 떨어지면, 누나한테 가지. 물론. 아니, 근데 나 재정 계획을 세워야 할 것 같긴 해.

Julie Well, let me see if I can help you. How much money do you spend on your apartment?
Julie 음, 내가 도울 수 있는지 좀 보자. 너 아파트에 얼마나 쓰니?

Gary Uh, I pay $910 on rent for the studio apartment downtown near my company... including utilities and cable TV. But the place has an awesome view of the city.

Gary 어, 회사 근처 시내에 있는 원룸 아파트에 집세로 910달러 내... **공과금**이랑 유선 TV 포함해서. 위치는 시내 전경이 보여서 멋지지.

Julie Uh, $910! Why are you paying through the nose for such a small place when you could find a cheaper one somewhere outside the downtown area? And, you barely stay at home except when you sleep at night, don't you? You're always busy hanging around after work with your friends. I don't think you need that awesome view.

Julie 910달러라고! 시내에서 좀만 나가면 더 저렴한 곳도 찾을 수 있을 텐데 왜 그 작은 데를 **바가지를 쓰고** 지내? 너 밤에 잘 때 빼고는 집에 거의 있지도 않잖아, 안 그래? 일 끝나면 친구들이랑 어울린다고 항상 바쁘잖아. 그렇게 멋진 전망도 필요 없을 것 같은데.

Gary Yeah, I guess.

Gary 응, 그러네.

Julie Okay. How much money do you spend on food a month?

Julie 그래. 한 달에 식비로는 얼마나 쓰니?

Gary Hmmm. I'm not really sure. I think I spend around $550. Well, I go out to eat almost every day, so those expenses add up. I just don't enjoy eating alone, and I don't have a knack for cooking like you do. And when I eat out, I can save a lot of time. That's because I don't need to go to the grocery stores to buy things and clear things after cooking. I think that's really time-consuming.

Gary 음... 진짜 확실하지가 않아. 내 생각에 550달러 정도 써. 뭐, 거의 매일 나가서 먹으니까, 그렇게 지출하는 게 조금씩 늘어나지. 혼자 밥 먹는 거 즐기지 않을 뿐더러, 누나처럼 요리에 **재주**도 없어. 나가서 먹으면 시간도 많이 절약돼. 재료들 사러 식료품점에 안 가도 되고 요리하고 안 치워도 되고. 진짜 시간 많이 걸리잖아.

Julie Well, I can understand that, but perhaps you can buy some microwaveable meals you could prepare at home in a very short time.

Julie 그래. 이해할 수 있지만, 집에서 짧은 시간에 준비할 수 있는 전자레인지 조리 식품 좀 살 수 있잖아.

Gary Well, I guess I could.

Gary 뭐, 그럴 수 있겠네.

Julie And entertainment?

Julie 그리고 여흥비는?

Gary Well, I spend a few dollars here and there. I think I spend a lot on baseball, basketball, and soccer tickets. As you know, I'm a big fan of sports. Umm... What else... Oh, I sometimes go to a movie or a concert. And I signed up for yoga and swimming classes this month. All of them are just for fun. I need those things to relieve my stress from work. So, don't tell me to stop those things.

Gary 뭐, 여기저기서 몇 달러씩 쓰지. 야구, 농구, 그리고 축구표 사는데 많이 쓰는 것 같아. 알잖아, 나 스포츠 열혈 팬 인거. 음... 또 뭐가 있을까. 오, 가끔 영화나 콘서트도 보러 가. 그리고 이번 달에는 요가와 수영 강좌도 등록했어. 그것들 모두 재미를 위해서야. 일하면서 받는 스트레스 풀려면 그런 게 좀 필요해. 그러니까 하지 말라고 하지 마.

Julie Uh, OK, but exactly how much do you spend on all of these? Just a "few" dollars?
Julie 어. 그래. 근데 이것들 다 하는데, 정확히 얼마나 쓰는데? 그냥 "몇" 달러야?

Gary Well, oh... about $500 or so.
Gary 뭐, 오... 대략 500달러 정도?

Julie How can you spend that much money on only those things?
Julie 고작 그거 하는데 그렇게 많은 돈을 쓴다고?

Gary Oh, I forgot to say about parties. I host parties almost every Friday at home. And when I host a party, I have to prepare food, drinks, fruits, dessert and many things... That means I have to spend a lot of money.
Gary 오, 파티 얘기하는 거 깜빡했다. 나 집에서 매주 금요일마다 파티 열어. 그리고 파티 열 때, 음식, 음료, 과일, 후식 같은 거 준비해야 해. 그러니까 돈이 많이 들어간단 얘기지.

Julie No wonder you're having money problems. You can't just <u>blow your money on</u> things like that! And what about transportation? Oh, you don't spend on that. Because you just moved near your company. That's not bad.
Julie 돈 문제가 있는 게 당연하네. 너 그렇게 <u>돈을 펑펑 쓰면</u> 안 돼! 그러면, 교통비는 어떤데? 아, 교통비에는 돈 안 쓰겠구나. 회사 근처로 막 이사 왔으니까. 나쁘지 않네.

Gary Oh, No. I <u>commute</u> to work every day in my new sports car, but I got a great deal, and my monthly payments are only $550. Come outside and take a look. We can go for a spin!
Gary 아니지. 나 새로 산 스포츠카 타고 매일 <u>출퇴근하는</u>데, 나 완전 싸게 잘 샀어. 매달 내는 돈이 550달러밖에 안 해. 밖에 나와서 봐봐. 우리 드라이브 갔다 오자.

Julie No way! You don't need a car. And you always said you don't want to have a car. What made you change your mind? It's because of your girlfriend?
Julie 말도 안 돼! 너 차 필요 없잖아. 그리고 너 차 없어도 된다고 항상 말했잖아. 뭐 때문에 마음이 바뀐 거야? 네 여자친구 때문이야?

Gary To be honest, yes. At first, she wanted me to buy her expensive things. So, I just bought some famous designer bags, coats, shoes, and so on. And one day, she said that she wanted me to buy a sports car. I was kind of forced to buy it. You know. I just wanted to make her happy. I know I was an idiot.

Gary 솔직히 말해서, 그래. 처음에는 여자친구가 비싼 것들 사달라고 했어. 그래서 나는 그냥 유명한 디자이너 가방, 코트, 신발 같은 것들 좀 사줬지. 그러다가 어느 날, 내가 스포츠카 샀으면 좋겠다고 말하더라고. 그래서 뭐 약간 억지로 산거지. 알잖아. 나는 그냥 여자친구 행복하게 해주고 싶었어. 내가 바보였단 거 알아.

Julie So, it works? I mean she is happier now?

Julie 그래서, 효과가 있었어? 내 말은 그녀가 지금 더 행복하대?

Gary No... We just broke up a few days ago. I don't know. She has another boyfriend now. I saw some photos on her Instagram.

Gary 아니... 며칠 전에 깨졌어. 나도 모르겠어. 지금 다른 남자친구 생겼더라고. 인스타그램에서 사진 봤어.

Julie I'm so sorry to hear that. It doesn't make any sense. But you've seriously got to curb your spending, or you'll end up broke. I suggest you get rid of your credit cards, cut back on your entertainment expenses, and sell your car. Take public transportation from now on.

Julie 유감이다 정말. 납득이 안 가. 근데, 너 심각하게 지출을 **제한해야** 해, 안 그러면 결국에는 너 빈털터리 될 거야. 너 신용카드들 좀 없애고, 유흥에 쓰는 지출은 좀 줄이고 차는 파는 게 어떨까 싶은데. 앞으로는 대중교통 이용해.

Gary Sell the car? But I need it to meet someone else. I can't date without a car. What am I going to say? "Uh, could you meet me downtown at the bus stop at 7:00?" Come on!

Gary 차를 팔라고? 나 근데 다른 사람 만나려면 차 필요한데. 차 없이는 데이트 못 해. 뭐라고 말해? "어, 7시에 시내에 있는 버스 정류장에서 만날까요?" 제발!

Julie How dare you think about going on a date with someone? You're in trouble with money. Anyway, you need to create a budget for yourself and stick to it, and start with paying off your bills, starting with me. You owe me 65 dollars.

Julie 감히 누구와 데이트할 생각을 하니? 너 지금 돈 문제 있어. 어쨌든, 너는 스스로 예산을 세우고 지켜야 할 필요가 있어. 그리고 빚진 거 갚는 것부터 시작하자. 내 거부터. 너 나한테 65달러 빚졌어.

Gary Fifty dollars! Wait, I only borrowed $30 from you last week. How did you come up with $65?

Gary 50달러잖아! 기다려봐. 나 지난주에 누나한테 30달러밖에 안 빌렸어. 어떻게 65달러가 된 거야?

Julie Financial consulting fees. My advice is at least worth $35!

Julie 재정 상담 수수료. 내 충고가 적어도 35달러는 되겠다.

Vocabulary and Sample Sentences

어휘 그리고 예제 문장들

단어	의 미
buck (noun) dollar	달러 (명사) 달러 **예문** Could you load me a buck or two until tomorrow? 내일까지 1, 2 달러만 빌려줄 수 있어?
be strapped for cash (idiom) have no money available	돈에 쪼들리다 (숙어) 쓸 수 있는 돈이 없다 **예문** He has really been strapped for cash because he lost his job two weeks ago. 그는 2주 전에 직장을 잃었기 때문에 돈에 쪼들려 왔다.
pinch pennies (idiom) be careful with money	절약하다, 최대한 아끼다 (숙어) 돈을 쓰는데 주의하다 **예문** That young couple had to pinch pennies, so they can live. 저 젊은 커플은 그들이 살 수 있도록 돈을 절약해야 했다.
in the hole (idiom) in debt	적자로, 빚을 져서 (숙어) 빚을 진 **예문** My brother has charged so some many purchases to his credit cards that he's is the hole. 내 남동생은 신용카드로 너무 많이 사서 빚을 진 상태이다.

단어	의미
make ends meet (idiom) make enough money to live	수지타산을 맞추다, 먹고 살다 (숙어) 살기에 충분한 돈을 벌다 **예문** When I was a student, I had to work three part-time jobs to make ends meet. 학생 때는 먹고살기 위해 세 개의 아르바이트를 해야 했다.

단어	의미
land (verb) find	차지하다, 획득하다, 구하다 (동사) 찾다 **예문** I need to land a good job where I can earn a lot of money. 나는 많은 돈을 벌 수 있는 좋은 직장을 얻어야 한다.

단어	의미
be loaded (adjective) having a lot of money	돈이 많은, 아주 부자인 (형용사) 많은 돈을 가지고 있는 **예문** Don't let him borrow money off you because, in reality, he's loaded. His rich parents give him $2,500 in spending money a month! 그가 너에게 돈을 빌리게 하지 마라, 왜냐하면 실제로 그는 돈이 많다. 그의 부유한 부모님이 한 달에 2,500달러를 주신다.

단어	의미
budget (noun) a financial plan of expenses and income	예산 (명사) 지출과 수입의 재정 계획 **예문** You should create a budget of your expenses. 너는 너의 지출예산을 작성해야 한다.

단어	의미
keep track of (idiom) keep a record of	기록하다 (숙어) 기록에 남기다 **예문** Any business should keep track of its earnings. 어떤 사업이든 소득을 기록해야 한다.

단어	의미
run out (phrasal verb) use up or exhaust	다 써버리다 (구동사) 다 써버리거나 소진하다 **예문** If you don't keep a budget, you might run out of money before your next paycheck. 만약에 예산을 세우지 않는다면, 다음 월급 전에 돈을 다 써버릴지도 모른다.

단어	의미
utilities (noun) services provided by gas, power, and water companies	공익사업 (명사) 가스, 전기, 그리고 수도 회사가 제공하는 서비스 **예문** The rent for this apartment includes the cost of utilities. 이 아파트의 임대료는 공과금을 포함한다.

단어	의미
pay through the nose (idiom) pay an excessive amount of money	크게 바가지를 쓰다, 터무니없이 많은 돈을 주다 (숙어) 과도한 금액을 지불하다 **예문** Car insurance is so expensive that you have to pay through the nose to get any type of coverage these days. 자동차 보험은 너무 비싸서 요새 어떤 보험을 들든지 간에 많은 돈을 지불해야 한다.

단어	의미
knack (noun) a special way or ability of doing something	**재주, 요령** (명사) 어떤 일을 하는 특별한 방법이나 능력 **예문** My mother has a real knack for saving money on her low salary. 어머니는 적은 월급으로 돈을 저축하는 데 정말 재주가 있다.
blow (verb) spend thoughtlessly or wastefully; throw away	**(돈을) 펑펑 쓰다, 날리다** (동사) 생각 없이 혹은 사치스럽게 돈을 쓰다; 허비하다 **예문** People sometimes blow money on things that have no lasting value. 사람들은 때때로 지속적인 가치가 없는 것들에 돈을 펑펑 쓴다.
commute (verb) travel back and forth between work and home	**통근하다** (동사) 직장과 집 사이를 왔다 갔다 하다 **예문** I commute by bus every day. 나는 매일 버스를 타고 출퇴근한다.
curb (verb) lessen or reduce	**제한하다** (동사) 줄이거나 낮추다 **예문** Unless you curb your spending, you're going to run out of money before the week is over. 지출을 제한하지 않는다면, 이번 주가 끝나기 전에 돈이 바닥날 것이다.

정답 01. (b) 02. (c) 03. (b) 04. (a) 05. (c) 06. (b) 07. (a)

01

영어문제

What is Gary asking of Julie and why?
(a) to pay him back his money
(b) to borrow a few bucks because he has no money available
(c) to give assistance for moving house
(d) to check if his budget plan is efficient

문제 한글 해석

Gary가 Julie에게 어떤 것을 무엇 때문에 요구하는가?
(a) 그의 돈을 돌려줄 것
(b) 그는 돈이 없기 때문에 돈을 조금 빌리기
(c) 이사할 때 도와주기
(d) 그의 예산 계획이 효율적인지 체크하기

문제해설

Gary는 월급날 전까지 돈을 빌려도 되는지 묻고 있다. 그는 돈에 쪼들린다고 말한다.

> Uh, could I borrow a few bucks until payday? I'm a little strapped for cash. To be honest, I'm really in the hole, and I can't seem to make ends meet these days.

02

영어문제

According to Gary, why is it important to look good?
(a) because of his parents
(b) because of his colleagues
(c) because of his occupation
(d) because of competitions

문제 한글 해석

Gary에 의하면, 왜 멋지게 보이는 것이 중요한가?
(a) 그의 부모님들 때문에
(b) 그의 동료들 때문에
(c) 그의 직업 때문에
(d) 그의 경쟁자들 때문에

문제해설

Gary는 판매원이기 때문에 겉으로 보이는 모습이 중요하다라고 설명하고 있다.

> Well, I do have a job, but I need to buy a lot of things like suits, shoes, ties, and bags for my work. As I'm a sales person, it's important how I look.

03 영어문제 | 문제 한글 해석

What does Julie think about the amount of money that Gary spends on his apartment?

(a) understandable because having a nice view at home is pleasing
(b) not understandable because Gary could find a cheaper place outside the downtown
(c) She thinks he is saving much money by living his apartment.
(d) She believes the amount of money that Gary spends is reasonable.

Gary가 그의 아파트에 지출하는 금액에 대해서 Julie는 어떻게 생각하는가?

(a) 좋은 전망이 있는 집에 있는 것은 즐거운 일이기 때문에 이해할 수 있다.
(b) Gary가 시내 밖에 있는 곳에 더 싼 집들을 알아볼 수 있기 때문에 이해할 수 없다.
(c) 그녀는 그가 그의 아파트에 살고 있음으로 많은 돈을 절약한다고 생각한다.
(d) 그녀는 그가 집에 쓰는 돈이 합리적이라고 생각한다.

문제해설

Gary가 시내 밖에 있는 곳에 더 싼 집들을 알아볼 수 있는데 왜 작은 장소에 터무니없이 많은 돈을 주냐고 묻는다. Gary가 집에서 전망을 즐길 만큼 많은 시간이 없기 때문에 Julie는 Gary가 그렇게 좋은 전망의 집이 필요가 없다고 생각한다.

> Uh, $910! Why are you paying through the nose for such a small place when you could find a cheaper one somewhere outside of the downtown area? And, you barely stay at home except when you sleep at night, don't you? You're always busy hanging around after work with your friends. I don't think you need that awesome view.

04 영어문제 | 문제 한글 해석

Based on the talk, how does Gary eat meals?

(a) He usually goes out to eat.
(b) He likes cooking, and he invites his friends home to dine together.
(c) He is lazy to cook, so he buys some microwaveable meals.
(d) He seldom eats.

이야기에 따르면, Gary는 어떻게 식사를 하는가?

(a) 그는 보통 밖에서 식사를 해결한다.
(b) 그는 요리하기를 좋아하고 친구들을 집에 불러 함께 식사한다.
(c) 그는 요리하기 귀찮아서 전자레인지로 요리할 수 있는 음식들을 구매한다.
(d) 그는 거의 식사를 하지 않는다.

문제해설

Gary는 식사에 550달러 정도를 쓴다. 거의 매일 나가서 먹기 때문에 지출이 늘어난다. 그는 혼자 먹는 것을 즐기지 않고 요리하는 것에 재주가 없다. 나가서 먹으면 시간을 많이 절약할 수 있다고 말한다.

> Hmmm. I'm not really sure. I think I spend around $550. Well, I go out to eat almost every day, so those expenses add up. I just don't enjoy eating alone, and I don't have a knack for cooking like you do. And when I eat out, I can save a lot of time.

05 영어문제 | 문제 한글 해석

How much does Gary spend for entertainment?

(a) He spends too much money on drinks.
(b) He spends a little money for cooking class.
(c) He spends a lot of money on baseball, basketball, and soccer tickets.
(d) Instead of spending money on entertainment, he saves money for the future.

Gary는 유흥비로 얼마를 지출하는가?

(a) 그는 음주에 너무 많은 돈을 지출한다.
(b) 그는 요리 수업에 약간의 돈을 지출한다.
(c) 그는 야구, 농구, 축구 티켓을 구매하는데 상당한 돈을 지출한다.
(d) 유흥비에 지출하는 대신 미래를 위해 돈을 저축한다.

문제해설

Gary는 유흥비에 여기저기 몇 달러씩 지출한다. 그가 생각하기에 야구, 농구, 축구 티켓에 많은 돈을 지출한다. 그가 운동 광팬이기 때문이다. 가끔은 영화나 콘서트를 보러 나가기도 한다. 또한 이번 달에는 요가와 수영 레슨을 신청했다고 한다.

> Well, I spend a few dollars here and there. I think I spend a lot on baseball, basketball, and soccer tickets. As you know, I'm a big fan of sports. Umm... What else... Oh, I sometimes go to a movie or a concert. And I signed up for yoga and swimming classes this month. There are for fun.

06 영어문제 | 문제 한글 해석

How does Gary commute to work?

(a) on foot
(b) by his sports car
(c) by public bus
(d) by subway

Gary는 직장까지 어떻게 통근하는가?

(a) 걸어서
(b) 그의 스포츠카로
(c) 대중 버스로
(d) 지하철로

문제해설

Gary는 새로운 스포츠카를 타고 출퇴근한다.

> Oh, No. I commute to work every day in my new sports car, but I got a great deal, and my monthly payments are only $550. Come outside and take a look. We can go for a spin!

07 영어문제

What did Gary's ex-girlfriend ask him to do?

(a) to buy her expensive things
(b) to request Gary to buy a house
(c) to save money for his future
(d) to buy himself a nice suit

문제 한글 해석

Gary의 전 여자 친구는 그에게 무엇을 하라고 하였는가?

(a) 그녀에게 비싼 것들을 사주는 것
(b) 집을 사달라는 것
(c) 미래를 위해 돈을 저축하는 것
(d) 좋은 정장을 사 입는 것

문제해설

Gary의 전 여자 친구는 비싼 것을 사줄 것을 원했다고 한다. 그래서 유명한 디자이너 가방, 코트, 신발과 같은 것들을 샀다고 한다. 어느 날 그녀는 그가 스포츠카를 사길 바란다고 말해서 어느 정도 강제로 사게 되었다.

> To be honest, yes. At first, she wanted me to buy her expensive things. So, I just bought some famous designer bags, coats, shoes, and so on. And one day, she said that she wanted me to buy a sports car. I was kind of forced to buy it. You know. I just wanted to make her happy. I know I was an idiot.

 **문제를 잘 듣고 받아쓰기 연습을 미리 해보세요.**

기억하세요! 3단어가 넘어가면 안 됩니다.

1.
2.
3.
4.
5.
6.

Part 4. You will hear a lecturer talking to a group of people. First you will hear questions 1 through 6. Then you will hear the talk. Choose the best answer to each question in the time provided.

01
(a) the homelessness
(b) the gender-gap
(c) the child labor abuse
(d) the aging society

02
(a) criminal records
(b) a traumatic event such as a natural disaster that damages or destroys a family's home
(c) a disappearance from home
(d) no motivation to find a job to afford a house

03
(a) All homeless people suffer from mental health issues.
(b) In the United States, half of the women who are homeless suffer from sexual abuse.
(c) All the victims suffer from domestic violence.
(d) In the United States, over half a million people are homeless, with about a third of those being children.

04
(a) Most of the homeless people had a house, but they lost it due to fraud.
(b) About one of five people suffer from a mental health issue.
(c) Around a quarter of the homeless are employed, but the cost of living is beyond their means and current income.
(d) More than a quarter of the homeless are unemployed, and they have no income to live.

05
(a) by inviting a homeless man to join for dinner
(b) by donating money for the homeless in the restaurant.
(c) by giving the man a scarf that she was wearing
(d) by giving the homeless man a room in her house

06
(a) The speaker wishes to show off people how great he and his wife are.
(b) He wants to say that we can make a small difference.
(c) The speaker wants to encourage people to donate money.
(d) He wants his audiences to understand how lucky they are.

스크립트 해석

Homelessness 노숙자

Today I'd like to talk about a social issue that we tend to ignore. What do you think about homelessness? It is a concern in almost every place you go around the world. However, we often don't think much about it unless it touches our lives in a personal way.

오늘, 저는 우리가 간과하기 쉬운 사회적 문제에 관한 이야기를 하고 싶습니다. 여러분은 노숙자에 대해서 어떻게 생각하시나요? 이는 여러분이 세계 곳곳을 돌아다니는 거의 모든 곳에서의 걱정거리입니다. 하지만, 노숙자 문제가 여러분의 삶에 개인적으로 미치지 않는다면, 이것에 대해 별로 생각하지 않곤 합니다.

Unfortunately, as human beings, we often come up with overly-simplistic reasons why some people do not have their own house to live. Why do they live on the streets or in homeless shelters? I guess most of you would take this question too lightly.

유감스럽게도, 인간으로서, 우리는 종종 어떤 사람들은 살기 위한 자신의 집을 왜 가지지 않는지에 대해 지나치게 단순한 이유를 떠올리곤 합니다. 왜 그들은 길이나 노숙자 쉼터에서 사는 걸까요? 여러분 대부분은 이 질문을 너무 가볍게 여길 거라 생각합니다.

This **perception** often limits our abilities to have real compassion for others. Actually, there are some other reasons including loss of employment, poverty, mental illness, substance abuse, and so on. Also, a **traumatic** event such as a natural disaster that damages or destroys a family's home can be the reason.

이러한 **인식**은 종종 다른 사람들에 대해 진정한 연민을 가지는 우리의 능력을 제한합니다. 실제로, 실업, 가난, 정신질환, 약물 남용 등을 포함한 몇 가지 다른 이유들이 있습니다. 또한, 가정을 파괴하거나 피해를 준 자연재해와 같은 **큰 정신적 충격을 준** 사건들이 이유가 될 수 있습니다.

As you can see, the facts on homelessness are **stark**. And I know there are a lot of countries suffering from those problems. But this time, I'm going to discuss the United States where I live.

보시다시피, 노숙자에 대한 현실은 **냉혹합니다**. 그리고 그러한 문제들로 고통받는 많은 나라들이 있다는 것을 압니다. 하지만 이번에 저는 제가 살고 있는 미국에 관해 이야기할 것입니다.

Which city has the most homeless people in the USA? It is the capital city, Washington, D.C. It has 103.3 homeless per 10,000 people. Boston follows at 101.8, New York at 101.5, San Francisco at 94.3 and Santa Rosa in California at 59.8.

미국에서 어떤 도시에 노숙자들이 가장 많을까요? 바로 수도인 워싱턴 DC입니다. 워싱턴에는 10,000명당 103.3명의 노숙자가 있습니다. 보스턴이 101.8명으로 그 뒤를 따르고, 뉴욕은 101.5명, 샌프란시스코는 94.3명, 그리고 캘리포니아주의 산타 로사는 59.8명의 노숙자가 있습니다.

Then, let's take a closer look.
Number one, in just the United States alone, over half a million people are homeless, with about a third of those being children.
Number two, about one of five people suffer from a mental health issue.

자, 더 자세히 살펴봅시다.
첫 번째, 미국 내에서만, 50만 이상이 노숙자이고 그 중, 3분의 1은 아이들입니다.
두 번째, 5명 중 약 1명꼴로 정신건강 문제로 고통 받고 있습니다.

Number three, about half of women who are homeless have been the victims of domestic abuse. And number four, around a quarter of the homeless are employed, but, unfortunately, the cost of living for many people is just beyond their means and current income.
세 번째, 노숙자 여성들의 절반은 **가정 내** 폭력의 피해자입니다.
그리고 네 번째, 노숙자의 약 4분의 1은 직업이 있지만, 불행히도 많은 이들의 생활비가 그들의 재산과 현 수입을 능가합니다.

Of course, I understand that people may feel uncomfortable in helping the homeless. But there are a number of things that we can do to alleviate the pain and suffering of those who are in desperate need of help. We can make their lives more comfortable and even save their lives! Even though it is a small help, it will be absolutely fine.
물론, 사람들이 노숙자들을 돕는 데에 불편함을 느낀다는 것은 이해합니다. 하지만, **필사적으로** 도움이 필요한 사람들의 고통과 괴로움을 **완화하기** 위해서 우리가 할 수 있는 일은 여러 가지가 있습니다. 우리는 그들의 삶을 더 편하게 만들 수 있고 심지어는 그들의 목숨을 살릴 수도 있습니다! 작은 도움이라도 물론 괜찮습니다.

For me, I just assume that people need help, and I give it to them. I try not to assume that a person's plight has been self-inflicted every time. One time, my wife and I were about to enter a restaurant when a homeless man approached us for money.
저는 사람들이 도움이 필요하다고 생각하고, 그들에게 도움을 줍니다. 저는 한 사람의 **역경**이 항상 본인이 자초한 것은 아니라고 생각하려 합니다. 한 번은, 제 아내와 같이 식당에 들어가려는데 한 노숙자가 접근해서 돈을 요구한 적이 있습니다.

Trying to set aside any prejudice or preconceived feeling about his intentions, my wife simply invited him to join us for dinner. As it turned out, it was a nice evening. The man shared with us his hopes and dreams, and when our meal was over, we expressed well wishes to him and went home, not really knowing if he had a home to return to as well.
그 사람의 **의도**에 대한 **선입견적인** 감정이나 **편견**은 제치려고 노력하며, 저의 아내는 그저 우리와 함께 저녁 식사를 하도록 그를 초대했습니다. 결론적으로, 훌륭한 저녁 식사였습니다. 그 남자는 우리에게 그의 희망과 꿈을 공유했고 식사가 끝났을 때, 우리는 그에게 염원을 표하고 그에게도 돌아갈 집이 있는지는 알지 못한 채 집으로 갔습니다.

To conclude, my intention in telling this story isn't to show how great we were for helping the man. I just want to show that other people serve humbly and anonymously in far greater ways than we do, and I realize that there have been times that I haven't been compassionate as I could have been.
결론적으로, 이 이야기를 하는 제 의도는 저와 제 아내가 그 남자를 도와준 것에 대해 얼마나 훌륭했는지를 말하려는 것이 아닙니다. 저는 그저 다른 사람들은 저희보다 훨씬 더 훌륭한 방법으로 겸손하게 **익명으로** 도움을 준다는 것을 알려주고 싶습니다. 그리고 제가 할 수 있었던 것처럼 자비롭지 못했던 순간들이 있었다는 것을 실감하게 되었습니다.

I know another impressive story about treating a homeless person in a nice way. One day, a famous musician Lady Gaga met a homeless man. He was a fan of her, so he was waiting for her in line with other fans outside of Lady Gaga's hotel. When he saw her, he gave her an engagement ring.

노숙자를 친절하게 대했던 또 다른 감동적인 이야기가 있는데요. 어느 날, 유명한 가수 Lady Gaga는 한 노숙자를 만납니다. 그는 그녀의 팬이었기 때문에 Lady Gaga가 묵었던 호텔 밖에서 다른 팬들과 함께 줄 서서 그녀를 기다리고 있었습니다. 그는 그녀를 보자 그녀에게 약혼반지를 주었습니다.

Many fans who were there said Gaga graciously accepted the ring he gave. And when she approached him to take photos, the homeless man said "But I smell." What she said to him, "Don't worry, I smell too." She gave him a rose in return, and posed for several pictures with him. Isn't it an amazing story?

현장에 있던 많은 팬들은 Gaga가 그가 준 반지를 정중하게 받았다고 말했습니다. 그리고 그녀가 사진을 찍으려고 그에게 다가갔을 때, 그 노숙자는 "하지만 저한테 냄새나는데요." 라고 말했습니다. 그리고 그녀가 그에게 한 말은, "걱정 마요, 저도 냄새나요" 이었습니다. 그녀는 그에게 답례로 장미 한 송이를 주었고 그와 함께 여러 사진을 찍으려고 자세를 취했습니다. 놀라운 이야기 아닌가요?

It shows that we should not have a prejudice against the homeless, and treat them with respect like Lady Gaga did to the man.

What I would like to say through these stories is that we can make a small difference in the small acts of generosity. What we do each day can be helpful to the homeless.

이 이야기는 우리가 노숙자에 대해서 편견을 갖지 말고 Lady Gaga가 그 남자에게 했던 것처럼 그들을 존중해야 한다는 것을 보여줍니다.
이러한 이야기들을 통해 제가 말하고 싶은 것은 작은 관용의 행동으로 작은 변화를 만들 수 있다는 것입니다. 우리가 매일 하는 행동이 노숙자들에게 도움이 될 수 있습니다.

Vocabulary and Sample Sentences

어휘 그리고 예제 문장들

단어	의 미
perception (noun) the way you think about or understand someone or something	인식, 이해, 지각, 생각 (명사) 당신이 어떤 사람이나 사물을 생각하거나 이해하는 방식 We need to change people's perceptions of the homeless to build batter understanding. 우리는 더 나은 이해를 위해 노숙자들에 대한 사람들의 인식을 바꿀 필요가 있다.

단어	의 미
traumatic (adjective) causing someone to become emotionally upset, angry, or hurt	외상성의, 큰 정신적 충격을 준 (형용사) 누군가가 감정적으로 화나고 혼란스럽거나 다치도록 하는 For many youth, living homeless on the streets can be a very traumatic experience. 많은 젊은이들에게 길거리에서 노숙자로 사는 것은 정신적으로 큰 충격을 주는 경험일 수도 있다.

단어	의 미
stark (adjective) a very plain, unpleasant, or difficult to accept	삭막한, 냉혹한, 극명한, 엄격한 (형용사) 받아들이기에 매우 분명하게 불쾌하거나 어려운 Many homeless face the stark reality of living without food and shelter for long periods of time. 많은 노숙자는 장시간 동안 음식이나 주거지가 없는 냉혹한 삶의 현실을 마주하게 됩니다.

단어	의미
domestic (adjective) related to a person's home or family	가정의, 집안의 (형용사) 집이나 가정과 관련된 **예문** Steve wasn't happy at all with his domestic life, so he left home to live on his own. Steve는 그의 가정생활에 전혀 행복하지 않아서 혼자 살기 위해 집을 떠났다.

단어	의미
alleviate (verb) reduce the pain or discomfort of something	완화하다, 편하게 하다 (동사) 어떤 것으로 인한 고통이나 불편함을 줄이다. **예문** What can citizens do to alleviate hunger and poverty? 기근이나 가난을 완화하기 위해서 시민들은 무엇을 할 수 있을까요?

단어	의미
desperate (adjective) very sad or upset and having little hope	절박한, 필사적인, 자포자기의 (형용사) 매우 슬프거나 화난 그리고 희망이 거의 없는 **예문** The holidays are very desperate times for many homeless because they sometimes have no family around to visit. 많은 노숙자에게 휴일은 때때로 주변에 방문할 가족이 없어서 매우 절망적인 시간이다.

단어	의미
plight (noun) a very bad or difficult situation	곤경, 역경, 처지 (명사) 매우 나쁘거나 어려운 상황 **예문** The city needs to do more to address the plight of the homeless in our community. 도시는 우리 지역 사회 노숙자들의 처지를 해결하기 위해서 더 많은 것들을 해야 한다.

단어	의미
prejudice (noun) an unfair feeling of dislike for a person or group because of race, religion, or sexual identity	편견, 선입견 (명사) 인종, 종교 혹은 성 정체성 때문에 개인이나 집단에 대한 불공평한 불호의 감정 **예문** Some people experience prejudice because of the color of their skin. 일부 사람들은 피부색으로 인한 편견을 경험한다.
preconceived (adjective) having an opinion or idea that you form beforehand	미리 생각한, 예상한, 선입견의 (형용사) 당신이 사전에 형성한 의견이나 생각을 가지는 **예문** It is unfortunate that so many people hold a number of preconceived ideas that are just not true about the homeless. 매우 많은 사람이 노숙자들에 대해 사실이 아닌 선입견적인 사고를 많이 가지고 있다는 것은 유감스러운 일이다.
intention (noun) plan or goal	의도, 의향, 의지, 취지 (명사) 계획이나 목표 **예문** What is the city's intention on building a new homeless shelter in the downtown area? Many citizens want to understand the plans better. 시내의 새로운 노숙자 쉼터를 짓는 도시의 취지는 무엇인가요? 많은 시민은 이 계획을 더 잘 이해하고 싶어 합니다.
anonymously (adverb) something done by someone who is not named or identified	익명으로, 특색 없이 (부사) 이름이나 신원을 밝히지 않은 사람에 의해 행해지는 것 **예문** Our family would like to give some food and clothing anonymously. 우리 가족은 익명으로 음식과 옷을 기부하기를 원한다.

정답 01. (a) 02. (b) 03. (d) 04. (c) 05. (a) 06. (b)

01 영어문제

What is the social issue that the speaker addresses?

(a) the homelessness
(b) the gender-gap
(c) the child labor abuse
(d) the aging society

문제 한글 해석

발표자가 연설하는 사회적 문제는 무엇인가?

(a) 노숙자
(b) 성별 격차
(c) 아동 노동 착취
(d) 고령화 사회

문제해설

사회자는 우리가 간과하기 쉬운 사회적 문제에 관한 이야기를 하고 싶어 한다. 노숙자 문제가 청중들의 삶에 개인적으로 영향을 미치지 않는다면, 많이 생각하지 않는다고 문제점을 이야기한다.

> Today I'd like to talk about a social issue that we tend to ignore. Homelessness is a concern in almost every place you go around the world, but we often don't think much about it unless it touches our lives in a personal way.

02 영어문제

What is not an overly-simplistic reason for homelessness mentioned by the speaker?

(a) criminal records
(b) a traumatic event such as a natural disaster that damages or destroys a family's home
(c) a disappearance from home
(d) no motivation to find a job to afford a house

문제 한글 해석

사회자가 말한 노숙 문제에 대해 지나치게 단순화된 이유가 아닌 것은 무엇인가?

(a) 범죄 경력
(b) 가족의 집에 손상을 주거나 파괴하는 자연재해와 같은 외상적 사건
(c) 가출
(d) 집을 살 여유가 될 만한 직업을 찾을 동기 부여가 없는 것

문제해설

우리는 노숙 문제에 대하여 지나치게 단순한 이유를 대고, 이런 인식이 다른 사람들에게 갖는 진짜 연민을 한정시킨다. 이런 이유는 실직, 가족의 집에 손상을 주거나 파괴하는 자연재해와 같은 외상적 사건, 약물 중독과 같은 것들이 포함될 수 있기 때문이다.

> Unfortunately, as human beings, we often come up with overly-simplistic reasons why people live on the streets or in homeless shelters, and this perception often limits our abilities to have real compassion for others. Some reasons can include loss of employment, a traumatic event such as a natural disaster that damages or destroys a family's home and substance abuse, and the list goes on and on.

03 영어문제 | 문제 한글 해석

According to the speech, what is the first fact mentioned about homelessness?

(a) All homeless people suffer from mental health issues.
(b) In the United States, half of the women who are homeless suffer from sexual abuse.
(c) All the victims suffer from domestic violence.
(d) In the United States, over half a million people are homeless, with about a third of those being children.

연설에 의하면, 노숙에 대해 언급된 첫 번째 사실은 무엇인가?

(a) 모든 노숙인들은 정신 건강 문제로 고통 받는다.
(b) 미국에서 노숙자인 여성 절반은 성적 학대에 시달리고 있다.
(c) 모든 피해자는 가정 내 폭력으로 시달리고 있다.
(d) 미국에서 50만 명이 이상의 사람들은 노숙자이고, 그 중 약 3분의 1은 아이들이다.

문제해설

미국 내에서만, 50만 이상이 노숙자이고 그 중, 3분의 1은 아이들이라고 말하고 있다.

> As you can see, the facts on homelessness are stark. And I know there are a lot of countries suffering from those problems. But this time, I'm going to discuss the United States where I live. Number one, in just the United States alone, over half a million people are homeless, with about a third of those being children.

04 영어문제 | 문제 한글 해석

What is the fourth fact mentioned about homelessness?

(a) Most of the homeless people had a house, but they lost it due to fraud.
(b) About one of five people suffer from a mental health issue.
(c) Around a quarter of the homeless are employed, but the cost of living is beyond their means and current income.
(d) More than a quarter of the homeless are unemployed, and they have no income to live.

노숙에 대해 언급된 네 번째 사실은 무엇인가?

(a) 노숙인 대부분이 집이 있었지만 사기를 당해 집을 잃었다.
(b) 약 5분의 1의 사람들은 정신 건강 문제로 시달리고 있다.
(c) 약 4분의 1의 노숙자들은 취직했지만, 생활비가 그들의 현재 재산과 소득보다 많다.
(d) 노숙자 중 4분의 1 이상이 실업자로 생활할 소득이 없다.

문제해설

노숙자의 약 4분의 1은 직업이 있지만, 불행히도 많은 이들의 생활비가 그들의 재산과 현 수입을 능가한다.

> And number four, around a quarter of the homeless are employed, but, unfortunately, the cost of living for many people is just beyond their means and current income.

05 영어문제 | 문제 한글 해석

How did the speaker's wife help the homeless?

(a) by inviting a homeless man to join for dinner
(b) by donating money for the homeless in the restaurant
(c) by giving the man a scarf that she was wearing
(d) by giving the homeless man a room in her house

연설가의 아내는 그 노숙자를 어떻게 도와주었는가?

(a) 노숙자를 저녁 식사에 초대함으로써
(b) 식당에 있는 노숙자를 위해 돈을 기부함으로써
(c) 그녀가 하고 있던 스카프를 남자에게 줌으로써
(d) 노숙자에게 그녀의 집에 있는 방 한 칸을 줌으로써

문제해설

연설가가 아내와 같이 식당에 들어가려는데 한 노숙자가 접근해서 돈을 요구한 적이 있다고 한다. 그 사람의 의도에 대한 선입견적인 감정이나 편견은 제쳐둔 채, 그와 아내는 그저 함께 저녁 식사를 하도록 그를 초대했다.

One time, my wife and I were about to enter a restaurant when a homeless man approached us for money. Trying to set aside any prejudice or preconceived feeling about his intentions, my wife simply invited him to join us for dinner.

06 영어문제 | 문제 한글 해석

What is the speaker's intention for his story?

(a) The speaker wishes to show off people how great he and his wife are.
(b) He wants to say that we can make a small difference.
(c) The speaker wants to encourage people to donate money.
(d) He wants his audiences to understand how lucky they are.

그의 이야기에 대한 연설자의 의도는 무엇인가?

(a) 연설가는 그와 그의 아내가 얼마나 대단한지 뽐내고 싶어 한다.
(b) 그는 우리가 작은 변화를 만들 수 있다는 것을 말하고 싶어 한다.
(c) 연설자는 사람들에게 돈을 기부하기를 격려하고 싶어 한다.
(d) 그는 그의 관중들이 얼마나 행운인가를 이해하길 원한다.

문제해설

이러한 이야기들을 통해 연설가가 말하고 싶은 것은 작은 관용의 행동으로 작은 변화를 만들 수 있다는 것이다. 우리가 매일 하는 행동이 노숙자들에게 도움이 될 수 있다고 말하고 있다.

What I would like to say through these stories is we can make a small difference in the small acts of generosity. What we do each day can be helpful to the homeless.

 **필수 단어, 표현, 숙어 암기노트**

단어, 표현, 숙어	의미

필수 단어, 표현, 숙어 암기노트

단어, 표현, 숙어	의미

리스닝 만렙을 위한 원포인트 레슨

3

리스닝 섹션에서는 각 파트별로 버리고 가는 문제가 1-2문제씩 있다.

질문 자체가 너무 길거나 전혀 학습이 되어 있지 않은 단어나 표현이 나오는 문제들이 있다. 과감히 1-2문제는 버리고 가라. 그 질문에 집착하다가 바로 이어서 나오는 질문을 2문제까지도 놓치게 된다. 기억하라! 리스닝 섹션은 만점이 목표가 아니다.

SIGNATURE

3 회

 문제를 잘 듣고 받아쓰기 연습을 미리 해보세요.

기억하세요! 3단어가 넘어가면 안 됩니다.

1.
2.
3.
4.
5.
6.
7.

Part 1. You will hear a conversation between two people. First you will hear questions 1 through 7. Then you will hear the conversation. Choose the best answer to each question in the time provided.

01

(a) He cared of his mom because she was also sick.
(b) He couldn't attend her dad's funeral because he was in another country.
(c) He stayed with her to help her go through hard time.
(d) He did nothing because she didn't tell him about her dad's death.

02

(a) because his mom looked healthy when she saw his mom last year
(b) because it has been years since she saw his mom
(c) because when she talked to his mom on the phone, his mom said she was so healthy
(d) because his mom didn't tell anyone that she was sick

03

(a) She had financially prepared for her family.
(b) She had made a will about money for each family member.
(c) She had donated part of her possessions to society.
(d) She had saved a great deal of money to give her husband.

04

(a) about Robert's dad's financial ability
(b) about Robert's dad's health condition
(c) about Robert's dad's emotional state
(d) about the relationship between Robert's dad and them

05

(a) Robert moved to Japan with Florence.
(b) Robert's aunt died.
(c) Florence's dad passed away.
(d) Florence attended Robert's mom's funeral.

06

(a) There will be a private memorial service for the late Robert's mom.
(b) Robert family will gather for an upcoming holiday.
(c) One of Robert's uncles will be giving the eulogy.
(d) Florence will sing a musical number.

07

(a) that Robert would not tell Florence about her death
(b) that Florence would take care of Robert's dad
(c) that Florence would invite her family to a musical
(d) that Florence would sing for her at the funeral

Funerals: Expressing Condolences 장례식 : 조의 표하기

Florence Hi, Robert. I'm really sorry to hear about your mom. My sincerest condolences go out to you and your family. I loved her so much. She was such a kind, beautiful woman. I just want you to know that she will be greatly missed.

Florence Robert 안녕. 어머니 일은 정말 유감이야. 너와 가족 분들에게 진심으로 애도의 뜻을 전해. 너희 어머니 정말 좋아했는데. 친절하시고 아름다운 분이셨어. 너희 어머니가 정말 그리울 거라는 것만 그냥 알아줬으면 좋겠어.

Robert Thank you so much to be here, Florence. How is staying in Japan going? I know it would be a long flight from Japan to California here, but I thought I should let you know about my mom. So I just called you last night and asked you to come... And you know, I really appreciate that you are here.

Robert 이렇게 와줘서 너무 고마워 Florence. 일본에서 지내는 건 어때? 일본에서 캘리포니아까지 오래 걸릴 거란 거 알았는데 너한테 어머니 소식은 전해야 할 것 같았어. 그래서 어젯밤에 전화해서 와달라고 부탁했어. 알지, 네가 여기 와줘서 정말 고마운 거.

Florence Don't say such things. If you had not told me about her, I would have regretted not coming to see her. And whenever I have hard time, you are always with me. Do you remember when my dad passed away? You helped me to go through everything at the time. It was so comforting. Without you, I couldn't have dealt with it. And you know, your mom means a lot to me. She was my best music teacher ever. When I wanted to quit learning music, she was the one who made me keep singing. She taught me not only music but also life lessons. Thanks to her, I'm still singing even now. She was really important to me, so I'm supposed to be here.

Florence 그런 말 마. 어머니 돌아가신 거 말 안 해줬으면 뵈러 오지 못 한 거 후회했을 거야. 그리고 내가 힘들어할 때마다 너는 항상 내 옆에 있어 주잖아. 우리 아버지 돌아가셨을 때 기억나? 그때 네가 하나하나 다 도와줬잖아. 얼마나 위로가 됐다고. 너 아니었으면 못 해냈을 거야. 그리고 알잖아. 너희 어머니가 나한테 얼마나 소중했는지. 내 최고의 음악 선생님이셨어. 내가 음악 배우는 거 관두고 싶었을 때 내가 계속 노래하도록 해주신 분이야. 음악뿐 아니라 인생에 대해서도 가르쳐 주셨어. 어머님 덕분에 아직도 노래하고 있잖아. 나한텐 정말 중요한 분이시니까 내가 여기 있는 게 당연하지.

Robert She also loved you so much. She always talked about you. I was kind of jealous of you. And I can't forget when mom and you sang together. That sounded so beautiful. And you two looked like angels. I wish I could listen to that again. But, it's not possible any more.

Robert 어머니도 너를 정말 많이 좋아하셨어. 항상 네 얘기를 하셨어. 약간 질투까지 났다니깐? 그리고 어머니랑 네가 같이 노래 불렀을 때는 잊을 수가 없어. 정말 아름다웠는데. 어머니랑 너 마치 천사 같았어. 다시 들을 수 있으면 좋을 텐데. 이젠 불가능하겠지.

Florence Of course, I remember. I can't forget that time, either. But you know, it was so unexpected to me. I mean your mom's death. She looked healthy the last time I saw her. It was her birthday last year. We had a party together in her house. And she made every single food for everyone by herself. So I could not expect her death to happen so suddenly.

Florence 당연히 기억하지. 나도 그때는 잊을 수가 없지. 나는 전혀 예상하지 못했어. 그러니까 어머니 돌아가신 거 말이야. 마지막으로 뵀을 때 건강해 보이셨는데. 작년 어머님 생신이었지. 어머니 댁에서 생일파티 했잖아. 손수 음식도 다 만들어주셨는데. 그래서 어머님이 이렇게 갑자기 돌아가실 줄은 예상도 못 했어.

Robert Actually not really for us. Sorry that I could not tell you about this. She had been sick for some time before she passed away, so we were kind of prepared.

Robert 사실 우리한텐 그렇지 않아. 너한테 이 얘기를 못 해서 미안해. 어머니가 **돌아가시기** 얼마 전부터 아프셔서 우리는 어느 정도 마음의 준비가 되어 있었어.

Florence She had? Oh... How long had she been sick? Oh, sorry to hear that... What about your dad? Is he OK? How's your dad taking it?

Florence 아프셨다고? 오. 얼마나 오래 아프셨는데? 오, 유감이야. 아버지는 어떠셔? 괜찮으셔? 잘 견뎌내고 계셔?

Robert Oh, it's been really hard on him. He is struggling to go through it. But, you know it's such a difficult thing. And I don't think you get over something like that.

Robert 어. 아버지한텐 정말 **힘든** 시간이었지. 이겨내려고 노력하고 계셔. 근데 알다시피 정말 힘든 일이잖아. 이런 일은 **극복하기** 어려운 것 같아.

Florence It's sad to hear that. My heart really goes out to him. Uh, then your dad is going to manage things alone? Or somebody else is going to help him?

Florence 그 얘기 들으니 마음이 아프다. 아버님 심정이 정말 이해가 가. 어, 그러면 아버님이 혼자 지내시는 거야? 아니면 누가 도와드리나?

Robert He can handle everything himself. Financially, dad will be able to live a secure life like forever. I mean, Mom had life insurance and substantial investments in property and stocks. She always worried about things after her death. That's why she decided to do such things to make us still have a mortgage, go to college, and afford other big expenses. And returns on those should take care of him. But our main concern at this moment is his emotional state. He's really down. And he can't eat anything these days. That's why we're worried about him a lot. Actually, it has been only 2 months since his sister passed away. He almost broke his heart at that time. And now he let his two beloved women. I don't even dare to imagine how sad he is now. So only thing what I can do for him is to call now and again, and it brightens his day.

Robert 혼자 감당하실 수 있을 거야. 재정적으로는 거의 평생 안정적으로 지낼 수 있으실 거야. 내 말은 어머니가 생명 보험에 들어 놓으시고 부동산이랑 주식에 투자를 많이 하셨거든. 항상 돌아가시고 난 후를 걱정하셨어. 어머님이 그런 결정을 하셔서 우리가 아직도 주택 담보 대출도 있고 대학도 다니고 큰 지출을 감당할 수 있는 거야. 그리고 거기서 나오는 수익으로 아버지가 생활하실 수 있어. 근데 우리가 지금 제일 걱정하는 건 아버지의 감정 상태야. 아버지가 정말 **기운이 없으셔**. 며칠 동안 아무것도 못 드셨어. 그래서 우리가 많이 걱정하는 거야. 사실 아버지 누님이 돌아가신 지도 2달밖에 안 됐거든. 그땐 거의 비탄에 잠겨 계셨어. 이제 사랑했던 두 분이 떠나신 거야. 얼마나 슬프실지 감히 상상도 안 가. 그래서 아버지를 위해서 해드릴 수 있는 거라곤 가끔 전화해서 하루를 즐겁게 해드리는 거야.

Florence It would be the most difficult time for him, I guess. So, how about the funeral arrangements? The obituary in the paper didn't mention much about the funeral.

Florence 아버님에게 가장 힘든 시간일 거야. 그래서 **장례** 절차는 어떻게 돼? 신문 부고에는 장례식에 대해서는 언급이 많이 안 되어 있던데.

Robert Well, some of the family members will gather on Monday morning for a private memorial service. And there will be a viewing in the afternoon from 3:00 to 4:00 p.m., followed by the funeral service. One of my uncles will be giving the eulogy.

Robert 음, 가족들끼리 월요일 아침에 모여서 비공개 추도식 지내려고. 그리고 영결식 이후에 오후 3시에서 4시 사이에 **조문객**을 받을 거야. 삼촌 중 한 분이 **추도 연설**하실 거야.

Florence I already miss her a lot. And I wish there was something I could do for you.

Florence 어머님이 벌써 많이 그립네. 그리고 내가 할 수 있는 게 뭐라도 있었으면 좋겠어.

Robert Well, actually, there is. You know, Mom admired you so much when she was alive. And she asked something before she died. She asked if you'd sing a musical number at the funeral. And it's going to be a great help to relieve our sorrow. I know it could be some burden to you. But if you are fine, I want you to do that for us. What do you say to it?

Robert 음, 사실 있는데. 알지? 어머니 살아생전에 네 칭찬 정말 많이 하신 거. 돌아가시기 전에도 네 얘기 물어보셨어. 네가 장례식에서 뮤지컬 수록곡을 불러줄 수 있는지 물어보셨어. 우리의 슬픔을 위로하는 데 큰 도움이 될 거야. 너한텐 부담이 될 수 있는 거 알아. 근데 너만 괜찮으면 네가 해줬으면 좋겠는데. 어떻게 생각해?

Florence Of course, I can. I'd be a great honor to me. I'm so happy that I can help you this way.

Florence 당연히 할 수 있지. 나한테도 정말 영광이야. 이렇게라도 도울 수 있어서 정말 기뻐.

Robert It would really mean a lot to my family.

Robert 우리 가족에게 정말 큰 힘이 될 거야.

Florence I'll do everything that helps you and your family. Then, see you on Monday.

Florence 너랑 가족 분들 도울 수 있는 건 뭐든지 할게. 그러면 월요일에 보자.

Robert Thank you for everything. Okay, see you then.

Robert 다 고마워. 좋아. 그때 만나.

Vocabulary and Sample Sentences

어휘 그리고 예제 문장들

단어	의미
condolences (noun) expressions of sympathy with another's sadness	애도, 조의 (명사) 누군가의 슬픔에 공감의 표현 **예문** We're sorry to hear about your brother. Please give our condolences to his wife and children. 당신의 동생 소식에 유감입니다. 부디 그의 아내와 아이들에게 우리의 애도를 전해 주세요.
hard (adjective) difficult	힘든 (형용사) 어려운, 힘든 **예문** Greg went through some very hard times after his wife died in a car accident. Greg는 그의 아내가 차 사고로 죽은 후에 힘든 시간을 보냈다.
get over (verb) recover from	극복하다, (불행을) 잊다 (동사) 회복하다, 극복하다 **예문** It took Sarah over a year to get over the loss of her baby. Sarah가 그녀의 아이를 잃은 것을 극복하는 데 1년이 넘게 걸렸습니다.
down (adjective) low in spirits	기운 없는, 풀이 죽은 (형용사) 기운이 없는, 처진 **예문** I'm feeling so down now that I can hardly concentrate on my work. 저는 오늘 기운이 너무 없어서 일에 거의 집중할 수 없어요.

단어	의미
funeral (noun) a ceremony where a person is buried or cremated	장례식 (명사) 사람을 매장하거나 화장하는 의식 **예문** My boss took the day off to attend the funeral of a close friend. 저의 사장님은 가까운 친구의 장례식에 참석하시느라 휴가를 내셨습니다.
viewing (noun) a period before the funeral when family and friends view the dead body and sometimes share memories about the person	조문, 고인과의 대면 (명사) 장례식 전에 가족과 친구들이 고인을 보고 때로는 고인에 대한 추억을 공유하는 시간 **예문** Only the immediate family is invited to attend the viewing. 근친만이 조문에 참석하도록 초대되었습니다.
eulogy (noun) a speech of praise given at a funeral for someone who has recently died	추모 연설 (명사) 최근에 돌아가신 누군가를 위한 장례식에서 주어지는 찬사 연설 **예문** The minister offered the eulogy on behalf of the family. 목사님이 가족을 대신해서 추모 연설을 하셨습니다.

정답 01. (c) 02. (a) 03. (a) 04. (c) 05. (b) 06. (a) 07. (d)

01

영어문제

What did Robert do when Florence's dad passed away?

(a) He cared of his mom because she was also sick.
(b) He couldn't attend her dad's funeral because he was in another country.
(c) He stayed with her to help her go through hard time.
(d) He did nothing because she didn't tell him about her dad's death.

문제 한글 해석

Robert는 Florence의 아빠가 돌아가실 때 무엇을 했는가?

(a) 그는 그의 엄마 또한 아팠기 때문에 그녀를 돌봤다.
(b) 그는 다른 나라에 있었기 때문에 그녀의 아빠 장례식에 참석할 수 없었다.
(c) 그는 그녀가 힘든 시간을 잘 보낼 수 있도록 돕기 위해 그녀 옆에 있었다.
(d) 그는 그녀가 그녀의 아빠의 죽음에 대해서 말하지 않았기 때문에 아무것도 하지 않았다.

문제해설

Robert가 자신의 엄마 장례식에 와줘서 고맙다고 하는 말에, Florence는 그도 자신이 힘들 때마다 자신 옆에 있었다고 말한다. 특히 자신의 아빠가 돌아가셨을 때 그가 그 시간을 견딜 수 있게 도왔다고 이야기하고 있다.

> And whenever I have hard time, you are always with me. Do you remember when my dad passed away? You helped me to go through everything at the time. It was so comforting.

02

영어문제

Why is Robert's mom's death so unexpected to Florence?

(a) because his mom looked healthy when she saw his mom last year
(b) because it has been years since she saw his mom
(c) because when she talked to his mom on the phone, his mom said she was so healthy
(d) because his mom didn't tell anyone that she was sick

문제 한글 해석

Florence에게 Robert의 엄마의 죽음은 왜 예기치 못한 것인가?

(a) 그녀가 그의 엄마를 작년에 봤을 때 그의 엄마는 건강해 보였기 때문에
(b) 그녀가 그의 엄마를 본 지 매우 오래됐기 때문에
(c) 그녀가 그의 엄마와 통화할 때 그의 엄마는 자신이 건강하다고 말했기 때문에
(d) 그의 엄마가 자신이 아팠다는 걸 아무한테도 말하지 않았기 때문에

문제해설

Florence가 Robert의 엄마를 마지막으로 봤던 작년 그녀의 생일 때를 이야기하며, 그때 그녀는 건강해 보였고 그래서 그녀의 죽음이 예기치 못하다고 하고 있다.

> But you know, it is so unexpected to me. I mean your mom's death. She looked healthy the last time I saw her. It was her birthday last year.

03 영어문제 | 문제 한글 해석

What had Robert's mom done when she was alive?

(a) She had financially prepared for her family.
(b) She had made a will about money for each family member.
(c) She had donated part of her possessions to society.
(d) She had saved a great deal of money to give her husband.

Robert의 엄마는 살아생전에 무엇을 해왔는가?

(a) 그녀는 그녀의 가족을 위해 재정적으로 준비를 해왔다.
(b) 그녀는 각 가족 구성원에게 돈에 대한 유언을 써왔다.
(c) 그녀는 그녀의 재산 일부를 사회에 기부해왔다.
(d) 그녀는 그녀의 남편에게 주기 위해 엄청난 돈을 모아 왔다.

문제해설

그녀는 직접 돈을 모으지는 않았지만, 생명 보험을 들고, 상당한 투자를 하면서 자신이 죽고 나서 이후에 가족들이 잘 살 수 있게 재정적으로 준비를 해왔음을 알 수 있다.

> Financially, dad will be able to live a secure life like forever. I mean, Mom had life insurance and substantial investments in property and stocks. She always worried about things after her death. That's why she decided to do such things to make us still have a mortgage, go to college, and afford other big expenses.

04 영어문제 | 문제 한글 해석

What is Robert's family's main concern at the moment?

(a) about Robert's dad's financial ability
(b) about Robert's dad's health condition
(c) about Robert's dad's emotional state
(d) about the relationship between Robert's dad and them

현재 Robert의 가족들의 주요 걱정이 무엇인가?

(a) Robert 아빠의 재정 능력
(b) Robert 아빠의 건강
(c) Robert 아빠의 감정 상태
(d) Robert 아빠와 그들 간의 관계

문제해설

지금 Robert의 가족들은 재정적으로는 Robert의 엄마가 준비를 했기 때문에 걱정이 없지만, 감정 상태가 걱정된다고 이야기하고 있다.

> But our main concern at this moment is his emotional state.

05 영어문제 | 문제 한글 해석

What happened two months ago?

(a) Robert moved to Japan with Florence.
(b) Robert's aunt died.
(c) Florence's dad passed away.
(d) Florence attended Robert's mom's funeral.

2달 전에 무슨 일이 있었는가?

(a) Robert가 Florence와 함께 일본으로 이사 갔다.
(b) Robert의 고모가 돌아가셨다.
(c) Florence의 아빠가 돌아가셨다.
(d) Florence가 Robert의 엄마의 장례식에 참석했다.

문제해설

Robert의 아빠를 지금 더 힘들게 하는 것은 사랑하는 두 사람을 보냈다는 것이다. 한 명은 자신의 아내이고, 한 명은 두 달 전에 그의 누나, 즉 Robert의 고모가 돌아가셨기 때문이다.

> Actually, it has been only 2 months since his sister passed away. He almost broke his heart at that time. And now he let his two beloved women go.

06 영어문제 | 문제 한글 해석

What will happen this Monday morning?

(a) There will be a private memorial service for the late Robert's mom.
(b) Robert family will gather for an upcoming holiday.
(c) One of Robert's uncles will be giving the eulogy.
(d) Florence will sing a musical number.

월요일 아침에 무슨 일이 일어날 것인가?

(a) 고인이 된 Robert의 엄마를 위한 추모식이 있을 것이다.
(b) Robert의 가족이 다가오는 연휴를 위해 모일 것이다.
(c) Robert의 삼촌들 중 한 분이 추도 연설을 할 것이다.
(d) Florence가 뮤지컬 수록곡을 부를 것이다.

문제해설

일부 가족이 월요일 아침에 모여 추모식을 진행할 것을 알 수 있다. 추도 연설이나 Florence가 노래 부르는 것은 월요일 오후에 일어날 일들이다.

> Well, some of the family members will gather on Monday morning for a private memorial service. And there will be a viewing in the afternoon from 3:00 to 4:00 p.m., followed by the funeral service. One of my uncles will be giving the eulogy.

07 영어문제

What did Robert's mom ask before she died?
(a) that Robert would not tell Florence about her death
(b) that Florence would take care of Robert's dad
(c) that Florence would invite her family to a musical
(d) that Florence would sing for her at the funeral

문제 한글 해석

Robert의 엄마가 그녀가 죽기 전에 부탁한 것은 무엇인가?
(a) Robert가 Florence에게 그녀의 죽음에 대해서 말하지 말라는 것
(b) Florence가 Robert의 아빠를 돌봐달라는 것
(c) Florence가 그녀의 가족을 뮤지컬에 초대해달라는 것
(d) Florence가 장례식에서 그녀를 위해 노래를 불러달라는 것

문제해설

Robert의 엄마는 Florence의 음악 선생님이자, 서로 소중했던 사이였다. 살아생전에도, 그녀를 칭찬할 만큼 그의 엄마는 Florence의 노래를 좋아했고, 그래서 장례식에서 뮤지컬 수록곡을 불러달라고 부탁한 것이다.

> Mom admired you so much when she was alive. And she asked something before she died. She asked if you'd sing a musical number at the funeral.

 **문제를 잘 듣고 받아쓰기 연습을 미리 해보세요.**

기억하세요! 3단어가 넘어가면 안 됩니다.

1.

2.

3.

4.

5.

6.

Part 2. You will hear a presentation. First you will hear questions 1 through 6. Then you will hear the talk. Choose the best answer to each question in the time provided.

01
(a) going on a diet to reduce the amount of food you eat
(b) living with parents to save the living expenses
(c) coming up with a detailed yearly budget plan
(d) cutting the amount of money you spend on food

02
(a) not to limit the amount of money on entertainment if it makes you happy
(b) to cancel all the subscriptions and don't enjoy entertainment that costs you money
(c) to spend less on entertainment by checking the promotion period or special offers
(d) to use illegal web sites to enjoy entertainment and save money

03
(a) selling the car and buy a cheaper car for cash
(b) riding a bike or walk to your destinations
(c) applying for card plans that give you a special discount on transportation
(d) using carpool to save money and talk with your colleagues

04
(a) to spend less on housing and related costs like utility expenses
(b) to search for the goods that people no longer use
(c) to lower costs for entertainment
(d) to make a grocery list and buy ingredients to cook

05
(a) They always cook at home to save money for dining out.
(b) They exchange goods with family members and reuse clothes for kids.
(c) They live in a small house since grown-up kids live independently.
(d) They use public transportation instead of driving a car.

06
(a) It is logical and a good way to save money.
(b) The speaker was disappointed when the speaker had to wear sisters' hand-me-downs.
(c) The speaker understands the importance of recycling but wants new clothes.
(d) The speaker thinks recycling clothes is not common.

Ways to Save Money 돈을 절약하는 방법들

Whether you are an office worker or a student receiving an allowance, a lot of people feel that they are lacking money or they want to have some more money. In this talk, I want to address 5 ways to save money, specifically for people who earn salaries.
여러분이 회사원이건 용돈을 받는 학생이건 많은 이들은 돈이 부족하거나 조금 더 필요하다고 느낍니다. 이번 강연에서 저는 돈을 절약하는 다섯 가지 방법, 특히나 월급을 받는 분들을 위해서 이야기해보려고 합니다.

First of all, cut the amount of money you spend on food. On average, the American family spends about $800 a month on food. You can spend less than that. To do so, you need to make a plan for your food budget. Of course, you can go out to dine out for a special occasion. But, if you go out every day to eat outside, you are likely to end up broke. Instead, you can make a grocery list and buy ingredients to cook.
첫 번째로 여러분이 음식에 지출하는 돈을 줄이세요. 미국의 가정은 한 달에 식비로 평균 800달러를 지출합니다. 여러분은 그보다 덜 지출할 수 있습니다. 그렇게 하기 위해서는 식비 예산에 대한 계획을 세워야 합니다. 물론 여러분은 특별한 경우에 외식하러 나갈 수도 있습니다. 하지만 만약 매일 나가서 먹는다면 결국 빈털터리가 될 것입니다. 대신에 식료품 목록을 작성하고 요리할 재료를 구매하세요.

Here are a few tips to save money on groceries:
1. Use the food you already have. Don't waste the money on buying the same products you already have. Before you go to a grocery shop, I would suggest you clear out your refrigerators, cupboards, freezer, and pantry. Maybe you might be able to cook something delicious tonight with the ingredients you already have.
여기 식료품에 드는 비용을 절약하는 몇 가지 방법이 있습니다:
이미 가지고 있는 식품을 사용하세요. 이미 가지고 있는 똑같은 제품을 사는 데 돈을 낭비하지 마세요. 식료품점에 가기 전에 여러분의 냉장고, 찬장, 냉동실 그리고 창고를 정리해보시기를 제안합니다. 아마 그날 밤 여러분은 이미 집에 있는 재료들로 맛있는 것을 만들 수 있을지도 모릅니다.

2. Shop at discount grocery stores. See if there is a discount grocery shop near your place. Compared to buying in the regular shop, buying at a discount store would enable you to save a lot more!
2. 할인 식료품점에서 쇼핑하세요. 여러분이 사는 곳 근처에 할인 식료품점이 있는지 찾아보세요. 일반 상점에서 사는 것과 비교했을 때 할인 식료품점에서 구매하면 더 절약할 수 있을 거예요.

3. Purchase products that are on sale. Keep track of grocery advertisements and plan that week's meals around that.
3. 할인 중인 제품을 구매하세요. 식료품점 광고를 계속 확인하고 그 주간의 식단을 계획하세요.

Second, spend less on entertainment. The American family, on average, spends close to $300 a month on entertainment. Try to spend less on cable or satellite, expensive mobile phone data plans, movies, music concerts, sports, video gaming, subscriptions, and membership. I know that it would be very soulless to live without entertainment, but you need to find a way to balance out between adequateness and overspending.

두 번째로 여흥에 쓰이는 지출을 줄이세요. 평균적인 미국 가정은 여흥비로 한 달에 300달러를 씁니다. 케이블이나 위성 방송, 비싼 휴대폰 데이터, 영화, 콘서트, 스포츠, 비디오 게임, 정기구독 그리고 멤버십에 더 적게 지출하려고 노력하세요. 물론 저도 여흥 없이 사는 것이 매우 **시시하다**는 것은 알고 있습니다만 **충분함**과 **과소비** 사이의 균형을 잡는 방법을 찾을 필요가 있습니다.

If it is difficult for you to limit the amount you spend on the entertainment, you may try to purchase tickets during the promotion period or check whether your credit cards provide you some special discount offers. For entertainment subscriptions like Netflix, you may try to share the accounts with your friends. That way, you can save a lot more than what you spend by paying the full amount.

만일 여흥에 지출하는 비용을 제한하는 것이 어렵다면 홍보 기간에 표를 사거나 여러분이 사용하는 신용카드가 특별할인을 제공하는지 확인해 보세요. Netflix와 같은 유흥을 위한 정기구독의 경우 친구들과 계정을 공유할 수 있습니다. 이러한 방법으로 여러분은 전액을 지불 하는 것보다 더 많이 절약할 수 있습니다.

Third, lower your transportation costs. Statistically, Americans spend about $400 a month. You may own a cheaper, paid-for car. If you have car loans, think about selling the car and buying a cheaper car for cash. If the distance is near, consider riding a bike or walking to your destinations.

세 번째는 교통비를 줄이세요. 통계상 미국인들은 한 달에 대략 400달러를 지출합니다. 물론 여러분이 싸게 산 차를 소유하고 있을 수도 있습니다. 만일 자동차 대출이 있다면 그 차를 팔고 현금으로 더 싼 차를 구매하세요. 거리가 가깝다면 목적지까지 자전거를 타거나 걷는 것을 고려해보세요.

Try to drive less because the gas price is expensive. Instead, you may use the public bus or carpool to work and school. Carpool means sharing of car journeys which more than one person travels in a car. Carpooling gives you a chance to save money as well as time for you to talk with your colleagues. It is also environmentally friendly!

기름 값이 비싸니 덜 운전하려고 하세요. 대신에 출근하거나 등교하기 위해 대중 버스를 타거나 카풀을 이용하세요. **카풀**은 여러 명이 차로 이동할 때 차를 공유하는 것을 의미합니다. 여러분은 카풀을 하면 돈과 시간을 절약할 수 있을 뿐 아니라 동료들과 대화할 수도 있습니다. 또한, 환경 친화적이기도 합니다.

Fourth, spend less on housing and related costs like utility expenses. For most people, housing is the largest expense they have to deal with. To cut down the expenses, you may think about doing business through Airbnb to rent out your spare bedrooms. From doing business, you could earn well over the cost of your monthly mortgage or rent payment.

네 번째로 주택비와 공과금과 같은 관련 비용에 대한 지출을 줄이세요. 많은 사람에게 주택비는 해결해야 하는 가장 큰 지출입니다. 이 지출을 줄이기 위해서는 Airbnb를 이용해 집에 남는 방을 빌려주는 일에 대해서 생각해 볼 수 있습니다. 이러한 사업을 통해 여러분은 월마다 나가는 **주택 담보대출** 비용이나 집세 이상을 벌 수 있습니다.

If your situation does not allow you to do such business, then you may try to rent a cheaper place, live with your family or friends, get a roommate, refinance your home if interest rates have dropped significantly, and sell your home to get a less expensive home. For utility expenses, balance electricity use by using appliances strategically.

만일 사정상 그러한 사업을 할 수 없다면 더 저렴한 장소에 세 들어 살거나 가족 혹은 친구와 함께 살거나 룸메이트를 구하든지, 만일 금리가 눈에 띄게 떨어졌다면 **이자가 더 낮은 담보대출로 바꾸고** 덜 비싼 집을 얻기 위해서 집을 매각할 수 있습니다. 공과금 지출에 대해서는 **가전제품**을 전략적으로 이용해서 전기 사용의 균형을 유지하세요.

Lastly, spend less on clothing. Many people spend so much on clothing. To save money, you could try to swap children's clothes with your nieces and nephews. When I was young, I got my sisters' hand-me-downs and my sisters' clothes were also exchanged with my cousins' clothes.
마지막으로 옷 구매에 지출을 줄이세요. 많은 사람들이 옷 사는 데 너무 많은 돈을 씁니다. 돈을 절약하기 위해서는 여러분의 조카들과 아이 옷을 바꿔 입히려고 노력해 보세요. 제가 어렸을 때는 제 누나의 옷을 **물려받아서** 입었고 누나의 옷도 제 친척 옷과 바꾼 것이었습니다.

I never complained about recycling clothes. I think it is logical and a good way to save money. You can also use sites like eBay to buy second-hand clothes. Most of the clothes are in good quality despite them being second-handed. By reusing the clothing, you can save money and the environment. It serves two ends!
저는 옷을 재활용해 입는 것에 불만을 가져 본 적이 없습니다. 이렇게 하는 것은 돈을 절약하는 **논리적이고** 훌륭한 방법이라고 생각합니다. 중고 옷을 사기 위해서 eBay 같은 사이트를 사용할 수도 있습니다. 대부분의 옷은 그것들이 중고임에 불구하고 품질이 좋습니다. 옷을 재사용해서 돈을 절약하고 환경을 지킬 수 있습니다. 일거양득입니다.

Apart from the tips I provided, there are far more ways for you to save money. If you follow some of my suggestions, you will be able to save up a lot in the end. Good luck with your financial journey to save more money!
제가 드린 조언들 이외에도 여러분이 돈을 절약할 수 있는 훨씬 더 많은 방법이 있습니다. 저의 제안 중 몇 개만 실천해 보신다면 **결국에는** 많이 절약할 수 있을 겁니다. 더 많은 돈을 절약하기 위한 여러분의 재정 여정에 행운을 빕니다.

Vocabulary and Sample Sentences

어휘 그리고 예제 문장들

단어	의미
allowance (noun) money that you are given regularly, especially to pay for a particular thing	용돈, 수당 (명사) 정기적으로 받는 돈, 특히 특정한 것에 대가를 치르기 위해서 **예문** I couldn't have managed at college if I hadn't had an allowance from my parents. 제가 부모님으로부터 용돈을 받지 않았다면 저는 대학을 끝마치지 못했을 것입니다.
budget (noun) the amount of money you have available to spend	예산 (명사) 당신이 가지고 있는 쓸 수 있는 돈의 양 **예문** She managed to complete her last film well within budget. 그녀는 예산 내에서 마지막 영화를 잘 마무리 지을 수 있었습니다.
occasion (noun) a particular time, especially when something happens or has happened	행사, 경우, 기회 (명사) 특별한 시간, 특히 어떤 것이 발생하거나 발생해온 때 **예문** We met on several occasions to discuss the issue. 우리는 그 문제를 논의하기 위해 여러 번 만났습니다.
grocery (noun) a store that sells food and small things for the home	식료품점 (명사) 집에 필요한 음식과 작은 것들을 파는 상점 **예문** America's largest grocery store chain will be bringing two new stores to Oakland. 미국의 가장 큰 식료품 체인점은 Oakland에 두 개의 새로운 지점을 세울 것입니다.

단어	의 미
pantry (noun) a small room or large cupboard in a house where food is kept	창고, 저장실, 찬장 (명사) 집에 식품을 저장하는 작은 공간이나 큰 찬장 **예문** My sensors indicate trace amounts of chocolate in the pantry. 제 감지기가 찬장에 소량의 초콜릿이 있다고 하네요.
soulless (adjective) showing no human influence or qualities	시시한, 혼이 없는 (형용사) 인간미 있는 영향력이나 자질을 보이지 않는 **예문** It is just a painted face, pretty in a way, shallow and soulless. 그것은 어떤 면에서는 아름답지만, 얕고 영혼이 없는 얼굴의 그림이다.
adequateness (noun) the state of being satisfactory, acceptable, or suitable in quality or quantity; adequacy	충분함, 적절함 (명사) 질이나 양적으로 만족스럽고 받아들일 수 있거나 적절한 상태; 적절함 **예문** Evaluation of the adequateness and safety level are not accurate. 적절함과 안전 수준에 대한 평가는 정확하지 않다.
overspending (noun) the action of spending more money than you should	과소비 (명사) 당신이 써야 하는 것보다 더 많은 돈을 지출하는 행동 **예문** The study showed overspending was more prevalent among women than men. 연구에 따르면 과소비는 남성보다 여성들 사이에 더 만연한 것으로 나타났습니다.
subscription (noun) an arrangement for providing, receiving, or making use of something of a continuing or periodic nature on a prepayment plan	정기구독 (명사) 선불 요금제로 지속적이거나 정기적인 것을 제공, 수령 또는 이용하는 약정 **예문** I decided to take out a subscription to a gardening magazine. 저는 원예 잡지 정기구독을 신청하기로 했습니다.

단어	의미
carpool (noun) a group of people who travel together, especially to work or school, usually in a different member's car each day	카풀, 승용차 함께 타기 (명사) 보통 매일 다른 회원의 차로 함께 이동하는 사람들의 집단. 특히나 직장이나 학교에 갈 때 **예문** We organized a carpool to make getting to work easier and more efficient. 저희는 더 쉽고 효율적으로 출근하기 위해서 카풀을 계획했습니다.
mortgage (noun) an agreement that allows you to borrow money from a bank or similar organization, especially in order to buy a house, or the amount of money itself	주택 담보대출, 저당, 융자 (명사) 집을 사기 위해서 은행이나 유사 기관에서 돈을 빌리도록 하는 계약 혹은 금액 그 자체 **예문** You take out a mortgage on your home at a fixed rate of interest. 당신은 고정 금리로 주택 담보대출을 받습니다.
refinance (verb) to change the terms of a mortgage or loan, usually by increasing the amount of it in order to be able to borrow more money	차환하다, 저금리로 담보대출을 바꾸다 (동사) 더 많은 돈을 빌릴 수 있기 위해서 대개 금액을 증가시켜서 담보대출이나 융자의 조건을 변경하는 것 **예문** He got the money to buy more property by refinancing his original house. 그는 본가의 담보대출을 바꿔서 더 많은 부동산을 사기 위한 돈을 벌었다.
appliance (noun) a device, machine, or piece of equipment, especially an electrical one that is used in the house, such as a cooker or washing machine	가전제품 (명사) 장치, 기계 혹은 장비. 특히 밥솥이나 세탁기처럼 집에서 사용되는 전자제품 **예문** We stock a wide range of domestic appliances, including refrigerators, freezers, and dishwashers. 저희는 냉장고, 냉동고 그리고 식기 세척기를 포함한 다양한 가전제품을 취급합니다.

단어	의미
hand-me-down (noun) a piece of clothing that someone has given to a younger person because they no longer want it	물려받은 옷, 헌 옷 (명사) 누군가가 더 이상 원하지 않기 때문에 더 어린 사람에게 주는 옷 **예문** I got fed up with having to wear my sister's hand-me-downs. 저는 제 언니에게서 물려받은 옷을 입는 것에 진절머리가 나요.

단어	의미
logical (adjective) using reason	논리적인 (형용사) 논리를 사용하는 **예문** You need to be logical when it comes to singing on the contract. 그 계약서에 사인하는 것에 관해서는 당신은 논리적일 필요가 있다.

정답 01. (d)　02. (c)　03. (c)　04. (a)　05. (b)　06. (a)

01 영어문제

According to the speech, what is the first suggestion made by the speaker?

(a) going on a diet to reduce the amount of food you eat
(b) living with parents to save the living expenses
(c) coming up with a detailed yearly budget plan
(d) cutting the amount of money you spend on food

문제 한글 해석

연설에 의하면, 화자가 말한 첫 번째 제안은 무엇인가?

(a) 다이어트를 해서 당신이 먹는 음식의 양을 줄이는 것
(b) 부모님과 함께 지내 생활비를 절약하는 것
(c) 상세한 연간 예산 계획을 세우는 것
(d) 음식에 지출하는 비용을 줄이는 것

문제해설

화자는 물론 여러분은 특별한 경우에 외식하러 나갈 수도 있지만 만약 매일 나가서 먹는다면 결국 빈털터리가 될 것이라고 경고하고 있다. 대신에 식료품 목록을 작성하고 요리할 재료를 구매하기를 권장하고 있다.

> First of all, cut the amount of money you spend on food. On average, the American family spends about $800 a month on food. You can spend less than that. To do so, you need to make a plan for your food budget. Of course, you can go out to dine out for a special occasion. But, if you go out every day to eat outside, you are likely to end up broke. Instead, you can make a grocery list and buy ingredients to cook.

02 영어문제

What does the speaker suggest about spending on entertainment?

(a) not to limit the amount of money on entertainment if it makes you happy
(b) to cancel all the subscriptions and don't enjoy entertainment that costs you money
(c) to spend less on entertainment by checking the promotion period or special offers
(d) to use illegal web sites to enjoy entertainment and save money

문제 한글 해석

화자는 유흥비 지출에 대해 무엇을 제안하는가?

(a) 만약 유흥이 당신을 행복하게 만든다면 유흥에 지출하는 비용을 한정시키지 않는것
(b) 모든 구독을 취소하고 돈이 드는 오락을 즐기지 않는 것
(c) 홍보기간이나 특가를 체크해서 유흥비를 절약하는 것
(d) 유흥을 즐기고 돈을 아끼기 위해 불법 웹사이트를 이용하는 것

문제해설

홍보기간 동안 티켓을 구매하거나, 당신의 신용카드사가 특별 할인을 제공하는지 확인함으로써 유흥비를 줄이라고 제안하고 있다.

> If it is difficult for you to limit the amount you spend on the entertainment, you may try to purchase tickets during the promotion period or check whether your credit cards provide you some special discount offers. For entertainment subscriptions like Netflix, you may try to share the accounts with your friends. That way, you can save a lot more than what you spend by paying the full amount.

03 영어문제 | 문제 한글 해석

Based on the speech, what is not the way of reducing transportation costs?

(a) selling the car and buy a cheaper car for cash
(b) riding a bike or walk to your destinations
(c) applying for card plans that give you a special discount on transportation
(d) using carpool to save money and talk with your colleagues

연설에 의하면, 교통비를 줄이기 위한 방법이 아닌 것은 무엇인가?

(a) 차를 팔고 그 돈으로 좀 더 값싼 차를 구매하는 것
(b) 자전거를 타거나 걸어서 목적지까지 가는 것
(c) 교통비에 특별 할인을 주는 카드를 신청하는 것
(d) 카풀을 해서 돈을 절약하고 동료들과 대화를 나누는 것

문제해설

교통비를 줄이기 위해서는 만약 자동차 대출이 있다면 그 차를 팔고 현금으로 더 싼 차를 구매하고 거리가 가깝다면 목적지까지 자전거를 타거나 걷는 것을 고려하라고 조언한다. 또한 버스나 카풀을 이용할 것을 권하고 있다.

> Third, lower your transportation costs. Statistically, Americans spend about $400 a month. You may own a cheaper, paid-for car. If you have car loans, think about selling the car and buying a cheaper car for cash. If the distance is near, consider riding a bike or walking to your destinations. Try to drive less because the gas price is expensive. Instead, you may use the public bus or carpool to work and school. Carpool means sharing of car journeys which more than one person travels in a car. Carpooling gives you a chance to save money as well as time for you to talk with your colleagues. It is also environmentally friendly!

04 영어문제 | 문제 한글 해석

What is the fourth suggestion mentioned by the speaker?

(a) to spend less on housing and related costs like utility expenses
(b) to search for the goods that people no longer use
(c) to lower costs for entertainment
(d) to make a grocery list and buy ingredients to cook

화자가 말한 네 번째 제안은 무엇인가?

(a) 주택비와 공과금과 같은 관련 비용에 대한 지출을 줄이는 것
(b) 사람들이 더 이상 사용하지 않는 물건들을 찾아보는 것
(c) 유흥에 쓰이는 지출을 줄이는 것
(d) 식료품 목록을 작성하고 요리할 재료를 구매하는 것

문제해설

네 번째 제안은 주택비와 공과금과 같은 관련 비용에 대한 지출을 줄이는 것이다. 많은 사람에게 주택비는 해결해야 하는 가장 큰 지출이다. 이 지출을 줄이기 위해서는 Airbnb를 이용해 집에 남는 방을 빌려주는 일에 대해서 생각해 볼 수 있다. 이러한 사업을 통해 여러분은 집세나 월마다 나가는 주택담보대출 비용 이상을 벌 수 있다.

> Fourth, spend less on housing and related costs like utility expenses. For most people, housing is the largest expense they have to deal with. To cut down the expenses, you may think about doing business through Airbnb to rent out your spare bedrooms. From doing business, you could earn well over the cost of your monthly mortgage or rent payment.

05 영어문제 | 문제 한글 해석

What can be inferred about the ways that the speaker's parents save money?
(a) They always cook at home to save money for dining out.
(b) They exchange goods with family members and reuse clothes for kids.
(c) They live in a small house since grown-up kids live independently.
(d) They use public transportation instead of driving a car.

화자의 부모님이 돈을 절약하는 방법에 대해 무엇을 추론할 수 있는가?
(a) 항상 집에서 요리를 해서 외식비를 절약한다.
(b) 가족 구성원들과 물건을 주고받고 아이들의 옷을 재사용한다.
(c) 아이들이 다 자라 독립하기 때문에 작은 집에서 산다.
(d) 운전을 하는 대신 대중교통을 이용한다.

문제해설

화자가 어렸을 때는 누나의 옷을 물려받아서 입었고 누나의 옷도 본인의 친척의 옷과 바꾼 것이었다.

> Lastly, spend less on clothing. Many people spend so much on clothing. To save money, you could try to swap children's clothes with your nieces and nephews. When I was young, I got my sisters' hand-me-downs and my sisters' clothes were also exchanged with my cousins' clothes.

06 영어문제 | 문제 한글 해석

What is the speaker's opinion about recycling clothes?
(a) It is logical and a good way to save money.
(b) The speaker was disappointed when the speaker had to wear sisters' hand-me-downs.
(c) The speaker understands the importance of recycling but wants new clothes.
(d) The speaker thinks recycling clothes is not common.

화자는 옷을 재활용하는 것에 대해 어떻게 생각하는가?
(a) 논리적이고 돈을 절약하는 훌륭한 방법이라고 생각한다.
(b) 화자는 누나가 물려준 옷을 입어야 했을 때 실망했다.
(c) 화자는 재활용의 중요성을 이해하지만 새로운 옷을 원한다.
(d) 화자는 옷을 재활용하는 것이 보편화 되어 있지 않다고 생각한다.

문제해설

그는 옷을 재활용해 입는 것에 불만을 가져 본 적이 없고 이렇게 하는 것은 돈을 절약하는 논리적이고 훌륭한 방법이라고 생각한다.

> I never complained about recycling clothes. I think it is logical and a good way to save money. You can also use sites like eBay to buy second-hand clothes. Most of the clothes are in good quality despite them being second-handed. By reusing the clothing, you can save money and the environment. It serves two ends!

 문제를 잘 듣고 받아쓰기 연습을 미리 해보세요.

기억하세요! 3단어가 넘어가면 안 됩니다.

1.
2.
3.
4.
5.
6.
7.

Part 3. You will hear a conversation between two people. First you will hear questions 1 through 7. Then you will hear the conversation. Choose the best answer to each question in the time provided.

01
(a) to check the house instead of her brother
(b) to look around the house before she moves in
(c) to hold a housewarming party
(d) to repair the washing machine in his kitchen

02
(a) He will sell his house because he runs out of money.
(b) He will hire someone who takes care of his house while he is away from home.
(c) He will share his house with someone because he has been strapped for cash.
(d) He will remodel his whole house before he moves in.

03
(a) the living room
(b) the kitchen
(c) the bathroom
(d) the bedroom

04
(a) by buying a new one
(b) by replacing it with Linda's refrigerator
(c) by temporarily pushing a box against it
(d) by locking it and not using it

05
(a) The toilet is clogged.
(b) The sink has a few leaks.
(c) The window pane is gone.
(d) The hot water doesn't come out.

06
(a) She is thankful for it.
(b) She is indifferent about it.
(c) She is mad about it.
(d) She is skeptical to it.

07
(a) She would meet her brother with.
(b) She would stay at Pete's house for a while because she likes it.
(c) She would tell her brother how nice Pete's house is.
(d) She would let her brother know that Pete's house is terrible.

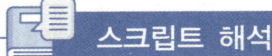
스크립트 해석

Home Repairs 집수리

Linda Um..Excuse me. Hi, I'm Linda. And I'm here to look around the house instead of my brother. He said that he found your house on the house sharing site. And it said that you are looking for a roommate, right? He was supposed to be here to see your house, but he had a small accident on his way. So he asked me to go and check everything. So is it OK for me to look around your house?

Linda 음..실례합니다. 안녕하세요, 저는 Linda예요. 제 남동생 대신에 집 좀 둘러보려고 왔는데요. 남동생이 말하기론 집 공유 사이트에서 이 집을 봤다고 하던데. 그리고 룸메이트를 찾고 계신다고 들었어요. 맞나요? 원래는 남동생이 집 보러 오기로 되어 있었는데 오는 길에 작은 사고가 나서요. 그래서 저한테 가서 확인해 달라고 부탁했어요. 괜찮으시면 제가 집을 좀 둘러봐도 되나요?

Pete Yeah. Fine. He called me and explained everything. Come on in. And I'm Pete.

Pete 네. 괜찮습니다. 남동생분이 저한테 전화해서 다 설명해 주셨어요. 들어오세요. 저는 Pete라고 해요.

Linda Nice to meet you. And the pictures my brother sent me are so good. You have a really nice house. And I just want to make sure the house is just like the pictures.

Linda 만나서 반가워요. 남동생이 저한테 보내준 사진들이 너무 좋던데요. 정말 멋진 집을 가지고 있으시네요. 그냥 집이 사진에서 본 거랑 똑같은지만 확인하고 싶어서요.

Pete I understand. But I didn't expect someone to come over to my house and look around today... So my place is not kind of ready. There are some problems in my house, but they are going to be fixed within a month. So just keep that mind. OK? I know it's a personal matter. But ever since I cut back on my working hours to go to school, I've **been strapped for cash**. So I decided to **share** the house with somebody.

Pete 알겠습니다. 그런데 오늘 누가 집에 와서 둘러볼 거라고 예상을 못해서. 그래서 약간 준비가 안 되어 있는데. 집에 문제가 좀 있는데 한 달 안에 고쳐질 거예요. 그러니까 그것만 기억해 주세요. 아시겠죠? 개인적인 문제라는 건 아는데 학교 다니려고 일하는 시간을 줄인 이래로 **돈이 정말 부족하거든요**. 그래서 다른 사람이랑 집을 **공유하기**로 결정했어요.

Linda Cool. Can you show me the place now?

Linda 좋네요. 이제 집 좀 보여주시겠어요?

Pete Yeap. First, let me show you the living room.

Pete 네. 거실 먼저 보여드릴게요.

Linda Oh. It looks like you could use a new carpet... and those stains?

Linda 오.. 새로운 카펫 쓰셔야 할 것 같은데. 그리고 저 얼룩들은?

Pete	Well. I just spilt something over the carpet a few days ago when having a party. I know it needs to be cleaned, but I just don't have the money to do it right now. I'll do it next month.
Pete	그게. 며칠 전에 파티할 때 카펫에 뭘 좀 흘렸어요. 세탁해야 하는 거 아는데 지금 당장 할 돈이 없어서요. 다음 달에 할 거예요.
Linda	Oh. And what about the kitchen? My brother likes to cook, so he said he would consider the kitchen the most important part in the house.
Linda	오. 부엌은 어때요? 제 남동생이 요리하는 걸 좋아해서 집에서 부엌을 가장 중요한 부분으로 생각한다고 했거든요.
Pete	I'm sure he's going to really like this. Right this way. Look. It's completely furnished with all the latest appliances. But here is a tiny problem.
Pete	그럼 여기 정말 좋아하실 거예요. 바로 이쪽이에요. 보세요. 완전히 최신 **가전제품**들로만 **갖춰져 있어요**. 근데 아주 작은 문제가 하나 있어요.
Linda	A tiny problem? What is that?
Linda	아주 작은 문제요? 그게 뭔데요?
Pete	Well, the refrigerator door is broken... a little bit... and it won't shut all the way. It needs fixing, but don't worry. I've just improvised by pushing a box against it to keep it shut.
Pete	그, 냉장고 문이 약간 망가져서 완전히 닫히진 않을 거예요. 고쳐야 하는데 걱정하지 마세요. 일단 **임시방편으로** 상자를 밀어서 닫아 놨어요.
Linda	No way... Oh, my...
Linda	그건 좀. 저런.
Pete	Ah. It isn't that bad. Except for the refrigerator, the kitchen is really nice, isn't it? You know, I'm proud of my kitchen. The new oven, the new microwave, the new dishwasher... Oh, I almost forgot to say this. We can't use the dishwasher at night. The one who lives next door complained a lot about the noise from the machine. I mean when you use the dishwasher, it makes a lot of noise. So...
Pete	아. 그렇게 나쁘진 않아요. 냉장고 빼면 부엌은 정말 좋지 않아요? 아시다시피 저는 제 부엌에 자부심이 있어요. 새 오븐, 전자레인지, 그리고 새로운 식기 세척기까지. 오, 까먹고 말 안 할 뻔했네요. 밤에는 식기 세척기를 못 써요. 옆집에 사시는 분이 기계에서 나는 소음에 불만이 많으셨어요. 제 말은 식기 세척기 쓸 때 소음이 많이 나거든요. 그래서..
Linda	Fine. Well, how about the bathroom?
Linda	알았어요. 그러면 화장실은 어때요?
Pete	Well...
Pete	그게..

Linda   No, no. Are there any problems in the bathroom, too? Don't tell me that the toilet is clogged or the sink has a few leaks?

Linda   잠깐만요. 화장실에도 문제가 있나요? 설마 변기가 막혔다거나 세면대가 새는 건 아니겠죠?

Pete   No, those work fine, but, uh, the tile in the shower needs to be replaced, and the window needs fixing.

Pete   아니에요. 그건 괜찮은데. 어. 샤워실에 있는 타일을 좀 교체해야 하고 창문도 고쳐야 해요.

Linda   Let me see. The tile... what? The window? Where's the window pane?

Linda   어디 보자. 타일이... 뭐죠? 창문은? **창유리**는 어디 있는 거죠?

Pete   Well, that's another slight problem. I've put up a piece of cardboard to keep out the rain and snow, and if it gets a little cold, you can always turn up the heat. Well, I wait until the central heating goes out.

Pete   아, 그게 또 다른 사소한 문제인데. 눈이랑 비 안 들어오게 판지로 붙여놨는데 그리고 약간 추워지면 언제든지 온도 높이면 돼요. 뭐, 저는 중앙난방이 꺼질 때까지 기다려요.

Linda   Oh boy. It seems like that everyone can see me taking a shower or something. How can you just live under like these conditions? Are you sure you can fix all these things within a month? I heard he's planning to move in next month. Anyway, where is his room?

Linda   오 저기요. 모든 사람이 제가 샤워하거나 뭐 하는 걸 볼 것 같아요. 이런 상황에서 어떻게 그냥 이렇게 사세요? 한 달 안에 확실히 다 수리할 순 있는 거예요? 제가 듣기론 남동생이 다음 달에 이사 들어오려고 계획했던데. 어쨌든, 남동생이 쓸 방은 어디에요?

Pete   This way. Before you see the room, you should be aware that this room is not totally ready. I mean...

Pete   이쪽이요. 보시기 전에 이 방이 아직 완전히 준비가 안 됐단 걸 아셔야 해요. 제 말은...

Linda   Is there any room being ready? It's OK. Just show it. There will be nothing worse than the bathroom, I think. What is this? How come it is so freezing in here? It seems like nobody can sleep here. Are you sure this is his room? Oh! Did you see them? What were those moving things? It looked like a mouse or something. Oh, again! Please tell me the truth. What were they? They were mice, weren't they?

Linda   준비된 방이 있긴 한가요? 괜찮아요. 그냥 보여주세요. 제 생각에 화장실보다 심한 곳은 없을 것 같아요. 이게 뭐예요? 어떻게 이렇게 추울 수 있어요? 사람이 잘 수 있을 것 같지 않은데요. 여기가 제 남동생이 쓸 방 맞아요? 오! 저거 보셨어요? 움직이는 저것들은 뭐예요? 쥐같이 생겼어요. 오, 또! 제발 사실대로 말해주세요. 뭐였어요? 쥐였어요. 그렇죠?

Pete   To be honest, you are right. I sometimes can see the mice around this room.

Pete   솔직히 말하면 맞아요. 저도 가끔 이 방에서 쥐 돌아다니는 거 봐요.

Linda Are you kidding me? He would make a big mistake unless I visited here. I think I've seen enough. I can't believe you've survived under these conditions.

Linda 장난해요? 제가 방문하지 않았더라면 남동생이 큰 실수할 뻔했네요. 저 충분히 본 것 같아요. 이런 환경에서 당신이 살아남았단 걸 믿을 수가 없네요.

Pete So what do you think? Nobody really can beat a place like this for $350 a month. So it has a few problems, but we can fix those.

Pete 그래서 어떻게 생각해요? 한 달에 350달러 내고 이 집보다 더 나은 집은 못 구하세요. 그래서 약간 문제는 있는데 저희가 고치면 돼요.

Linda Uh, no thank you. I won't let my brother live here.

Linda 어, 아니 괜찮아요. 제 남동생이 여기에 살게 두진 않을 거예요.

Vocabulary and Sample Sentences

어휘 그리고 예제 문장들

단어	의 미
share (verb) use together	공유하다, 함께 사용하다 (동사) 같이 사용하다. **예문** My son didn't want to share his toys. 제 아들은 그의 장난감을 공유하기 원하지 않습니다.
furnished (adjective) having furniture and appliances	가구가 비치된 (형용사) 가구와 가전제품을 갖춘 **예문** I'm looking for a furnished apartment. 저는 가구가 비치된 아파트를 찾고 있습니다.
appliances (noun) electronic devices often used in the kitchen including the stove, microwave, blender, dishwasher, and refrigerator	가전제품 (명사) 가스레인지, 전자레인지, 믹서, 식기세척기 그리고 냉장고를 포함해 부엌에서 주로 사용되는 가전제품들 **예문** This store sells excellent appliances. 이 상점은 훌륭한 가전제품을 팝니다.
improvise (verb) to use another way of doing something to accomplish your goal	즉흥적으로 하다, 임시로 마련하다. (동사) 당신의 목적을 달성하기 위해 무언가를 하는 또 다른 방법을 사용하다. **예문** I didn't have the right brushes to paint the living room, so I had to improvise. 저는 거실을 도색할 적절한 붓이 없어서 임시로 마련해야 했습니다.

단어	의미
window pane (noun) the glass part of the window	창유리 (명사) 창문의 유리 부분 **예문** The window pane in the bedroom needs replacing. 침실에 있는 창유리는 교체가 필요하다.

단어	의미
beat (verb) be better than	~을 능가하다, 이기다 (동사) -보다 더 낫다. **예문** I've looked around the best prices on paint, and this store beats any other place around. 저는 가장 좋은 가격의 페인트를 찾아다니고 있었고 이 상점은 어떤 다른 곳보다 낫습니다.

정답 01. (a)　02. (c)　03. (b)　04. (c)　05. (c)　06. (d)　07. (d)

01

영어문제

Why did Linda come to Pete's house?

(a) to check the house instead of her brother
(b) to look around the house before she moves in
(c) to hold a housewarming party
(d) to repair the washing machine in his kitchen

문제 한글 해석

Linda는 Pete의 집을 왜 갔는가?

(a) 그녀의 남동생 대신에 집을 확인하기 위해
(b) 그녀가 이사 오기 전에 집을 둘러보기 위해
(c) 집들이를 하기 위해
(d) 부엌에 있는 세탁기를 수리하기 위해

문제해설

원래는 Linda의 남동생이 Pete의 집을 둘러보기로 되어 있었지만, 중간에 작은 사고가 생겨서 그녀가 대신 왔다.

> And I'm here to look around the house instead of my brother. He said that he found your house on the house sharing site. And it said that you are looking for a roommate.

02

영어문제

What will Pete do with his house?

(a) He will sell his house because he runs out of money.
(b) He will hire someone who takes care of his house while he is away from home.
(c) He will share his house with someone because he has been strapped for cash.
(d) He will remodel his whole house before he moves in.

문제 한글 해석

Pete는 그의 집으로 무엇을 할 것인가?

(a) 그는 돈이 떨어져서 그의 집을 팔 것이다.
(b) 그가 집에 없는 동안 그의 집을 관리할 누군가를 고용할 것이다.
(c) 그는 돈이 부족해서 누군가와 그의 집을 공유할 것이다.
(d) 그가 이사 오기 전에 집 전체를 리모델링할 것이다.

문제해설

Pete는 학교에 가기 위해 일하는 시간을 줄였고, 그 이후 돈이 부족하다. 그래서 자신의 집을 다른 사람과 공유하여, 돈을 받기로 결심했다.

> But ever since I cut back on my working hours to go to school, I've been really strapped for cash. So I decided to share the house with somebody.

03 영어문제

According to Linda's brother, which room is the most important to him?

(a) the living room
(b) the kitchen
(c) the bathroom
(d) the bedroom

문제 한글 해석

Linda의 남동생에 따르면, 어떤 공간이 그에게 가장 중요한가?

(a) 거실
(b) 부엌
(c) 화장실
(d) 침실

문제해설

Linda에 따르면 그녀의 남동생은 요리하는 것을 좋아하기 때문에, 집에서 부엌을 가장 중요하게 여긴다고 한다.

> And what about the kitchen? My brother likes to cook, so he said he would consider the kitchen the most important part in the house.

04 영어문제

How does Pete deal with his broken refrigerator?

(a) by buying a new one
(b) by replacing it with Linda's refrigerator
(c) by temporarily pushing a box against it
(d) by locking it and not using it

문제 한글 해석

Pete는 고장 난 냉장고를 어떻게 다루는가?

(a) 새로운 것을 구매함으로써
(b) Linda의 냉장고로 그것을 대체함으로써
(c) 임시적으로 그곳에 박스를 대고 있음으로써
(d) 그것을 잠가 사용하지 않음으로써

문제해설

Pete는 Linda에게 부엌을 보여주면서, 냉장고가 고장 나서 닫히지 않는다고 한다. Linda가 음식은 어떻게 보관하냐고 묻자, 임시변통으로 박스를 이용한다고 한다.

> I've just improvised by pushing a box against it to keep it shut.

05 영어문제 | 문제 한글 해석

What is the problem in the bathroom?
(a) The toilet is clogged.
(b) The sink has a few leaks.
(c) The window pane is gone.
(d) The hot water doesn't come out.

화장실의 문제는 무엇인가?
(a) 변기가 막혀 있다.
(b) 세면대가 약간 새고 있다.
(c) 창유리가 없다.
(d) 뜨거운 물이 안 나온다.

문제해설

Pete는 화장실을 보여주기 전에 화장실에도 문제가 있다고 한다. 그 문제는 창유리가 없어서 비나 눈이 올 때 판지로 막아야 하고, 추워지면 난로를 더 세게 틀어야 하는 것이다. 변기가 막히고, 세면대가 새는 문제는 Linda가 추측한 것이다.

> No, those work fine, but, uh, the tile in the shower needs to be replaced, and the window needs fixing. I've put up a piece of cardboard to keep out the rain and snow, and if it gets a little cold, you can always turn up the heat.

06 영어문제 | 문제 한글 해석

How does Linda react about Pete's fixing all the problems in his house?
(a) She is thankful for it.
(b) She is indifferent about it.
(c) She is mad about it.
(d) She is skeptical to it.

Linda는 Pete가 그의 집에 있는 모든 문제를 고친다고 하는 것에 대해 어떻게 반응하는가?
(a) 그녀는 그것에 대해 감사해 한다.
(b) 그녀는 그것에 대해 무관심하다.
(c) 그녀는 그것에 대해 화가 난다.
(d) 그녀는 그것에 대해 회의적이다.

문제해설

Linda는 자신의 남동생이 이사 올지도 모를 Pete의 집에 너무 많은 문제가 있자, 한 달 안에 그것들을 다 고칠 수 있는지 물으며 의심한다.

> Are you sure you can fix all these things within a month? I heard he's planning to move in next month.

07 영어문제 | 문제 한글 해석

What would Linda do after the conversation?
(a) She would meet her brother with Pete.
(b) She would stay at Pete's house for a while because she likes it.
(c) She would tell her brother how nice Pete's house is.
(d) She would let her brother know that Pete's house is terrible.

대화 후에, Linda는 무엇을 할 것 같은가?
(a) 그녀는 Pete와 함께 그녀의 남동생을 만날 것이다.
(b) 그녀는 Pete의 집이 마음에 들어서 잠시 동안 그곳에 머물 것이다.
(c) 그녀는 그녀의 남동생에게 Pete의 집이 얼마나 좋은지 말할 것이다.
(d) 그녀는 그녀의 남동생에게 Pete의 집이 엉망이라고 알려줄 것이다.

문제해설

Pete는 Linda에게 저렴한 값으로 들어오려면, 집에 이 정도 문제는 있을 수 있다고 한다. 하지만 Linda는 자신의 남동생이 절대 여기 못 살게 할 것이라고 하며 대화가 끝난다. 그녀는 대화가 끝나고 아마 남동생에게 Pete의 집은 엉망이라는 것을 알려줘서, 이곳에 못 들어오게 할 것이다.

> Uh, no thank you. I won't let my brother live here.

 **문제를 잘 듣고 받아쓰기 연습을 미리 해보세요.**

기억하세요! 3단어가 넘어가면 안 됩니다.

1.
2.
3.
4.
5.
6.

Part 4. You will hear a lecturer talking to a group of people. First you will hear questions 1 through 6. Then you will hear the talk. Choose the best answer to each question in the time provided.

01
(a) extinction due to impairment in the body function
(b) broken food chain due to lack of prey
(c) survival in the animal population
(d) impossibility in independent survival as a specific population reduced

02
(a) high temperature and dry weather
(b) low temperature and dry weather
(c) high temperature and humid weather
(d) low temperature and humid weather

03
(a) It might be the major cause of the Australian bush fire.
(b) It causes almost no harm to Australia.
(c) It is the only cause of global warming.
(d) It circulates the ocean worldwide.

04
(a) Victoria
(b) New South Wales
(c) Queensland
(d) Tasmania

05
(a) It decreases the number of coals.
(b) It raises the chance of people getting sick.
(c) It increases the frequency of earthquakes.
(d) It may give a bad influence on the global climate.

06
(a) It donated handcrafted goods.
(b) It organized an organization to donate money.
(c) It sprinkled vegetables using helicopters and airplanes.
(d) It gathered a number of volunteers worldwide to rescue animals.

스크립트 해석

Australia Bush fire 호주 산불

Thank you for inviting me here today. Have you seen the photos of burnt kangaroos on social media? As most of you know, Australia is experiencing a hard time. It is expected that at least a billion of Australian animals including koalas and kangaroos died and people are concerned about animal extinction.

오늘 이 자리에 저를 초대해 주셔서 감사합니다. 여러분은 매체에서 화상을 입은 캥거루들의 사진을 본 적이 있으신가요? 여러분 대부분이 아시다시피 호주는 힘든 시기를 겪고 있습니다. 코알라와 캥거루를 포함해서 적어도 10억 마리의 호주 동물들이 죽을 것이라고 예상되며 사람들은 동물 멸종에 대해 우려하고 있습니다.

Statistically, 30% of koalas died based in New South Wales. Experts also refer to these koalas as "functionally extinct" because 80% of eucalyptus forests, which are the habitat of koalas, are burned. Functionally extinct means impossibility in independent survival due to a reduction in specific animal's population. Local Australian news has reported that at least 28 people died.

통계적으로 뉴사우스웨일스 주에 서식하던 코알라의 30%가 죽었습니다. 전문가들은 또한 코알라들의 서식지였던 유칼립투스 숲의 80%가 불에 타면서 이 코알라들이 "기능적 **멸종**" 상태라고 말합니다. 기능적으로 멸종된 상태란 특정 동물의 개체 수가 감소하여 독자적으로 생존할 수 없게 됨을 뜻합니다. 호주 지역 뉴스는 적어도 28명의 사람이 목숨을 잃었다고 보도했습니다.

Every year, Australia experiences many major and minor forest fires due to high temperature and low humidity during the summer with casualties resulting in more than 800 to 1,850 deaths in recent years. However, the recent fire, for the first time ever, caused the whole of Australia to come under the influence of fire.

매년, 호주는 여름 동안 높은 온도와 낮은 **습도**로 인해 많은 크고 작은 산불을 겪으며 1850년에서 현재에 이르기까지 800명 이상의 사망자를 낳았습니다. 하지만 사상 처음으로 이번 산불로 인해 호주 전역이 화재의 영향을 받고 있습니다.

Most of the experts claim that the cause of record-breaking bush fire to be climate change. Due to Indian Ocean Dipole (IOD) phenomenon, the weather gets warmer and drier every year. Starting from September last year, the fire continues until now.

전문가 대부분이 기록적인 **산불**의 원인으로 기후 변화를 꼽고 있습니다. 인도양 쌍극자 현상으로 인해 기후는 매년 덥고 건조해집니다. 작년 9월을 시작으로 화재는 현재까지 계속되고 있습니다.

Apart from the damage in animal population, there are many harms to Australia. People lost their living place and live in terror of possible bush fire. In New South Wales, almost 1,900 homes had been destroyed this fire season - with more than 300 razed in other states. Furthermore, the bush fire in Australia disturbed the opening of the season's first major tennis competition.

동물 개체 수의 손실 이외에도 호주에는 손해가 많이 있습니다. 사람들은 그들의 거주지를 잃고 또다시 산불이 발생할지도 모른다는 두려움 속에 지내고 있습니다. 뉴사우스웨일스 주에는 이번 화재 기간에 거의 1900채의 가구가 소실되었으며 다른 주에서도 300채 이상이 파괴되었습니다. 게다가 호주 산불의 여파는 시즌 첫 메이저 테니스 대회의 개막식에도 영향을 주었습니다.

Some athletes have abstained from participating in the competition as they feel difficulties in breathing. An emergency warning was also issued in Western Australia for several suburbs in the south of Perth. The hopeless news is that the scale of the conflagration is beyond imagination and it is still progressive. No one can predict when the fire will be extinct.

몇 선수는 호흡 곤란을 호소하며 경기 참여를 **기권하기도** 했습니다. 호주 서부의 퍼스 남쪽의 여러 근교 지역에도 비상사태가 선포되었습니다. 절망적인 소식은 **대규모 화재**의 규모가 상상을 초월하고 여전히 **진행 중**이라는 것입니다. 산불이 언제 끝날지 아무도 예측할 수 없습니다.

The bigger problem is that this disaster will have chain action with escalating global warming from greenhouse gas emission from the bush fire. Experts call this effect as 'feedback effect'. Australia is waiting for the much-needed rain so that the fire could be extinguished. Meanwhile, there needs to be some active actions to remedy the situation.

더 큰 문제는 이번 재앙이 온실가스를 배출시켜 지구 온난화를 가속시키는 연쇄적인 효과를 가질 거라는 점입니다. 전문가들은 이러한 효과를 '되먹임 현상'이라고 부릅니다. 호주는 단비가 내려 산불이 **진화되기**를 기다리고 있습니다. 한편으로는 현재 상황을 구제하기 위한 적극적인 조치가 필요합니다.

You may question how this issue is relevant to you. You may think that the Australian bush fire impacts only locally. Surprisingly, there is an analysis that the bush fire may give a bad influence to the global climate. In reference to NASA, the smoke from the bush fire rose up to a maximum 17m in the sky and has already circulated halfway round the world.

여러분은 이 문제가 어떻게 본인과 관련 있는지 의문을 가질 수도 있습니다. 호주 산불은 단지 해당 지역에만 영향을 준다고 생각하실 겁니다. 놀랍게도 산불은 전 세계 기후에 악영향을 끼칠 것이라는 분석이 있습니다. NASA에 따르면 호주 산불로 배출된 연기가 상공에서 최대 17m까지 올라가 이미 지구 반 바퀴를 **돌았다**고 합니다.

Global warming from industrial activity causes the environment to become hotter and drier, and bush fires happen more frequently, and the vicious cycle continues. Indeed, Australia is the world's top coal export country. As global warming gets worse, Australia needs to come up with a better policy in regards to coal mining.

산업 활동으로 인한 지구 온난화는 더 덥고 더 건조한 환경을 초래하고 이로 인해 산불이 더 빈번히 발생하며 **악순환**이 계속됩니다. 실제로 호주는 세계 최대의 석탄 수출국입니다. 지구 온난화가 심화되면서 호주는 석탄 채굴과 관련해 더 나은 정책을 고안해 내야 합니다.

Climatologists warn that there may be extreme weather events like bush fires and intense heat as global warming continues. I hope you remember that it is something that we can experience in the near future. Not only Australia, but other countries should also devise ways to reduce greenhouse gas.

기상학자들은 지구 온난화가 계속되면 산불이나 폭염 같은 기상 이변이 있을 것이라고 경고합니다. 저는 이것이 우리가 가까운 미래에 겪을 수도 있는 일임을 여러분이 기억해주시길 바랍니다. 호주뿐 아니라 다른 국가들 또한 온실가스를 줄일 방법을 고안해 내야 합니다.

Reducing the greenhouse gas is the long-term goal, and we need to think about the short-term goal to help out Australia. To save the animals and return the forest as of old, the Australian government, Australians, and the international communities are making efforts. State governments have committed money for the recovery effort.

온실가스를 줄이는 것은 장기적인 목표이며 우리는 호주를 도울 수 있는 단기적인 목표에 대해 생각해 볼 필요가 있습니다. 동물들을 구하고 숲을 예전처럼 되돌리기 위해서 호주 정부와 호주 국민 그리고 전 세계의 사람들이 노력하고 있습니다. 주 정부는 **복구** 작업을 위해 돈을 지원해 왔습니다.

New South Wales sprinkled about 4,800 pounds of vegetables using helicopter and airplane. This is the effort made by the Australian government to rescue the one billion endangered wildlife. Vegetables such as carrots and sweet potatoes have been distributed throughout various areas of Australia.

뉴사우스웨일스 주는 헬리콥터와 항공기를 사용해서 4800파운드의 채소를 **뿌렸습니다**. 이는 **멸종위기에 처한** 10억 마리의 야생동물들을 구조하기 위한 호주 정부의 노력입니다. 당근과 고구마 같은 채소가 호주 전역에 뿌려졌습니다.

The government says that they will provide food and water until the environment returns to normal. This effort is not enough to rescue the animals. As an international community, we need to work together. Even one penny will save the poor lives and your donation will play a significant role in recovering the burned habitats.

정부는 자연이 원래의 상태가 될 때까지 그들이 물과 식량을 제공할 것이라고 말했습니다. 이러한 노력은 동물들을 구하기에 충분치 않습니다. 국제 사회가 함께 노력해야 합니다. 단 한 푼이라도 불쌍한 생명을 구할 것이며 여러분의 기부가 불타버린 **서식지**를 복구하는 데 중요한 역할을 할 것입니다.

You can also help Australia by donating handcrafted goods. People from America, New Zealand, Hong Kong, France, and a few other countries have formed an organization and handcrafted quilt and knit aid for wildlife animals. The union has exceeded 100,000 members. Apart from what I mentioned, there are many ways that we can help them out. Let's take the initiative and save lives!

여러분은 또한 **수공예** 제품을 기부해서 호주를 도울 수 있습니다. 미국, 뉴질랜드, 홍콩, 프랑스 그리고 몇몇 다른 국가들에서 단체를 만들어 야생동물을 위한 수공예 덮개와 니트로 된 보조용품을 지원했습니다. 해당 단체는 십만 명 이상의 회원을 갖고 있습니다. 제가 언급한 것 이외에도 우리가 그들을 도울 방법은 많습니다. **솔선**하여 생명을 구합시다!

Vocabulary and Sample Sentences

어휘 그리고 예제 문장들

단어	의 미
extinct (adjective) no longer active	멸종된 (형용사) 더는 활동적이지 않은 **예문** Dinosaurs became extinct a long time ago. 공룡들은 오래 전에 멸종했습니다.
humidity (noun) a moderate degree of wetness especially of the atmosphere	습도 (명사) 특히 대기의 적정한 습기 정도 **예문** It depends on the temperature and humidity. 그것은 온도와 습도에 따라 좌우됩니다.
bush fire (noun) an uncontrolled fire in a bush area	산불 (명사) 숲 지역에 통제되지 않는 불 **예문** A bush fire broke out in Australia last month. 지난 달 호주에서 산불이 발생했습니다.
abstain (verb) to choose not to do or have something	자제하다, 삼가다, 기권하다 (동사) 무언가를 가지거나 하지 않기로 선택하는 것 **예문** Ten members voted for the proposal, six members voted against it, and two abstained. 회원 10명은 그 제안에 찬성, 6명은 반대했고 2명은 기권했습니다.

단어	의미
conflagration (noun) especially a large disastrous fire	큰 화재, 대화재 (명사) 특히 대규모의 피해가 큰 화재 **예문** The conflagration destroyed the entire town. 큰 화재로 전체 마을이 훼손 되었습니다.
progressive (adjective) moving forward or onward	진행하는, 진보적인 (형용사) 앞으로 계속해서 움직이는 **예문** We're making slow but steady progress with the decorating. 데코레이팅 작업은 느리지만 꾸준히 진행하고 있습니다.
extinguish (verb) to bring to an end; to cause to cease burning	진화하다, 끝내다 (동사) 마치다; 불타는 것을 멈추게 하다 **예문** It took three hours to extinguish the wildfire. 들불을 진화하는 데 3시간이 걸렸습니다.
circulate (verb) to pass from person to person or place to place	순환하다, 돌다, 퍼지다 (동사) 사람에서 사람으로 혹은 장소에서 장소로 지나가다 **예문** This medicine helps your blood circulate. 이 약품은 당신의 피가 순환하도록 도와줍니다.
vicious (adjective) dangerously aggressive	악의 있는, 타락한, 잔인한 (형용사) 위험할 정도로 공격적인 **예문** She has a vicious temper. 그녀는 포악한 성질을 가지고 있습니다.

단어	의미
recovery (noun) the process of combating a disorder (such as alcoholism) or a real or perceived problem	회복, 복구 (명사) (알코올 중독과 같은) 질병, 실제의 혹은 인지된 문제를 이겨내는 과정 **예문** This policy may slow the pace of economic recovery. 이 정책은 경제 회복 속도를 늦출지도 모릅니다.
sprinkle (verb) to scatter in drops or particles	뿌리다 (동사) 물방울이나 작은 조각들을 흩뿌리다. **예문** He sprinkled water on the plants. 그는 식물에 물을 뿌렸다.
endangered (adjective) in danger of being harmed, lost, unsuccessful	멸종위기에 처한, 위험한 (형용사) 훼손되고, 가망이 없고 성과가 나쁠 위험에 있는 **예문** The list of endangered species includes nearly 600 fishes. 멸종위기에 있는 종들의 목록에 거의 600종의 물고기가 포함되어 있습니다.
habitat (noun) the place or environment where a plant or animal naturally or normally lives and grows	서식지, 생태 (명사) 식물이나 동물이 자연적이고 정상적으로 살고 자라는 장소나 환경 **예문** The panda's natural habitat is the bamboo forest. 판다의 자연 서식지는 대나무 숲이다.
handcrafted (adjective) made using the hands rather than a machine	수공예의, 수제의 (형용사) 기계보다는 손을 사용해서 만들어진 **예문** A lot of our stuff is handcrafted and labour-intensive and so more expensive. 저희 제품의 대다수는 수공예로 만들어지고 많은 노동력을 요구하기 때문에 더 비쌉니다.

단어	의미
initiative (noun) an introductory step	주도권, 결단력, 진취성 (명사) 시작하는 단계 예문 She did it on her own initiative. 그녀는 자신의 결단력으로 그것을 했습니다.

정답 01. (d) 02. (a) 03. (a) 04. (b) 05. (d) 06. (c)

01

영어문제

According to the speech, what is the meaning of "functionally extinct"?

(a) extinction due to impairment in the body function
(b) broken food chain due to lack of prey
(c) survival in the animal population
(d) impossibility in independent survival as a specific population reduced

문제 한글 해석

연설에 의하면 "기능적 멸종"이란 무엇인가?

(a) 신체 기능의 문제로 인한 멸종
(b) 먹이 부족으로 인한 먹이 사슬 훼손
(c) 동물 개체 생존
(d) 특정 개체 수가 감소하여 독자적으로 생존할 수 없게 됨

문제해설

지문에 따르면 기능적으로 멸종된 상태란 특정 동물의 개체 수가 감소하여 독자적으로 생존할 수 없게 됨을 뜻한다.

> Experts also refer to these koalas as "functionally extinct" because 80% of eucalyptus forests, which are the habitat of koalas, are burned. Functionally extinct means impossibility in independent survival due to a reduction in specific animal's population. Local Australian news has reported that at least 28 people died.

02

영어문제

Referring to the speaker, what is the cause of many major and minor forest fires?

(a) high temperature and dry weather
(b) low temperature and dry weather
(c) high temperature and humid weather
(d) low temperature and humid weather

문제 한글 해석

연설가에 의하면 크고 작은 산불의 원인은 무엇인가?

(a) 높은 온도와 건조한 날씨
(b) 낮은 온도와 건조한 날씨
(c) 높은 온도와 습한 날씨
(d) 낮은 온도와 습한 날씨

문제해설

호주는 여름 동안 (12월에서 2월) 높은 온도와 낮은 습도로 인해 많은 크고 작은 산불을 겪는다고 말하고 있다.

> Every year, Australia experiences many major and minor forest fires due to high temperature and low humidity during the summer with casualties resulting more than 800 to 1,850 deaths to recent years. However, the recent fire, for the first time ever, caused the whole Australia come under the influence of fire.

03 영어문제 | 문제 한글 해석

What can be inferred about the Indian Ocean Dipole (IOD) phenomenon?

(a) It might be the major cause of the Australian bush fire.
(b) It causes almost no harm to Australia.
(c) It is the only cause of global warming.
(d) It circulates the ocean worldwide.

인도양 쌍극자 현상에 대해 무엇을 추론할 수 있는가?

(a) 호주 산불의 주요한 원인일 수 있다.
(b) 호주에 나쁜 영향을 거의 주지 않는다.
(c) 지구 온난화의 단 하나뿐인 원인이다.
(d) 전 세계 바다를 순환한다.

문제해설

전문가 대부분이 기록적인 산불의 원인으로 기후 변화를 꼽고 있다. 인도양 쌍극자 현상으로 인해 기후는 매년 덥고 건조해지기 때문에 이 현상이 산불의 주요 원인으로 여겨진다.

> Most of the experts claim that the cause of record-breaking bush fire to be climate change. Due to Indian Ocean Dipole (IOD) phenomenon, the weather gets warmer and drier every year. Starting from September last year, the fire continues until now.

04 영어문제 | 문제 한글 해석

What is the name of the territory in Australia where 1,900 homes were destroyed?

(a) Victoria
(b) New South Wales
(c) Queensland
(d) Tasmania

1,900채의 가구가 소실된 호주 지역의 이름은 무엇인가?

(a) 빅토리아
(b) 뉴사우스웨일스
(c) 퀸즐랜드
(d) 태즈메이니아

문제해설

지문에 따르면 뉴사우스웨일스 주에는 이번 화재 기간에 거의 1,900채의 가구가 소실되었으며 다른 주에서도 300채 이상이 파괴되었다. 그러므로 1,900채의 가구가 소실된 호주 지역의 명칭은 뉴사우스웨일스 주이다.

> Apart from the damage in animal population, there are many harm to Australia. People lost their living place and live in terror of possible bush fire. In New South Wales (NSW), almost 1,900 homes had been destroyed this fire season - with more than 300 razed in other states.

05 영어문제 | 문제 한글 해석

Based on the speech, how does the Australian bush fire impact the global community?

(a) It decreases the number of coals.
(b) It raises the chance of people getting sick.
(c) It increases the frequency of earthquakes.
(d) It may give a bad influence on the global climate.

연설에 의하면 호주 산불은 어떻게 세계 공동체에 영향을 주는가?

(a) 석탄의 숫자가 줄어든다.
(b) 사람들이 아플 확률을 높인다.
(c) 지진이 일어날 빈도를 높인다.
(d) 지구 기후에 악영향을 줄 수 있다.

문제해설

연설자에 따르면 놀랍게도 산불은 전 지구적인 기후에 악영향을 끼칠 것이라는 분석이 있다고 한다. NASA에 따르면 호주 산불로 배출된 연기가 상공에서 최대 17m까지 올라가 이미 지구 반 바퀴를 돌았다고 한다. 산업 활동으로 인한 지구 온난화는 건조하고 고온의 기후를 초래하고 이로 인해 산불이 더 빈번히 발생하며 악순환이 계속된다.

You may question how this issue is relevant to you. You may think that the Australian bush fire impacts only locally. Surprisingly, there is an analysis that the bush fire may give a bad influence to the global climate. In reference to Nasa, the smoke from the bush fire rose up to a maximum 17m in the sky and has already circulated halfway round the world. Global warming from industrial activity causes the environment to be hotter and drier and bush fires happen more frequently, and the vicious cycle continues.

06 영어문제 | 문제 한글 해석

How did New South Wales (NSW) try to save endangered wildlife?

(a) It donated handcrafted goods.
(b) It organized an organization to donate money.
(c) It sprinkled vegetables using helicopters and airplanes.
(d) It gathered a number of volunteers worldwide to rescue animals.

뉴사우스웨일스는 어떻게 멸종위기에 처한 야생동물들을 구하려고 했는가?

(a) 수공예 제품을 기부했다.
(b) 기관을 만들어 돈을 기부했다.
(c) 헬리콥터와 항공기를 사용해서 채소를 뿌렸다.
(d) 전 세계적으로 자원봉사자들을 모아 동물들을 구했다.

문제해설

지문에 따르면 뉴사우스웨일스 주는 헬리콥터와 항공기를 사용해서 4,800파운드의 채소를 뿌렸다고 한다. 이는 멸종위기에 처한 10억 마리의 야생동물들을 구조하기 위한 호주 정부의 노력이라고 전했다.

NSW(New South Wales) sprinkled about 4,800 pounds of vegetables using helicopter and airplane. This is the effort has been made by the Australian government to rescue the one billion endangered wildlife. Vegetables such as carrots and sweet potatoes have been distributed throughout various areas of Australia. The government says that they will provide food and water until the environment returns to normal with enough supply of food and water.

필수 단어, 표현, 숙어 암기노트

단어, 표현, 숙어	의미

필수 단어, 표현, 숙어 암기노트

단어, 표현, 숙어	의미

PREFACE

독해 만렙을 위한
실전모의고사
이 책의 인사말

안녕하세요. **4S G-TELP**의 **한사랑**입니다.

독해 만렙을 위한 실전모의고사 3회는 G-TELP시험의 독해 섹션 내
4개의 파트별 최근 기출 지문 주제와 길이, 난이도, 문제 유형 및 기출어휘를
분석하여 제작되었습니다.

각 파트별 지문의 주제는
PART 1 인물 또는 단체의 전기류의 글로 구성되어 있습니다.
PART 2 잡지에서 볼 수 있는 주제들인 사회의 변화나 우주, 기술 또는 과학과 환경에
관련된 지문으로 구성되어 있습니다.
PART 3 백과사전에 등제되어 있는 표제어에 관련된 지문으로 하나의 사물이나 현상의
유래, 역사 등에 관련된 지문입니다.
PART 4 비즈니스 관련 이메일이 주로 출제되며, 개인적인 편지 등이 출제되기도
합니다.

각 파트별로 내용이해문제 5문항과 어휘문제 2문항으로 총 7문항씩 28문항이며
2018년부터 섹션별 시간제한이 없어졌으므로 다른 섹션의 시간을 독해섹션에서
사용하실 수 있습니다.
독해에서 좀 더 높은 점수를 받을 수 있는 좋은 기회라고 생각합니다.
본 교재는 실제 시험에 나오는 지문의 길이와 난이도를 최대한 유사하게
제작하였습니다.
실전에서 고득점을 받을 수 있도록 시간배분 연습과 자주 출제되는 문제유형 및 지문의
순서 등을 익힐 수 있도록 제작된 이 교재와 함께 꼭 독해 만점을 받기를 기원합니다!

2020년 11월

한사랑

02

4S G-TELP

SIGNATURE

독해 만렙을 위한
실전모의고사

독해 섹션을 위한 사랑의 팁!

1 사람이름, 지위, 기관, 학교 명칭 등은 무시하고 다음 문장으로 넘어가라.

지문 내에 사람이름이나 기관 또는 대학의 이름이 이유 없이 길게 나오는 경우가 대부분이다. 그냥 A대학의 B교수 정도로 해석하고 문제를 푸는데 더 중요한 문장 해석으로 넘어가도록 한다.

ex.
1. It was conducted by a Turkish research team, led by Dr. Fatma Ulger at Ondokuz Mayis University.
   : 그것은 O대학의 F교수에 의해 이끌어 지는 T팀에 의해 행해졌다.

2. "It is a provocative paper," says immunologist Marco Colonna of Washington University School of Medicine in St. Louis.
   : "이 논문은 도발적인 논문입니다." W대학교 의과 대학의 면역 학자 M은 말한다.

3. Researchers led by Michael Heneka of the University of Bonn in Germany started by studying specks made of a protein called ASC that's produced as part of the inflammatory response.
   : B대학교의 M이 이끄는 연구자들은 염증 반응의 일부로 생성 된 ASC라는 단백질로 만들어진 얼룩을 연구하기 시작했다.

2 Said that, found that, announce that 구문이 보인다면
재빠르게 that이하의 문장을 주어 동사 목적어 순서로 해석하라.

ex.
1. They found that 95 percent of telephones were contaminated - often with more than one type of germ.
   : 그들은 발견했다-전화의 95 %가 오염 된 것을- 종종 여러 종류의 세균에 의해

2. On March 16, city officials announced that smoking will be prohibited in public areas in Seoul such as streets, major squares, parks and schools.
   : 3월 16일, 도시 관리들은 발표했다- 거리, 주요 광장, 공원 및 학교와 같은 서울의 공공 장소에서 흡연이 금지 될 것이라고

3. The report said that cell phones used by hospital workers are often contaminated with germs, including those that can cause illness in hospitalized patients.
   : 보고서에 따르면- 병원 직원들이 사용하는 휴대폰은 병원 입원 환자에게 질병을 일으 킬 수 있는 세균을 포함하여 세균에 오염되는 경우가 많다

독해 섹션을 위한 사랑의 팁!

3 수식어구나 절로 이어진 구문이 보인다면 괄호로 잘 묶어 바로 앞의 명사에 업혀준다.

ex.
1. on the street (which will be designed using granite.)
   : 화강암을 사용하여 디자인될 길 위에..
2. the Seoul citizens' walking festival (which will be held on May 16.)
   : 5월 16일에 열릴 서울 시민의 걷기 축제
3. Yuzo Yamamoto of Asahi Press, (which produced the best-selling text book.)
   : 베스트 셀링 교재를 출판하는 아사히신문의 Yuzo Yamamoto

4 There is/ there are로 시작하는 구문은 무조건 ~이/가 있다 라고 단순하게 해석한다.

ex.
1. There are/ many different kinds of restaurants /in the world.
   : 있다/ 많은 다른 종류의 식당들이/ 세상에는
2. there is no /real distinction /between smoking and non-smoking area.
   : 없다/ 확실한 구분이/ 흡연석과 비흡연석 사이에
3. there are /certain parks (where you can walk your dogs.)
   : 있다/ 특정한 공원들이/ 당신이 당신의 개들을 산책시킬 수 있는

5 Of는 항상 of 다음 단어먼저 해석 후 앞 단어를 해석한다.

ex. The purpose of this policy : 이 방침의 목적
the health of non-smokers : 비흡연자들의 건강
increasing numbers of apartment complexes : 아파트단지의 증가하는 숫자들
a variety of no-smoking campaigns : 금연 캠페인의 다양성

독해 만렙을 위한
실전모의고사

4S G-TELP

SIGNATURE

1 회

PART 1. 독해 만렙 실전모의고사

Part 1. Read the following biographical article and answer the questions. The underlined words in the article are for vocabulary questions.

Galileo

Galileo was born in Pisa, in the Tuscany region of Italy, in 1564. He was homeschooled through his early years and later attended the University of Pisa. Galileo soon became bored with his studies and eventually dropped out of the university. Nevertheless, he was offered a position as a mathematics professor there in 1589 after giving an impressive lecture.

While teaching at Pisa, Galileo conducted a legendary experiment in which he challenged Aristotle's law that states that heavier objects fall at a faster rate than lighter objects. According to legend, Galileo went to the top of the Tower of Pisa and dropped various balls of different material, size, and weight from the top. When they all hit the ground at the same time, Galileo had proven Aristotle wrong.

Galileo next taught geometry, mechanics, and astronomy at the University of Padua. It was at Padua where he made many of his amazing discoveries. In 1596, Galileo invented a military compass that could be used to properly aim cannonballs. In 1609, he learned that a Dutch spectacle-maker had invented a device called a spyglass. The spyglass (later called a telescope) made distant objects appear much closer. Before the Dutch inventor could secure a patent, Galileo quickly constructed his own 3-power telescope, and then a 10-power telescope to present to the senate in Venice. Galileo then used his telescope to document the surface of the moon, which he described as bumpy, cratered, and uneven. Galileo next created a 30-power telescope and observed Jupiter and three of its moons that seemed to rotate around the giant planet.

Galileo soon began taking up other scientific interests. In one particular paper he published, Galileo explained theories on ocean tides by using three characters engaging in a "dialogue." One character supported Galileo's views, another character was open-minded, and the last was stubborn and foolish and represented Galileo's enemies. He then wrote a similar book about the Earth rotating around the sun. Although the "dialogues" were very popular with the Italian public, the Pope believed that they were the model for the stubborn and foolish enemies of Galileo. The Pope ordered all of the "dialogues" banned and demanded that Galileo be tried for teaching the theory. Galileo was sentenced to house arrest and forced to confess that his views were flawed. He died in Florence in 1642.

01

Why did Galileo stop studying in the University of Pisa according to the first paragraph?

(a) He didn't have sufficient money to pay for his education.
(b) Studying in the university became boring to him.
(c) He wanted to study in another university.
(d) He needed to have a job to finance his study in the university.

02

What did Galileo try to prove through the experiment at the Tower of Pisa?

(a) The Aristotle's law related to the falling speed is correct.
(b) The heavier objects are, the faster objects fall.
(c) Weights of objects are a conclusive factor in determining the falling speed.
(d) Every object falls at the same speed.

03

Which of the following is NOT true about the telescopes invented by Galileo?

(a) After knowing of a spyglass created by a Dutch spectacle-maker, Galileo started to make the telescopes.
(b) One telescope was used to observe the surface of the moon.
(c) The telescopes had a function to point cannonballs well.
(d) Galileo gradually created the telescopes with higher power.

04

According to the last paragraph, how did people respond to Galileo's theory which was explained by using a "dialogue"?

(a) The Pope was not in favor of his theory.
(b) The "dialogue" didn't receive much attention by the Italian people.
(c) Everyone asked Galileo to teach the theory to the public.
(d) Most of people at that time supported one of three characters in the "dialogue."

05

Based on the passage, how can Galileo's scientific achievement be assessed?

(a) One of what he focused on was the way to follow the previous scientific rules.
(b) He constantly made a lot of efforts to create something new in terms of theory and invention.
(c) Many of scientists were affected by his experiment approach.
(d) He enjoyed provoking a conflict among people.

06

In the context of the passage, the word "construct" means

(a) disassemble
(b) arrange
(c) make
(d) fix

07

In the context of the passage, the word "ban" means

(a) remove
(b) stop
(c) approve
(d) prohibit

갈릴레오

Galileo는 이탈리아 Tuscany 지역의 Pisa에서 1564년에 태어났다. 그는 어린 시절에 홈스쿨링을 했고 후에 Pisa 대학교에 다녔다. Galileo는 그의 학업에 곧 지루함을 느꼈고 결국 대학교를 중퇴했다. 그럼에도 불구하고, 그는 인상적인 강의를 하고 나서 1589년 그곳에서 수학과 교수직을 제안 받았다.

Pisa에서 가르치는 동안, 가벼운 물체보다 무거운 물체가 더 빠른 속도로 떨어진다고 한 Aristotle의 법칙에 도전한 전설적인 실험을 수행했다. 전설에 따르면, Galileo는 Tower of Pisa(피사의 사탑)의 꼭대기로 가서 다른 재료, 크기, 무게의 다양한 공들을 꼭대기에서 떨어뜨렸다. 그것들 모두가 동시에 땅에 닿았을 때, Galileo는 Aristotle가 틀렸다는 걸 증명했다.

Galileo는 다음으로 Padua 대학교에서 기하학, 역학 그리고 천문학을 가르쳤다. 그가 많은 놀라운 발견을 한 곳이 Padua였다. 1596년에 Galileo는 포탄을 알맞게 조준하는 데 사용될 수 있는 군용 나침반을 발명했다. 1609년에 그는 네덜란드 출신의 어느 안경 제조가가 작은 망원경이라고 불리는 고안품을 발명했다는 것을 알았다. 작은 망원경(후에 망원경이라고 불림)은 멀리 있는 물체를 훨씬 가까이 보이게 만들었다. 네덜란드 발명가가 특허를 얻기 전에, Galileo는 Venice 상원에서 보여주기 위해서 3배율 망원경을, 그리고 나서 10배율 망원경을 곧 만들었다. Galileo는 그리고 나서 그가 울퉁불퉁하고 구멍이 있고 평평하지 않다고 묘사했던 달의 표면을 문서화하기 위해서 그의 망원경을 사용했다. Galileo는 다음에 30배율 망원경을 제작했고 목성과 거대한 행성 주위를 회전하는 것처럼 보이는 그것의 3개의 위성들을 관측했다.

Galileo는 곧 다른 과학적인 관심을 가지기 시작했다. 그가 출판했던 한 특정 논문에서, Galileo는 대화에 참여하는 세 명의 인물을 이용함으로써 해양 조류에 관한 이론을 설명했다.

한 인물은 Galileo의 관점을 지지하고 또 다른 인물은 개방적이고 마지막 사람은 완고하고 어리석고 Galileo의 적을 대변했다. 그는 그리고 나서 지구가 태양 주위를 회전하는 것에 대한 비슷한 책을 썼다. 비록 그 "대화"가 이탈리아 대중에게 매우 인기가 있었지만, 교황은 그 대화들이 Galileo의 완고스럽고 어리석은 적에 대한 표본이라고 믿었다. 교황은 모든 "대화"를 금지시키도록 명했고 Galileo가 그 이론을 가르친다는 혐의로 재판을 받아야 한다고 강력히 요구했다. Galileo는 가택연금을 선고받았고 그의 관점에 결함이 있다고 자백하도록 강요받았다. 그는 1642년 Florence에서 죽었다.

- drop out 자퇴하다
- military compass 군용 나침반
- spectacle-maker 안경 제조업자
- senate 상원, 원로원
- cratered 분화구가 있는
- take up 시작하다
- engage in 참여하다, 관여하다
- stubborn 완고한, 고집스러운
- sentence 선고하다
- legendary 전설적인
- cannonball 포탄
- spyglass 작은 망원경
- bumpy 울퉁불퉁한
- uneven 평평하지 않은
- ocean tides 해양 조류
- open-minded 마음이 열린
- ban 금지하다
- flawed 결함 있는, 흠 있는

정답 01. (b) 02. (d) 03. (c) 04. (a) 05. (b) 06. (c) 07. (d)

01 영어문제 | 문제 한글 해석

Why did Galileo stop studying in the University of Pisa according to the first paragraph?

(a) He didn't have sufficient money to pay for his education.
(b) Studying in the university became boring to him.
(c) He wanted to study in another university.
(d) He needed to have a job to finance his study in the university.

첫 번째 문단에 의하면, Galileo가 Pisa 대학교에서 공부하는 것을 그만둔 이유는?

(a) 그는 학비를 조달할 충분한 돈을 가지고 있지 않았다.
(b) 대학교에서 공부하는 것이 그에게 지루해졌다.
(c) 그는 다른 대학교에서 공부하기를 원했다.
(d) 그는 대학교에서 그의 공부에 자금을 대기 위해 직업을 가져야만 했다.

문제해설

첫 번째 문단을 보면, Galileo가 Pisa 대학교에 들어간 뒤 그의 학업에 지루함을 느끼고 대학교를 그만두었다는 사실을 알 수 있다.

> Galileo was born in Pisa, in the Tuscany region of Italy, in 1564. He was homeschooled through his early years and later attended the University of Pisa. Galileo soon became bored with his studies and eventually dropped out of the university. Nevertheless, he was offered a position as a mathematics professor there in 1589 after giving an impressive lecture.

02 영어문제 | 문제 한글 해석

What did Galileo try to prove through the experiment at the Tower of Pisa?

(a) The Aristotle's law related to the falling speed is correct.
(b) The heavier objects are, the faster objects fall.
(c) Weights of objects are a conclusive factor in determining the falling speed.
(d) Every object falls at the same speed.

Galileo가 피사의 사탑에서 한 실험을 통해 증명하고자 했던 것은?

(a) 하강 속도에 대한 Aristotle의 법칙이 옳다.
(b) 물체가 무거울수록, 물체는 더 빠르게 떨어진다.
(c) 물체의 무게는 하강 속도를 결정하는 결정적인 요소이다.
(d) 모든 물체는 똑같은 속도로 떨어진다.

문제해설

두 번째 문단을 보면 Galileo는 피사의 사탑에서 각각 재료, 크기, 무게 등이 다양한 공들을 떨어뜨리는 실험을 했고, 공들 모두가 같은 시간에 땅에 떨어졌다. 이를 통해 재료, 크기, 무게 등에 상관없이 사물은 같은 속도로 떨어진다는 것을 증명했다는 점을 알 수 있다.

> While teaching at Pisa, Galileo conducted a legendary experiment in which he challenged Aristotle's law that states that heavier objects fall at a faster rate than lighter objects. According to legend, Galileo went to the top of the Tower of Pisa and dropped various balls of different material, size, and weight from the top. When they all hit the ground at the same time, Galileo had proven Aristotle wrong.

03 영어문제

Which of the following is NOT true about the telescopes invented by Galileo?

(a) After knowing of a spyglass created by a Dutch spectacle-maker, Galileo started to make the telescopes.
(b) One telescope was used to observe the surface of the moon.
(c) The telescopes had a function to point cannonballs well.
(d) Galileo gradually created the telescopes with higher power.

문제 한글 해석

Galileo에 의해 발명된 망원경들에 대한 설명으로 바르지 않은 것은?

(a) Galileo는 한 네덜란드 안경사가 만든 작은 망원경이라고 불리는 장치를 개발한 것을 알게 된 이후 망원경들을 발명하기 시작했다.
(b) 한 망원경은 달의 표면을 관측하기 위하여 사용되었다.
(c) 그 망원경들은 포탄을 잘 조준하는 기능을 가지고 있었다.
(d) Galileo는 점차 더 높은 배율의 망원경을 발명하였다.

문제해설

(a) Galileo는 한 네덜란드 안경사가 작은 망원경이라고 불리는 장치를 개발한 것을 안 뒤에, 그 네덜란드 발명가가 특허를 얻기 전에 3배율 망원경을 만들었다.

> The spyglass (later called a telescope) made distant objects appear much closer. Before the Dutch inventor could secure a patent, Galileo quickly constructed his own 3-power telescope, and then a 10-power telescope to present to the senate in Venice.

(b) Galileo는 달의 표면을 문서화하기 위해 그의 망원경을 사용했다.

> Galileo then used his telescope to document the surface of the moon, which he described as bumpy, cratered, and uneven.

(c) 포탄을 올바르게 조준하기 위해 사용될 수 있었던 것은 망원경이 아니라, 그가 1596년에 발명했던 군용 나침반이다.

> In 1596, Galileo invented a military compass that could be used to properly aim cannonballs.

(d) 세 번째 문단을 보면, Galileo가 처음에는 3배율 망원경을, 그 다음에는 10배율 망원경을, 이후에는 30배율 망원경을 만들었다는 사실을 알 수 있다.

> Before the Dutch inventor could secure a patent, Galileo quickly constructed his own 3-power telescope, and then a 10-power telescope to present to the senate in Venice. Galileo then used his telescope to document the surface of the moon, which he described as bumpy, cratered, and uneven. Galileo next created a 30-power telescope and observed Jupiter and three of its moons that seemed to rotate around the giant planet.

04 영어문제

According to the last paragraph, how did people respond to Galileo's theory which was explained by using a "dialogue"?

(a) The Pope was not in favor of his theory.
(b) The "dialogue" didn't receive much attention by the Italian people.
(c) Everyone asked Galileo to teach the theory to the public.
(d) Most of people at that time supported one of three characters in the "dialogue."

문제 한글 해석

마지막 문단에 따르면, "대화"를 이용함으로써 설명된 Galileo의 이론에 대해 사람들은 어떻게 반응하였는가?

(a) 교황은 그의 이론을 지지하지 않았다.
(b) 그 "대화"는 이탈리아 대중들에게 많은 관심을 받지 못했다.
(c) 모두들 Galileo가 대중들에게 그 이론을 가르칠 것을 요청했다.
(d) 당시 대부분의 사람들은 그 "대화"의 세 명의 인물 중 한 명을 지지했다.

문제해설

마지막 문단에 따르면, 교황은 그 대화들을 Galileo의 완고스럽고 어리석은 적에 대한 표본이라고 믿었으며, 결국 그 모든 대화를 금지시켰다는 것을 통해, 교황이 그 대화를 통한 이론을 지지하지 않았음을 알 수 있다.

> Although the "dialogues" were very popular with the Italian public, the Pope believed that they were the model for the stubborn and foolish enemies of Galileo. The Pope ordered all of the "dialogues" banned and demanded that Galileo be tried for teaching the theory. Galileo was sentenced to house arrest and forced to confess that his views were flawed. He died in Florence in 1642.

05 영어문제 | 문제 한글 해석

Based on the passage, how can Galileo's scientific achievement be assessed?

(a) One of what he focused on was the way to follow the previous scientific rules.
(b) He constantly made a lot of efforts to create something new in terms of theory and invention.
(c) Many of scientists were affected by his experiment approach.
(d) He enjoyed provoking a conflict among people.

이 글에 따르면, Galileo의 과학적 업적은 어떻게 평가받을 수 있을까?

(a) 그가 집중했던 것 중 하나는 이전의 과학적 규칙들을 따르는 방법이었다.
(b) 그는 이론과 발명품 면에서 어떤 새로운 것을 창조하기 위해 많은 노력을 했다.
(c) 많은 과학자들이 그의 실험 접근방식에 의해 영향을 받았다.
(d) 그는 사람들 사이에 분쟁을 일으키기를 즐겼다.

문제해설

두 번째 문단을 통해 그가 피사의 사탑에서 한 실험을 통해 모든 물체는 같은 속도로 떨어진다는 새로운 이론을 만들었다는 것을 알 수 있다.

> According to legend, Galileo went to the top of the Tower of Pisa and dropped various balls of different material, size, and weight from the top. When they all hit the ground at the same time, Galileo had proven Aristotle wrong.

또한 세 번째 문단을 통해 그가 군용 나침반 및 여러 배율의 망원경을 만들었다는 것을 알 수 있다.

> Galileo next taught geometry, mechanics, and astronomy at the University of Padua. It was at Padua where he made many of his amazing discoveries. In 1596, Galileo invented a military compass that could be used to properly aim cannonballs. In 1609, he learned that a Dutch spectacle-maker had invented a device called a spyglass. The spyglass (later called a telescope) made distant objects appear much closer. Before the Dutch inventor could secure a patent, Galileo quickly constructed his own 3-power telescope, and then a 10-power telescope to present to the senate in Venice. Galileo then used his telescope to document the surface of the moon, which he described as bumpy, cratered, and uneven. Galileo next created a 30-power telescope and observed Jupiter and three of its moons that seemed to rotate around the giant planet.

마지막으로 네 번째 문단을 통해 해양 조류에 관한 이론을 설명했고, 지구가 태양 주위를 회전하는 것에 대한 책을 썼다는 점을 알 수 있다.

> Galileo soon began taking up other scientific interests. In one particular paper he published, Galileo explained theories on ocean tides by using three characters engaging in a "dialogue." One character supported Galileo's views, another character was open-minded, and the last was stubborn and foolish and represented Galileo's enemies. He then wrote a similar book about the Earth rotating around the sun. Although the "dialogues" were very popular with the Italian public, the Pope believed that he was the model for the stubborn and foolish enemy of Galileo. The Pope ordered all of the "dialogues" banned and demanded that Galileo be tried for teaching the theory. Galileo was sentenced to house arrest and forced to confess that his views were flawed. He died in Florence in 1642.

즉, 이를 통해 Galileo가 끊임없이 새로운 이론과 발명품을 만들었으며, 이를 위해 실험을 하고 책을 내는 등 많은 노력을 했다는 점을 알 수 있다. 따라서 그가 과거의 과학적 규칙들을 따랐다고 설명하는 보기 (a)는 그의 업적과 반대되는 내용을 담고 있다. 보기 (c)의 내용은 윗글의 내용만으로 판단하기가 어렵다. 또한 마지막 문단에 그가 대화를 통해 설명한 이론이 교황으로부터 비난을 받기는 했지만, 이 글의 내용만으로 그가 분쟁을 일으키기를 좋아했다는 사람이라고 볼 수는 없다. 따라서 보기 (d)도 틀린 내용이다.

06 영어문제 | 문제 한글 해석

In the context of the passage, the word "construct" means
(a) disassemble
(b) arrange
(c) make
(d) fix

이 글의 문맥상 "construct"은 무엇을 의미하는가?
(a) 분해하다
(b) 정리하다
(c) 만들다
(d) 수리하다

문제해설

이 글의 문맥상 "construct"는 이 지문에서 '만들다', '제작하다'를 의미한다. 따라서 가장 가까운 의미의 (c) make가 정답이 된다. construct는 이외에도 "공사하다" "건설하다"의 의미도 있으므로 함께 익혀둔다.

07 영어문제 | 문제 한글 해석

In the context of the passage, the word "ban" means
(a) remove
(b) stop
(c) approve
(d) prohibit

이 글의 문맥상 "ban"은 무엇을 의미하는가?
(a) 제거하다
(b) 멈추게 하다
(c) 승인하다
(d) 금지하다

문제해설

이 글에서 "ban"은 '금지하다'의 의미로, (d) prohibit과 가장 가까운 뜻을 가졌다. 그 외에 (a), (b), (c)는 ban과 상관 없는 의미의 단어들이다.

PART 2. 독해 만렙 실전모의고사

Part 2. Read the following magazine article and answer the questions.
The underlined words in the article are for vocabulary questions.

RoboCop joins Dubai police to fight real life crime

This story is not about the 1987 American cyberpunk action film. This is the real thing and it is happening. But you can't see it on the streets near you, unless of course you live in Dubai. As many avid manias of the film with recall, the plot is set in crime ridden Detroit in the future, and RoboCop centres on police officer Alex Murphy who is murdered by a gang of criminals and subsequently revived by the megacorporation Omni Consumer Products (OCP) as a superhuman cyborg law enforcer known as RoboCop. The film received rave reviews and was cited as one of the best films of 1987. It was followed by two sequels, a television series, a remake, two animated TV series.

The real thing in Dubai can help identify wanted criminals and collect evidence and is the latest recruit to the Dubai police service. The robot policeman will patrol busy areas in the city, as part of a government programme <u>aimed</u> at replacing some human crime- fighters with machines. Now although the Dubai "RoboCop" is clad in colours of the Dubai Police uniform, there is no mistaking that it still looks like a robot. But, do not be taken in by that; it can shake hands, salute in military style, can read vehicle licence plates, is equipped with cameras and facial recognition software and its video feed can help police watch for risks such as unattended bags in popular areas of Dubai, which are of course a financial and tourism hub.

The wheeled "RoboCop" will work for 24 hours per day, won't go on maternity leave, and as Brigadier Khalid Nasser Al Razooqi, director general of the Smart Services Department at Dubai Police, commented it will not go sick either; well unless there is any circuits <u>malfunction</u> of course! Members of the public can talk to "RoboCop" if they want to report a crime. They can also communicate with it using a touch screen computer embedded in its chest.

01

Which of the following is NOT true about the film according to the first paragraph?

(a) The setting of the movie was the region of Detroit.
(b) This film was based on the true story.
(c) Alex Murphy who had once been a police officer revived as RoboCop.
(d) Detroit was an area with a high incidence of crime.

02

In Dubai, what is the governmental aim of the robot policeman?

(a) for having a substitute for people combatting crimes
(b) to reduce costs related to criminal works
(c) in order to make the city safer and better
(d) for the purpose of developing state-of-the-art technology

03

Which of the following is NOT true about what the robot policeman is able to do?

(a) The robot policeman can help to gather the proofs.
(b) One of its roles is to guard some areas in the city.
(c) It has a function to identify vehicle license plates.
(d) All risks such as unattended bags can be removed by its help.

04

In which circumstance will the RoboCop be able to work all day?

(a) when it becomes more intelligent than any human
(b) in a situation where it maintains the ability to do its job properly
(c) in a case that it is updated regularly
(d) if there is no defect in its circuit

05

According to the passage, what does it mean to use the RoboCop in Dubai?

(a) an increasing conflict between human-beings and robots
(b) solving all of the problems happened in the city in a perfect way
(c) helping human policemen to do their jobs in some ways
(d) protecting the citizens from every potential danger

06

In the context of the passage, the word "aim" means

(a) intend   (b) mind
(c) forgive   (d) criticize

07

In the context of the passage, the word "malfunction" means

(a) role   (b) drawback
(c) equipment   (d) apparatus

RoboCop, 실제 범죄와 싸우기 위해 두바이 경찰에 합류하다

이 이야기는 1987년 미국 사이버 펑크 액션 영화에 관한 이야기가 아니다. 이건 실제의 이야기이며 지금 일어나고 있는 일이다. 물론 당신이 사는 곳에서는 이 광경을 볼 수는 없다. 당신이 두바이에 살고 있는 것이 아니라면 말이다. 많은 영화의 열렬한 매니아들이 기억하는 것처럼, 줄거리는 미래에 범죄가 들끓는 Detroit가 배경이고 RoboCop은 경찰관 Alex Murphy를 중심으로 진행되는데, 그는 범죄 조직에 의해 살해당하고 그 후 거대 기업 Omni Consumer Products(OCP)에 의해 RoboCop로 알려진 초인간적 사이보그 법 진행관으로 부활했다. 그 영화는 극찬을 받았고 1987년의 최고의 영화 중 하나로 꼽히는데, 이 작품 후로 2개의 속편, 하나의 텔레비전 시리즈, 리메이크, 두 개의 애니메이션 TV시리즈가 생겨났다.

Dubai에 실재하는 것은 지명 수배자의 신원을 확인하고 증거 수집하는 것을 도와줄 수 있고 Dubai 경찰서에 가장 최근에 들어온 신입 경찰이다. 그 로봇 경찰은 인간 범죄 수사대원을 기계로 대체하는 것을 목표로 한 정부 프로그램의 일부로서 도시의 번잡한 지역들을 순찰할 것이다. 비록 지금은 Dubai "RoboCop"이 Dubai 경찰복 색의 옷을 입고 있지만, 여전히 로봇처럼 보인다는 것은 틀림없다. 그러나 그 점에 넘어가지는 말라. 그것은 악수를 할 수 있고, 경례를 할 수 있고, 차량 번호판을 읽을 수 있고, 카메라와 얼굴 인식 소프트웨어가 장착되어 있으며, 그것의 영상 자료는 경제 및 관광 명소인 두바이의 인기 있는 지역에서 방치된 가방 등과 같은 위험 요소를 경찰이 경계하도록 도와줄 수 있다.

바퀴가 달린 로보캅은 하루에 24시간 일할 수 있고, 출산 휴가를 떠나지 않을 것이며, Dubai 경찰서의 Smart Services Department의 과장 Brigadier Khalid Nasser Al Razooqi가 언급한 바와 같이, 회로 오작동만 일으키지 않는다면 아플 일도 없을 것이다. 대중들은 그들이 범죄를 보고하기 원한다면 "RoboCop"에게 얘기할 수 있고, 가슴에 끼워져 있는 터치스크린을 사용해서 그것과 의사소통을 할 수 있다.

- ☐ **cyberpunk** 하이테크 공상 과학 소설
- ☐ **mania** 매니아
- ☐ **murder** 살인하다
- ☐ **subsequently** 나중에, 그 뒤에
- ☐ **law enforcer** 법 집행자, 경찰관
- ☐ **identify** 확인하다
- ☐ **recruit** 신입 경찰; 모집하다
- ☐ **replace A with B** A를 B로 대체하다
- ☐ **salute** 경례를 하다
- ☐ **facial recognition** 얼굴 인식
- ☐ **financial** 재정적인
- ☐ **maternity leave** 출산 휴가
- ☐ **embed** 끼워 넣다
- ☐ **avid** 열심인
- ☐ **ridden** 들끓는
- ☐ **gang** 갱, 범죄 조직
- ☐ **megacorporation** 거대 기업
- ☐ **rave reviews** 극찬하는 기사
- ☐ **wanted criminals** 지명 수배자
- ☐ **patrol** 순찰을 돌다
- ☐ **clad** ~을 입은, ~이 덮인
- ☐ **be equipped with** ~를 갖추다
- ☐ **unattended** 지켜보는 사람이 없는
- ☐ **tourism hub** 관광중심지
- ☐ **malfunction** 오작동

정답 01. (b) 02. (a) 03. (d) 04. (d) 05. (c) 06. (a) 07. (b)

01 영어문제 | 문제 한글 해석

Which of the following is NOT true about the film according to the first paragraph?

(a) The setting of the movie was the region of Detroit.
(b) This film was based on the true story.
(c) Alex Murphy who had once been a police officer revived as RoboCop.
(d) Detroit was an area with a high incidence of crime.

첫 번째 문단에 따르면, 영화에 대한 설명으로 바르지 않은 것은?

(a) 영화의 배경은 Detroit라는 지역이었다.
(b) 이 영화는 실화를 바탕으로 했다.
(c) 한때 경찰관이었던 Alex Murphy는 RoboCop으로 부활했다.
(d) Detroit는 범죄 발생률이 높은 지역이었다.

문제해설

첫 번째 문단을 통해 그 영화가 실화 바탕이라는 사실은 어디에도 나와 있지 않다.

This story is not about the 1987 American cyberpunk action film. This is the real thing and it is happening. But you can't see it on the streets near you, unless of course you live in Dubai. As many avid mania of the film with recall, (a) the plot is set (d) in crime ridden Detroit in the future, and (c) RoboCop centres on police officer Alex Murphy who is murdered by a gang of criminals and subsequently revived by the megacorporation Omni Consumer Products (OCP) as a superhuman cyborg law enforcer known as RoboCop. The film received rave reviews and was cited as one of the best films of 1987. It was followed by two sequels, a television series, a remake, two animated TV series.

02 영어문제

In Dubai, what is the governmental aim of the robot policeman?

(a) for having a substitute for people combatting crimes
(b) to reduce costs related to criminal works
(c) in order to make the city safer and better
(d) for the purpose of developing state-of-the-art technology

문제 한글 해석

Dubai에서 로봇 경찰에 대한 정부의 목표는?

(a) 범죄와 싸우는 사람들을 대체하기 위하여
(b) 범죄 업무와 관련된 비용을 줄이기 위하여
(c) 도시를 더 안전하고 더 좋게 만들기 위하여
(d) 첨단 기술을 개발할 목적으로

문제해설

두 번째 문단을 통해 로봇 경찰은 인간 범죄 수사대원을 기계로 대체하는 것을 목표로 한 정부 프로그램의 일부로서 배치되었음을 알 수 있다.

The real thing in Dubai can help identify wanted criminals and collect evidence and is the latest recruit to the Dubai police service. The robot policeman will patrol busy areas in the city, as part of a government programme aimed at replacing some human crime-fighters with machines. Now although the Dubai "RoboCop" is clad in colours of the Dubai Police uniform, there is no mistaking that it still looks like a robot. But, do not be taken in by that; it can shake hands, salute in military style, can read vehicle licence plates, is equipped with cameras and facial recognition software and its video feed can help police watch for risks such as unattended bags in popular areas of Dubai, which are of course a financial and tourism hub.

03 영어문제

Which of the following is NOT true about what the robot policeman is able to do?

(a) The robot policeman can help to gather the proofs.
(b) One of its roles is to guard some areas in the city.
(c) It has a function to identify vehicle license plates.
(d) All risks such as unattended bags can be removed by its help.

문제 한글 해석

로봇 경찰이 할 수 있는 일로 바르지 않은 것은?

(a) 로봇 경찰은 증거를 모으는 일을 도울 수 있다.
(b) 그 역할 중 하나는 도시의 일부 지역을 순찰하는 것이다.
(c) 그것은 차량 번호판을 식별하는 기능을 가지고 있다.
(d) 방치된 가방 등과 같은 모든 위험 요소를 그의 도움으로 제거할 수 있다.

문제해설

지켜보는 사람이 없는 가방과 같은 위험을 지켜보는 것을 도울 수는 있지만, 그러한 모든 위험을 제거할 수 있는 것은 아니다.

The real thing in Dubai can help identify wanted criminals and (a) collect evidence and is the latest recruit to the Dubai police service. (b) The robot policeman will patrol busy areas in the city, as part of a government programme aimed at replacing some human crime-fighters with machines. Now although the Dubai "RoboCop" is clad in colours of the Dubai Police uniform, there is no mistaking that it still looks like a robot. But, do not be taken in by that; it can shake hands, salute in military style, (c) can read vehicle licence plates, is equipped with cameras and facial recognition software and its video feed can help police watch for risks such as unattended bags in popular areas of Dubai, which are of course a financial and tourism hub.

04 영어문제

In which circumstance will the RoboCop be able to work all day?

(a) when it becomes more intelligent than any human
(b) in a situation where it maintains the ability to do its job properly
(c) in a case that it is updated regularly
(d) if there is no defect in its circuit

문제 한글 해석

어떤 상황에서 RoboCop은 하루 종일 일할 수 있는가?

(a) 어떤 사람보다 지능이 높아졌을 때
(b) 업무를 적절하게 수행할 수 있는 능력을 유지하는 상황에서
(c) 정기적으로 업데이트 받는 경우
(d) 그 회로에 결함이 없다면

문제해설

마지막 문단을 통해 RoboCop이 회로 오작동만 있지 않는다면 24시간 동안 일할 수 있으며, 출산 휴가나 병가를 내지 않을 것이라는 것을 알 수 있다.

The wheeled "RoboCop" will work for 24 hours per day, won't go on maternity leave, and as Brigadier Khalid Nasser Al Razooqi, director general of the Smart Services Department at Dubai Police, commented it will not go sick either; well unless there is any circuits malfunction of course! Members of the public can talk to "RoboCop" if they want to report a crime. They can also communicate with it using a touch screen computer embedded in its chest.

05 영어문제

According to the passage, what does it mean to use the RoboCop in Dubai?

(a) an increasing conflict between human-beings and robots
(b) solving all of the problems happened in the city in a perfect way
(c) helping human policemen to do their jobs in some ways
(d) protecting the citizens from every potential danger

문제 한글 해석

이 글에 따르면, 두바이에서 RoboCop을 사용한다는 것은 어떤 의미를 가지는가?

(a) 인간들과 로봇들 간의 증가하는 분쟁
(b) 도시에서 발생하는 모든 문제를 완벽하게 해결하는 것
(c) 여러 가지 면에서 인간 경찰관들이 직무를 수행할 수 있도록 도와주는 것
(d) 모든 잠재적인 위험에서 시민들을 보호하는 것

문제해설

두 번째 문단을 통해 RoboCop은 사람 경찰관이 하는 일의 일부를 도와줄 수 있는 여러 가지 기능을 가지고 있다. 따라서 어떤 면에서 인간 경찰관들이 그들의 일을 하는 데 도움을 줄 수 있다고 설명한 (c)가 정답이다.

The real thing in Dubai can help identify wanted criminals and collect evidence and is the latest recruit to the Dubai police service. The robot policeman will patrol busy areas in the city, as part of a government programme aimed at replacing some human crime-fighters with machines. Now although the Dubai "RoboCop" is clad in colours of the Dubai Police uniform, there is no mistaking that it still looks like a robot. But, do not be taken in by that; it can shake hands, salute in military style, can read vehicle licence plates, is equipped with cameras and facial recognition software and its video feed can help police watch for risks such as unattended bags in popular areas of Dubai, which are of course a financial and tourism hub.

06 영어문제

In the context of the passage, the word "aim" means

(a) intend
(b) mind
(c) forgive
(d) criticize

문제 한글 해석

이 글의 문맥상 "aim"은 무엇을 의미하는가?

(a) 의도하다
(b) 상관하다
(c) 용서하다
(d) 비판하다

문제해설

이 글의 문맥상 "aim"은 이 지문에서 '목표로 하다', '목적을 두다'를 의미한다. 따라서 가장 가까운 의미의 (a) intend '~을/를 의도하다'가 정답이 된다.

07 영어문제

In the context of the passage, the word "malfunction" means

(a) role
(b) drawback
(c) equipment
(d) apparatus

문제 한글 해석

이 글의 문맥상 "malfunction"는 무엇을 의미하는가?

(a) 역할
(b) 결점
(c) 장비
(d) 장치, 기구

문제해설

이 글에서 "malfunction"은 '결점, 결함'의 의미로, (b) drawback '결점, 결함'과 가장 가까운 뜻을 가졌다. 그 외에 error, downside 등의 유의어도 함께 익혀두자.

MEMO

PART 3. 독해 만렙 실전모의고사

Part 3. Read the following encyclopedia article and answer the questions.
The underlined words in the article are for vocabulary questions.

Groundhog's Day

Groundhog's Day occurs every February 2nd in the United States. According to tradition, when a groundhog comes out of its burrow on this day and sees that it is cloudy, spring will come early. If the groundhog comes out of its burrow and it is sunny, and thus sees its shadow, winter will persist for six more weeks and the groundhog will return to its burrow.

While Groundhog's Day may have first been celebrated in Pennsylvania Dutch Country in the early 1800s, it was first <u>celebrated</u> as a holiday in Punxsutawney, Pennsylvania, in 1886. The following year, the town crowned "Phil" as the official groundhog of Groundhog's Day. Phil would henceforth be known as Punxsutawney Phil. There have been many "Phils" over the years, but according to the Punxsutawney Groundhog Club website, Phil is 131 years old and counting! He has been able to live so long because he drinks a special formula called "Groundhog's Punch."

You might think that such a special rodent would have special <u>prediction</u> abilities. According to the Punxsutawney Groundhog Club, this is not the case. Phil's recorded predictions over the years have only yielded an accuracy rate of about 39%. Furthermore, in the 103 years in which Phil's predictions have been recorded, he has only predicted the coming of an early spring 17 times! Phil's poor predictive abilities, however, have not seemed to impact the importance of Groundhog's Day. Thousands of people descend upon Punxsutawney every February to help the city celebrate.

01

What can be inferred by the fact that the groundhog sees the shadow after coming out of its burrow?

(a) It can be inferred that spring will come soon.
(b) The fact implies that it is cloudy.
(c) We can infer that winter will not be over for a while.
(d) It means that the groundhog will stay on the ground, not returning to its burrow.

02

Which of the following is true about "Phil"?

(a) There has been only one Phil in the world.
(b) One Phil ended its life at the age of 131.
(c) Groundhog's Day was first celebrated as a holiday in the early 1800s.
(d) The special reason for Phil's longevity is on his food.

03

Which information does the Punxsutawney Groundhog Club provide?

(a) Phil became an official groundhog of Groundhog's Day.
(b) Phil has no special ability to predict the coming of the spring accurately.
(c) Another name of Phil is Punxsutawney Phil.
(d) Punxsutawaney is crowded by a lot of people every February.

04

What is the meaning of Phil to the people in the city?

(a) People can celebrate an event altogether every year regardless of its ability.
(b) Phil has a great meaning in terms of his outstanding prediction ability.
(c) He is an important tool for weather forecasting.
(d) Thousands of people are influenced by its ability as a special rodent.

05

Which of the following is NOT true about the Groundhog's Day?

(a) The date which is celebrated as Groundhog's Day is February 2nd.
(b) There is a tradition which is about predicting the coming of spring according to the groundhog's act.
(c) It became a holiday from the time when it had been first celebrated.
(d) People enjoy celebrating the Groundhog's Day regardless of Phil's prediction abilities.

06

In the context of the passage, the word "celebrate" means

(a) graduate
(b) decorate
(c) recognize
(d) commemorate

07

In the context of the passage, the word "prediction" means

(a) forecast
(b) observation
(c) prevention
(d) accuracy

입춘

Groundhog's Day은 미국에서 매년 2월 2일에 열린다. 전통에 따르면, 이날에 마멋이 굴 밖으로 나와서 날이 흐린 걸 본다면, 봄은 일찍 올 것이다. 만약에 마멋이 굴 밖으로 나와서 해가 비추어 그늘을 본다면, 겨울은 6주 더 지속될 것이고 마멋은 굴로 돌아갈 것이다.

Groundhog's Day가 1800년대 초기에 Pennsylvania Dutch Country에서 처음으로 기념되었을지 모르는 반면에, 이것은 1886년 Pennsylvania주 Punxsutawney에서 공휴일로 처음 기념되었다. 이듬해에, 그 마을은 "Phil"을 Groundhog's Day의 공식적인 마멋으로 등극시켰다. Phil은 이후로 Punxsutawney Phil로 알려졌다. 몇 년 동안 많은 "Phil"들이 있어 왔지만, Punxsutawney Groundhog Club 웹 사이트에 따르면, Phil은 131살이고 지금까지도 살고 있다! 그는 "Groundhog's Punch"라고 불리는 특별한 유동식을 마시기 때문에 그렇게 오래 살 수 있었다.

당신은 이 특별한 설치류가 특별한 예측 능력을 가졌을 것이라고 생각할지 모른다. Punxsutawney Groundhog Club에 따르면, 그것은 사실이 아니다. 몇 년 동안 기록된 Phil의 예측들은 오직 약 39%의 적중률을 냈다. 게다가, Phil의 예측들이 기록된 103년 동안, 그는 초기 봄이 오는 것을 단지 17번 예측해냈다! 그러나, Phil의 형편없는 예측 능력은 Groundhog's Day의 중요성에 영향을 미치는 것처럼 보이지 않았다. 수천 명의 사람들이 그 도시가 기념하는 것을 도와주기 위해서 매년 2월 Punxsutawney에 몰려온다.

- groundhog 마멋
- shadow 그늘
- celebrate 기념하다
- formula 유동식, 공식, 비법, 분유
- prediction 예측
- accuracy rate 적중률
- predictive 예측의, 예견의
- descend upon ~에 몰려오다
- burrow 굴; 굴을 파다
- persist 지속하다, 고집하다
- henceforth 이후로
- rodent 설치류
- yield 생산하다, 양보하다
- furthermore 게다가
- impact 영향, 충격

정답 01. (c)　02. (d)　03. (b)　04. (a)　05. (c)　06. (d)　07. (a)

01　영어문제

What can be inferred by the fact that the groundhog sees the shadow after coming out of its burrow?

(a) It can be inferred that spring will come soon.
(b) The fact implies that it is cloudy.
(c) We can infer that winter will not be over for a while.
(d) It means that the groundhog will stay on the ground, not returning to its burrow.

문제 한글 해석

마멋이 굴 밖으로 나와서 그림자를 본다는 사실을 통해 무엇을 추론할 수 있는가?

(a) 봄이 곧 올 것이라는 것을 추론할 수 있다.
(b) 그 사실은 구름이 꼈다는 것을 암시한다.
(c) 우리는 겨울이 한동안 끝나지 않을 것을 추론할 수 있다.
(d) 그것은 마멋이 굴에 돌아가지 않고, 지상에 머무를 것을 의미한다.

문제해설

첫 번째 문단을 통해 마멋이 굴 밖으로 나와서 해가 비추어 그림자를 본다면, 6주 동안은 더 겨울이 지속될 것이라는 사실을 알 수 있다.

> Groundhog's Day occurs every February 2nd in the United States. According to tradition, when a groundhog comes out of its burrow on this day and sees that it is cloudy, spring will come early. If the groundhog comes out of its burrow and it is sunny, and thus sees its shadow, winter will persist for six more weeks and the groundhog will return to its burrow.

02 영어문제 | 문제 한글 해석

Which of the following is true about "Phil"?

(a) There has been only one Phil in the world.
(b) One Phil ended its life at the age of 131.
(c) Groundhog's Day was first celebrated as a holiday in the early 1800s.
(d) The special reason for Phil's longevity is on his food.

"Phil"에 대한 설명으로 바른 것은?

(a) 이 세상에서 단 하나의 Phil이 있었다.
(b) 한 Phil은 131의 나이로 생을 마감했다.
(c) Groundhog's Day는 1800년대 초에 공휴일로 처음 기념되었다.
(d) Phil의 장생의 특별한 이유는 그의 음식에 있다.

문제해설

두 번째 문단의 마지막 문장을 통해, Phil이 오랫동안 살 수 있는 이유는 "Groundhog's Punch"라고 불리는 특별한 유동식을 마시기 때문이라는 것을 알 수 있다.

> While Groundhog's Day may have first been celebrated in Pennsylvania Dutch Country in the early 1800s, (c) it was first celebrated as a holiday in Punxsutawney, Pennsylvania, in 1886. The following year, the town crowned "Phil" as the official groundhog of Groundhog's Day. Phil would henceforth be known as Punxsutawney Phil. (a) There have been many "Phils" over the years, but according to the Punxsutawney Groundhog Club website,

(b) Phil is 131 years old and counting! He has been able to live so long because he drinks a special formula called "Groundhog's Punch."

(a) 몇 년 동안 많은 Phil이 존재했으므로, 단 하나의 Phil이 있었다는 설명은 틀린 내용이다.

(b) Phil은 131살이며 지금도 살고 있으므로, 생을 마감했다고 한 설명은 틀린 내용이다.

(c) Groundhog's Day는 1800년대 초가 아닌 1886년에 공휴일로 처음 기념되었다.

03 영어문제

Which information does the Punxsutawney Groundhog Club provide?

(a) Phil became an official groundhog of Groundhog's Day.
(b) Phil has no special ability to predict the coming of the spring accurately.
(c) Another name of Phil is Punxsutawney Phil.
(d) Punxsutawaney is crowded by a lot of people every February.

문제 한글 해석

Punxsutawney Groundhog Club은 어떤 정보를 제공하는가?

(a) Phil은 Groundhog's Day의 공식적인 마멋이 되었다.
(b) Phil은 봄이 오는 것에 대해 정확하게 예측할 특별한 능력이 없다.
(c) Phil의 또 다른 이름은 Punxsutawney Phil이다.
(d) Punxsutawaney는 매년 2월 많은 사람들로 붐빈다.

문제해설

마지막 문단을 통해, Punxsutawney Groundhog Club에 의하면 Phil은 특별한 예측 능력이 없다는 것을 알 수 있다.

> You might think that such a special rodent would have special prediction abilities. According to the Punxsutawney Groundhog Club, this is not the case. Phil's recorded predictions over the years have only yielded an accuracy rate of about 39%. Furthermore, in the 103 years in which Phil's predictions have been recorded, he has only predicted the coming of an early spring 17 times! Phil's poor predictive abilities, however, have not seemed to impact the importance of Groundhog's Day. Thousands of people descend upon Punxsutawney every February to help the city celebrate.

그 외에 다른 보기들의 내용이 사실일지라도, Punxsutawney Groundhog Club이 제공한 정보가 아니므로 정답이 될 수 없다.

04 영어문제

What is the meaning of Phil to the people in the city?
(a) People can celebrate an event altogether every year regardless of its ability.
(b) Phil has a great meaning in terms of his outstanding prediction ability.
(c) He is an important tool for weather forecasting.
(d) Thousands of people are influenced by its ability as a special rodent.

문제 한글 해석

Phil은 도시의 사람들에게 어떤 의미를 가지는가?
(a) 사람들은 그것의 능력과는 상관없이 매년마다 다 함께 행사를 기념한다.
(b) Phil은 그의 뛰어난 예측 능력의 면에서 중요한 의미를 가진다.
(c) 그는 기상 예측에 중요한 도구이다.
(d) 수천 명의 사람들은 특별한 설치류의 능력에 의해 영향을 받는다.

문제해설

마지막 문단에 의하면, Phil에게 특별한 예측 능력이 없더라도 Groundhog's Day의 중요성에 영향을 미치지 않으며, 수천 명의 사람들이 이 날을 기념한다는 사실을 알 수 있다.

You might think that such a special rodent would have special prediction abilities. According to the Punxsutawney Groundhog Club, this is not the case. Phil's recorded predictions over the years have only yielded an accuracy rate of about 39%. Furthermore, in the 103 years in which Phil's predictions have been recorded, he has only predicted the coming of an early spring 17 times! Phil's poor predictive abilities, however, have not seemed to impact the importance of Groundhog's Day. Thousands of people descend upon Punxsutawney every February to help the city celebrate.

05 영어문제

Which of the following is NOT true about the Groundhog's Day?

(a) The date which is celebrated as Groundhog's Day is February 2nd.
(b) There is a tradition which is about predicting the coming of spring according to the groundhog's act.
(c) It became a holiday from the time when it had been first celebrated.
(d) People enjoy celebrating the Groundhog's Day regardless of Phil's prediction abilities.

문제 한글 해석

Groundhog's Day에 대한 설명으로 바르지 않은 것은?

(a) Groundhog's Day로 기념되는 날은 2월 2일이다.
(b) 마멋의 행동을 통해 봄의 도래를 예측한다는 전통이 있다.
(c) 그것은 그것이 처음으로 기념된 때부터 공휴일이 되었다.
(d) 사람들은 Phil의 예측 능력에 상관없이 Groundhog's Day를 기념하기를 즐긴다.

문제해설

두 번째 문단을 통해, Groundhog's Day는 1800년대 초에 처음으로 기념되었지만, 1886년이 되어서야 공휴일로 기념되었다는 사실을 알 수 있다.

While Groundhog's Day may have first been celebrated in Pennsylvania Dutch Country in the early 1800s, it was first celebrated as a holiday in Punxsutawney, Pennsylvania, in 1886. The following year, the town crowned "Phil" as the official groundhog of Groundhog's Day. Phil would henceforth be known as Punxsutawney Phil. There have been many "Phils" over the years, but according to the Punxsutawney Groundhog Club website, Phil is 131 years old and counting! He has been able to live so long because he drinks a special formula called "Groundhog's Punch."

(a) Groundhog's Day occurs every February 2nd in the United States. (b) According to tradition, when a groundhog comes out of its burrow on this day and sees that it is cloudy, spring will come early. If the groundhog comes out of its burrow and it is sunny, and thus sees its shadow, winter will persist for six more weeks and the groundhog will return to its burrow.

You might think that such a special rodent would have special prediction abilities. According to the Punxsutawney Groundhog Club, this is not the case. Phil's recorded predictions over the years have only yielded an accuracy rate of about 39%. Furthermore, in the 103 years in which Phil's predictions have been recorded, he has only predicted the coming of an early spring 17 times! Phil's poor predictive abilities, (d) however, have not seemed to impact the importance of Groundhog's Day. Thousands of people descend upon Punxsutawney every February to help the city celebrate.

06 영어문제

In the context of the passage, the word "celebrate" means

(a) graduate
(b) decorate
(c) recognize
(d) commemorate

문제 한글 해석

이 글의 문맥상 "celebrate"가 무엇을 의미하는가?

(a) 졸업하다
(b) 장식하다
(c) 인식하다, 알아보다
(d) 기념하다, 축하하다

문제해설

이 글의 문맥상 "celebrate"는 '축하하다', '기념하다'를 의미한다. 따라서 가장 가까운 의미의 (d) commemorate가 정답이 된다.

07 영어문제

In the context of the passage, the word "prediction" means

(a) forecast
(b) observation
(c) prevention
(d) accuracy

문제 한글 해석

이 글의 문맥상 "prediction"은 무엇을 의미하는가?

(a) 예측
(b) 관찰
(c) 예방, 방지
(d) 정확성

문제해설

이 글에서 "prediction"은 '예측'의 의미로, (a) forecast와 가장 가까운 뜻을 가졌다. 그 외에 (b), (c)는 접미사가 같은 -tion으로 끝나는 함정이므로 유의하도록 한다.

PART 4. 독해 만렙 실전모의고사

Part 4. Read the following business letter and answer the questions.
The underlined words in the article are for vocabulary questions.

A recent purchase of widgets

Prime Company, Inc.
213 Alphabet Drive
Los Angeles, California 90002
15 October 2019

Mr. Jason Park
Customer Service Representative
Widgets Galore, Inc.
987 Widget Street
Miami, Florida 33111

Dear Mr. Jason Park:

I am writing you concerning a recent purchase of widgets. Approximately two weeks ago, on October 1, I ordered a total of 50 widgets for Prime Company, Inc. via the Widgets Galore client webpage. I received an email notification two days later confirming the receipt of payment and the shipment of the widgets. According to your website, shipments should reach their destination within 3-5 business days of being sent, but I have yet to receive the widgets. Do you have any information on what may have <u>happened</u> to delay the shipment or where the shipment is currently?

I have worked with Widgets Galore, Inc. before and have the greatest confidence in your products and customer service. However, we need the shipment of widgets soon, and I hoped you might be able to <u>provide</u> me with an idea of when I can expect them. Thank you in advance for any help you might be able to offer.

Sincerely,
Sam Brown
Vice President of Prime Company, Inc.
514-457-1633
s.brown@primecompanyinc.com

01

What is the purpose of the e-mail?

(a) to inform the seller of receipt of widgets
(b) to acquire information about the shipment's company
(c) to inquire whether the seller has sent an e-mail notification
(d) to ask about the status of the delayed shipment of widgets

02

Which is NOT true about Sam Brown?

(a) He purchased a total of 50 widgets recently on behalf of the Widgets Galore, Inc.
(b) He is in high position in the company which he belongs to.
(c) This email was written by Sam Brown in the middle of October.
(d) He checked information related to shipments via the Widgets Galore company's website.

03

According to the Widgets Galore client webpage, around when was Sam Brown supposed to receive widgets?

(a) October 1st
(b) October 3rd
(c) October 7th
(d) October 15th

04

What is the relationship between Prime Company, Inc. and Widgets Galore?

(a) They have made several transactions.
(b) Both companies have never been involved in business with each other.
(c) Prime Company, Inc. is in competition with Widgets Galore, Inc.
(d) Prime Company, Inc. and Widgets Galore, Inc. are a parent company and its subsidiary, respectively.

05

What made Sam Brown ask about the shipment of widgets?

(a) Sam Brown had been in the same situation before.
(b) Prime Company, Inc. is in need of widgets as soon as possible.
(c) He was asked to inquire about the shipment by his company.
(d) His company, Prime Company, Inc. is placed in a financially difficult situation.

06

In the context of the passage, the word "happen" means

(a) target
(b) involve
(c) occur
(d) behave

07

In the context of the passage, the word "provide" means

(a) offer
(b) contribute
(c) prepare
(d) prescribe

A recent purchase of widgets

Prime Company, Inc.
213 Alphabet Drive
Los Angeles, California 90002
15 October 2019

Mr. Jason Park
Customer Service Representative
Widgets Galore, Inc.
987 Widget Street
Miami, Florida 33111

친애하는 Jason Park 씨께

저는 최근 구매한 위젯에 대해서 귀하에게 편지를 드리게 되었습니다. 약 2주 전인 10월 1일에, 저는 Widgets Galore 고객 웹페이지를 통해서 Prime Company, Inc.를 위해 총 50개의 위젯을 주문했습니다. 2일 후에 지불 영수증과 위젯의 배송을 확인하는 이메일 알림을 받았습니다. 당신의 웹 사이트에 따르면, 배송은 배송 된지 영업일 3-5일 이내에 목적지로 도착해야 한다고 되어있지만 저는 아직 위젯을 받지 못했습니다. 혹시 무엇이 배송을 지연시켰는지, 현재 배송물이 어디에 있는지에 대한 정보를 가지고 있으신가요?

저는 Widgets Galore, Inc.과 이전에 거래한 경험이 있고, 귀사의 제품과 소비자 서비스에 가장 신뢰도가 높습니다. 그러나 우리는 곧 위젯의 배송이 필요하고, 제가 언제 그것들을 받을 수 있을지에 대한 정보를 제공해줄 수 있기를 희망합니다. 귀하가 제공할 수 있는 모든 도움에 대해 미리 감사드립니다.

안녕히 계십시오.
Sam Brown
Vice President of Prime Company, Inc.
514-457-1633
s.brown@primecompanyinc.com

- **concerning** ~에 관해서
- **widget** 작은 장치
- **order** 주문하다, 명령하다
- **receive** 받다
- **confirm** 확인하다
- **shipment** 배송
- **delay** 지연; 미루다
- **provide A with B** A에게 B를 제공하다
- **purchase** 구매하다
- **approximately** 대략
- **via** ~를 통해서
- **notification** 알림, 통지
- **receipt** 영수증
- **destination** 목적지
- **currently** 현재, 지금
- **in advance** 미리

정답 01. (d) 02. (a) 03. (c) 04. (a) 05. (b) 06. (c) 07. (a)

01 영어문제

What is the purpose of the e-mail?
(a) to inform the seller of receipt of widgets
(b) to acquire information about the shipment's company
(c) to inquire whether the seller has sent an e-mail notification
(d) to ask about the status of the delayed shipment of widgets

문제 한글 해석

이 메일의 목적은 무엇인가?
(a) 판매자에게 위젯 수령을 알리기 위하여
(b) 배송 회사에 대한 정보를 얻기 위하여
(c) 판매자가 이메일 알림을 보냈는지 문의하기 위하여
(d) 지연된 위젯 배송 상태에 대해 문의하기 위하여

문제해설

첫 번째 문단을 통해 메일을 쓴 Sam Brown은 최근에 Widgets Galore 고객 웹페이지를 통해 위젯을 구매했고 본래 3-5일 영업일 안에 배송이 되어야 하는데 위젯을 받지 못하여, 왜 배송이 지연되었는지와 현재 배송물이 어디에 있는지에 대해 문의하는 메일이라는 것을 알 수 있다.

> I am writing you concerning a recent purchase of widgets. Approximately two weeks ago, on October 1, I ordered a total of 50 widgets for Prime Company, Inc. via the Widgets Galore Client webpage. I received an email notification two days later confirming the receipt of payment and the shipment of the widgets. According to your website, shipments should reach their destination within 3-5 business days of being sent, but I have yet to receive the widgets. Do you have any information on what may have happened to delay the shipment or where the shipment is currently?

02 영어문제

Which is NOT true about Sam Brown?

(a) He purchased a total of 50 widgets recently on behalf of the Widgets Galore, Inc.
(b) He is in high position in the company which he belongs to.
(c) This email was written by Sam Brown in the middle of October.
(d) He checked information related to shipments via the Widgets Galore company's website.

문제 한글 해석

Sam Brown에 대한 설명으로 바르지 않은 것은?

(a) 그는 최근에 Widgets Galore, Inc.를 대신하여 총 50개의 위젯을 구매했다.
(b) 그는 그가 속해 있는 회사에서 높은 지위에 있다.
(c) 이 메일은 Sam Brown에 의해 10월 중순경에 작성되었다.
(d) 그는 Widgets Galore 회사의 웹사이트를 통해 배송에 대한 정보를 확인했다.

문제해설

첫 번째 문단을 통해 Sam Brown이 Widgets Galore 회사가 아닌, Prime Company, Inc. 회사를 위해 총 50개의 위젯을 구매했음을 알 수 있다.

> I am writing you concerning a recent purchase of widgets. Approximately two weeks ago, on October 1, I ordered a total of 50 widgets for Prime Company, Inc. via the Widgets Galore client webpage. I received an email notification two days later confirming the receipt of payment and the shipment of the widgets. According to your website, shipments should reach their destination within 3-5 business days of being sent, but I have yet to receive the widgets. Do you have any information on what may have happened to delay the shipment or where the shipment is currently?

(b) 메일 끝에 기재된 Sam Brown의 정보를 통해, 그가 부사장이라는 점을 알 수 있다.

> Sincerely,
> Sam Brown
> Vice President of Prime Company, Inc.
> 514-457-1633
> s.brown@primecompanyinc.com

(c) 첫 번째 문단을 통해 Sam Brown이 10월 1일쯤에 위젯을 구매했으며, 10월 1일을 2주 전이라고 표현하는 것을 통해 현재 메일을 쓰는 시점은 10월 15일쯤이라는 것을 알 수 있다.

(d) 메일에서 웹페이지에 의하면 배송이 3-5 영업일 이내에 배송되었어야 했다고 말하는 것을 보아, 그가 Widgets Calore 회사 고객 웹페이지를 통해 배송에 대한 정보를 확인했다는 점을 알 수 있다.

> I am writing you concerning a recent purchase of widgets. Approximately two weeks ago, on October 1, I ordered a total of 50 widgets for Prime Company, Inc. via the Widgets Galore client webpage. I received an email notification two days later confirming the receipt of payment and the shipment of the widgets. (d) According to your website, shipments should reach their destination within 3-5 business days of being sent, but I have yet to receive the widgets. Do you have any information on what may have happened to delay the shipment or where the shipment is currently?

03 영어문제 | 문제 한글 해석

According to the Widgets Galore client webpage, around when was Sam Brown supposed to receive widgets?

(a) October 1st
(b) October 3rd
(c) October 7th
(d) October 15th

Widgets Galore 고객 웹페이지에 따르면, Sam Brown은 언제쯤에 위젯을 받아야 했는가?

(a) 10월 1일
(b) 10월 3일
(c) 10월 7일
(d) 10월 15일

문제해설

첫 번째 문단에 따라 Sam Brown이 위젯을 구매한 시기는 대략 10월 1일이며, 이틀 뒤인 10월 3일쯤에 위젯 배송과 관련한 이메일 통지를 받았다고 했다. 또한 Widgets Galore 고객 웹페이지에 따르면 배송이 시작되고 3-5 영업일 이내에 물건을 받아야 한다고 했으므로, 10월 6일에서 10월 8일 사이에 받아야 한다. 따라서 정답은 (c) 10월 7일이 된다.

I am writing you concerning a recent purchase of widgets. Approximately two weeks ago, on October 1, I ordered a total of 50 widgets for Prime Company, Inc. via the Widgets Galore Client webpage. I received an email notification two days later confirming the receipt of payment and the shipment of the widgets. According to your website, shipments should reach their destination within 3-5 business days of being sent, but I have yet to receive the widgets. Do you have any information on what may have happened to delay the shipment or where the shipment is currently?

04 영어문제

What is the relationship between Prime Company, Inc. and Widgets Galore?

(a) They have made several transactions.
(b) Both companies have never been involved in business with each other.
(c) Prime Company, Inc. is in competition with Widgets Galore, Inc.
(d) Prime Company, Inc. and Widgets Galore, Inc. are a parent company and its subsidiary, respectively.

문제 한글 해석

Prime Company, Inc.와 Widgets Galore, Inc.과의 관계는 어떻게 되는가?

(a) 그들은 몇 번의 거래를 한 적이 있다.
(b) 두 회사는 서로 거래에 관련된 적이 한 번도 없다.
(c) Prime Company, Inc.는 Widgets Galore, Inc.과 경쟁 관계에 있다.
(d) Prime Company, Inc.와 Widgets Galore, Inc.은 각각 모회사, 자회사이다.

문제해설

두 번째 문단을 통해 Prime Company, Inc.의 부사장인 Sam Brown이 Widgets Galore와 일해본 적이 있다는 사실을 알 수 있으므로, 두 회사는 이전에도 거래를 한 적이 있다.

> I have worked with Widgets Galore, Inc. before and have the greatest confidence in your products and customer service. However, we need the shipment of widgets soon, and I hoped you might be able to provide me with an idea of when I can expect them. Thank you in advance for any help you might be able to offer.

05 영어문제

What made Sam Brown ask about the shipment of widgets?

(a) Sam Brown had been in the same situation before.
(b) Prime Company, Inc. is in need of widgets as soon as possible.
(c) He was asked to inquire about the shipment by his company.
(d) His company, Prime Company, Inc. is placed in a financially difficult situation.

문제 한글 해석

무엇이 Sam Brown이 위젯의 배송에 대해 묻게 만들었는가?

(a) Sam Brown은 이전에도 똑같은 상황에 놓인 적이 있다.
(b) Prime Company, Inc.는 위젯이 최대한 빨리 필요하다.
(c) 그는 회사로부터 배송에 대해 문의를 하라고 요구받았다.
(d) 그의 회사인 Prime Company, Inc.는 재정적으로 어려운 상황에 놓여 있다.

문제해설

두 번째 문단을 통해 Prime Company, Inc.가 곧 위젯의 배송이 필요하다는 점을 알 수 있다. 따라서 Sam Brown은 배송이 늦어지고 있다는 점에 대해 문의하기 위하여 이 메일을 쓴 것이다.

> I have worked with Widgets Galore, Inc. before and have the greatest confidence in your products and customer service. However, we need the shipment of widgets soon, and I hoped you might be able to provide me with an idea of when I can expect them. Thank you in advance for any help you might be able to offer.

06 영어문제 | 문제 한글 해석

In the context of the passage, the word "happen" means
(a) target
(b) involve
(c) occur
(d) behave

이 글의 문맥상 "happen"은 무엇을 의미하는가?
(a) 목표로 하다
(b) 개입하다
(c) 일어나다, 발생하다
(d) 행동하다

문제해설

이 글의 문맥상 "happen"은 '일어나다', '발생하다'를 의미한다. 따라서 가장 가까운 의미의 (c) occur이 정답이 된다. 나머지 보기들은 happen과 연관 없는 단어들이다.

07 영어문제 | 문제 한글 해석

In the context of the passage, the word "provide" means
(a) offer
(b) contribute
(c) prepare
(d) prescribe

이 글의 문맥상 "provide"는 무엇을 의미하는가?
(a) 제공하다, 제안하다
(b) 공헌하다
(c) 대비하다
(d) 규정하다

문제해설

이 글에서 "provide"는 '제공하다'의 의미로, (a) offer '제안하다, 제공하다'와 가장 가까운 뜻을 가졌다. 그 외에 (b), (c), (d)는 provide와 상관없는 의미의 단어들이다.

필수 단어, 표현, 숙어 암기노트

단어, 표현, 숙어	의미

필수 단어, 표현, 숙어 암기노트

단어, 표현, 숙어	의미

독해 만렙을 위한
실전모의고사

4S G-TELP

SIGNATURE

2 회

PART 1. 독해 만렙 실전모의고사

Part 1. Read the following biographical article and answer the questions.
The underlined words in the article are for vocabulary questions.

James Madison

James Madison was born on March 16, 1751, in King George County, Virginia. He graduated from Princeton University in 1771 at the age of 20. He served in the Virginia Constitutional Convention in 1776. In 1780, Madison served as a delegate to the Second Continental Congress. Madison served as the chief recorder at the Constitutional Convention in 1787. He is generally regarded as the "Father of the Constitution." Later in 1787, Madison teamed up with Alexander Hamilton (and to a small extent John Jay) to write the Federalist Papers, a series of persuasive essays designed to convince the states to ratify the Constitution. Written under the pen name "Publius," the Federalist Papers is considered one of the most important documents in American history.

In 1789, Madison was elected to the House of Representatives, where he helped draft the Bill of Rights and fought against the passage of the Alien and Sedition Acts. Madison married Dolley Payne Todd in 1794. He helped found the Democratic Party and was chosen as Thomas Jefferson's Secretary of State in 1801.

Madison was elected as America's fourth president in 1808. George Clinton was appointed vice president but died in office in 1812. Madison's first term was plagued by tensions with Great Britain and his foreign policy was widely criticized. Despite the problems that characterized his first term, Madison was re-elected in 1812 for the second term.

In 1817, after his second term, James Madison retired to his estate at Montpelier, Virginia. In 1829, he served as a delegate to the Virginia Constitutional Convention before his death on June 28, 1836. He was the last surviving signer of the Constitution. Madison was honored on the United States' $5,000 bill before it was taken out of circulation.

01

Which is NOT true about James Madison according to the first paragraph?

(a) After he had graduated from the university, he worked for the Virginia Constitutional Convention.
(b) He was responsible for taking notes at the Constitutional Convention.
(c) He co-worked with Alexander Hamilton for convincing the federal governments to ratify the Constitution.
(d) The Federalist Papers which he wrote have a great importance in American history.

02

Which is NOT true about the Federalist Papers?

(a) Madison played a role in writing the papers.
(b) The papers consisted of a series of essays.
(c) Its purpose was to persuade the states to approve the Constitution.
(d) It was written by a certain type of pen.

03

What did Madison do in 1789?

(a) He recommended a candidate for the House of Representatives.
(b) He supported the passage of the Alien and Sedition Acts.
(c) He married Dolley Payne Todd.
(d) He was involved in drafting the Bill of Rights.

04

What can be inferred about Madison's presidency according to the passage?

(a) His first term was judged as successful.
(b) During his first term he maintained an amicable relationship with Great Britain.
(c) He received unfavorable appraisal of his foreign policy.
(d) He served one term as the president of America and resigned.

05

What happened to Madison after his presidency according to the fourth paragraph?

(a) He served vice president.
(b) He stopped working.
(c) He worked as a delegate for where he had worked before.
(d) He was selected as the face of the $5,000 bill used at that time.

06

In the context of the passage, the word "consider" means

(a) appraise   (b) value
(c) evaluate   (d) regard

07

In the context of the passage, the word "elect" means

(a) appoint   (b) electric
(c) president   (d) element

James Madison은 Virginia주 King George County에서 1751년 3월 16일에 태어났다. 그는 1771년 20세의 나이에 Princeton University를 졸업했다. 그는 1776년에 Virginia Constitutional Convention(버지니아 헌법 회의)에 (참여)했다. 1780년에 Madison은 Second Continental Congress (제2차 대륙 회의)에서 대의원 (대표)을 역임했다. 1787년에 Madison은 Constitutional Convention에서 최고 기록관을 역임했다. 그는 일반적으로 "Father of the Constitution(헌법의 아버지)"로 불린다. 1787년 후반에, Madison은 Alexander Hamilton과 (그리고 가끔 John Jay와도) 협업하여 주 정부가 Constitution(헌법)을 비준하도록 설득하기 위해 고안된 에세이 시리즈인 Federalist Papers (연방주의자 논집)를 집필했다. "Publius"라는 필명으로 쓰인 Federalist Papers는 미국 역사에서 가장 중요한 문서 중 하나로 여겨진다.

1789년, 매디슨은 하원에 선출되어 권리장전 초안을 작성하고 외국인 및 보안법의 통과에 맞서 싸웠다. Madison은 1794년에 Dolley Payne Todd와 결혼했다. 그는 민주당을 설립하는 것을 도왔고, 1801년에 Thomas Jefferson의 국무장관으로 선발되었다.

Madison은 1808년에 미국의 4번째 대통령으로 선출되었다. George Clinton이 부통령으로 임명되었지만 1812년 재직 중에 사망했다. Madison의 첫 번째 임기는 영국과의 갈등에 의해 괴로웠고 그의 외교 정책은 널리 비판받았다. 그의 첫 번째 임기를 규정지었던 문제들에도 불구하고, Madison은 1812년 두 번째 임기에도 재 선출되었다.

두 번째 임기 후 1817년에 James Madison은 퇴직하고 Virginia주 Montpelier에 있는 그의 사유지로 물러갔다. 1829년에 그는 1836년 6월 28일 사망 전에 Virginia Constitutional Convention의 대표를 역임했다. 그는 가장 마지막까지 생존해있는 헌법 서명자였다. Madison은 미국 5000달러 지폐의 유통이 중단되기 전까지 그 위에 기려졌다.

- graduate from ~를 졸업하다
- Constitutional Convention 헌법 제정 회의
- Continental Congress 대륙 회의
- be regarded as ~로 간주되다, 여겨지다
- convince 확신시키다
- elect 선출하다
- Alien and Sedition Acts 이민법과 선동법
- vice president 부통령
- plague 괴롭히다
- criticize 비판하다
- serve as ~를 역임하다
- delegate 대표
- chief 주된, 최고자인
- persuasive 설득력 있는
- ratify 비준하다
- Representatives 대표자, 하원의원
- appoint 임명하다
- term 임기
- tension 긴장
- circulation 순환

정답

01. (c) 02. (d) 03. (d) 04. (c) 05. (c) 06. (d) 07. (a)

01 영어문제

Which is NOT true about James Madison according to the first paragraph?

(a) After he had graduated from the university, he worked for the Virginia Constitutional Convention.
(b) He was responsible for taking notes at the Constitutional Convention.
(c) He co-worked with Alexander Hamilton for convincing the federal governments to ratify the Constitution.
(d) The Federalist Papers which he wrote have a great importance in American history.

문제 한글 해석

첫 번째 문단에 따르면, James Madison에 대한 것 중 사실이 아닌 것은?

(a) 그는 대학교를 졸업한 뒤에, Virginia Constitutional Convention에서 일했다.
(b) 그는 Constitutional Convention에서 기록하는 것을 담당하였다.
(c) 그는 연방 정부가 헌법을 비준하도록 설득시키기 위해 Alexander Hamilton과 함께 일했다.
(d) 그가 작성한 Federalist Papers는 미국 역사에서 큰 중요성을 가진다.

문제해설

첫 번째 문단을 보면 Madison은 주 정부가 헌법을 비준하도록 설득시키기 위해 연방주의자 논집을 작성했다는 것을 알 수 있다.

> Madison teamed up with Alexander Hamilton (and to a small extent John Jay) to write the Federalist Papers, a series of persuasive essays designed to convince the states to ratify the Constitution.

(a) 그가 1771년 대학교를 졸업한 뒤에, 1776년에 Virginia Constitutional Convention에서 일했다는 것을 알 수 있다.

> He graduated from Princeton University in 1771 at the age of 20. He served in the Virginia Constitutional Convention in 1776.

(b) 그가 Constitutional Convention에서 최고 기록관으로 일했다는 사실을 알 수 있다.

> Madison served as the chief recorder at the Constitutional Convention in 1787.

(d) 연방주의자 논집은 미국 역사상 가장 중요한 문서 중 하나로 여겨진다는 것을 알 수 있다.

> Written under the pen name "Publius," the Federalist Papers is considered one of the most important documents in American history.

02 영어문제 / 문제 한글 해석

Which is NOT true about the Federalist Papers?
(a) Madison played a role in writing the papers.
(b) The papers consisted of a series of essays.
(c) Its purpose was to persuade the states to approve the Constitution.
(d) It was written by a certain type of pen.

Federalist Papers에 대한 것 중 사실이 아닌 것은?
(a) Madison은 그 논집을 쓰는 데 한몫했다.
(b) 그 논집은 에세이 시리즈로 구성되어 있다.
(c) 그것의 목적은 주 정부가 헌법을 수정하도록 설득시키기 위함이었다.
(d) 이는 특정한 유형의 펜으로 쓰였다.

문제해설
첫 번째 문단을 보면 Federalist Papers가 "Publius"라는 필명으로 쓰였다는 것을 알 수 있다. pen name에서 pen은 펜이 아닌 name과 함께 필명으로 해석해야 한다. 따라서 특정 펜이 쓰였다는 것은 내용상 관련이 없다.

> Madison teamed up with Alexander Hamilton (and to a small extent John Jay) to write the Federalist Papers, a series of persuasive essays designed to convince the states to ratify the Constitution.
>
> (a) ~ later in 1787, Madison teamed up with Alexander Hamilton (and to a small extent John Jay) to write the Federalist Papers, (b) a series of persuasive essays designed (c) to convince the states to ratify the Constitution. (d) Written under the pen name "Publius," the Federalist Papers is considered one of the most important documents in American history.

03 영어문제 / 문제 한글 해석

What did Madison do in 1789?
(a) He recommended a candidate for the House of Representatives.
(b) He supported the passage of the Alien and Sedition Acts.
(c) He married Dolley Payne Todd.
(d) He was involved in drafting the Bill of Rights.

Madison이 1789년에 한 일은 무엇인가?
(a) 그는 미국 하원 의원의 후보를 추천했다.
(b) 그는 이민법과 선동법의 통과를 지지했다.
(c) 그는 Dolley Payne Todd와 결혼했다.
(d) 그는 권리 장전의 초안을 작성하는 일에 참여했다.

문제해설
두 번째 문단을 보면 Madison은 1789년에 미국 하원 의원에 선출되었고, 그곳에서 권리 장전의 초안을 작성하는 것을 도왔다는 것을 알 수 있다.

> In 1789, Madison was elected to the House of Representatives, where he helped draft the Bill of Rights and fought against the passage of the Alien and Sedition Acts.

04 영어문제

What can be inferred about Madison's presidency according to the passage?

(a) His first term was judged as successful.
(b) During his first term, he maintained an amicable relationship with Great Britain.
(c) He received unfavorable appraisal of his foreign policy.
(d) He served one term as the president of America and resigned.

문제 한글 해석

이 글에 따르면, Madison의 대통령 임기에 대해 추론할 수 있는 것은?

(a) 그의 첫 번째 임기는 성공적이라는 평가를 받았다.
(b) 그의 첫 번째 임기 동안, 그는 영국과 우호적인 관계를 유지했다.
(c) 그는 그의 외교 정책에 대해 비판적인 평가를 받았다.
(d) 그는 미국의 대통령으로서 한 번의 임기를 역임하고 나서 사임했다.

문제해설

세 번째 문단을 보면 Madison의 대통령직 첫 임기 동안 그의 외교 정책이 많은 비판을 받았음을 알 수 있다.

> Madison's first term was plagued by tensions with Great Britain and his foreign policy was widely criticized.

05 영어문제

What happened to Madison after his presidency according to the fourth paragraph?

(a) He served vice president.
(b) He stopped working.
(c) He worked as a delegate for where he had worked before.
(d) He was selected as the face of the $5,000 bill used at that time.

문제 한글 해석

네 번째 문단에 따르면, Madison의 대통령 임기가 끝난 이후 그에게 일어났던 일은 무엇인가?

(a) 그는 부통령을 역임했다.
(b) 그는 일을 그만두었다.
(c) 그는 전에 일했던 곳을 위해 대표로 일했다.
(d) 그는 당시 사용되고 있던 5000달러 지폐의 인물로 선정되었다.

문제해설

첫 번째 문단을 보면 Madison이 1776년에 Virginia Constitutional Convention에서 일한 적이 있으며, 그의 대통령직의 두 번째 임기가 끝난 후에 그가 죽기 전까지 Virginia Constitutional Convention에서 다시 일했다는 것을 알 수 있다.

> James Madison was born on March 16, 1751, in King George County, Virginia. He graduated from Princeton University in 1771 at the age of 20. He served in the Virginia Constitutional Convention in 1776. In 1780, Madison served as a delegate to the Second Continental Congress. Madison served as the chief recorder at the Constitutional Convention in 1817, after his second term, James Madison retired to his estate at Montpelier, Virginia. In 1829, he served as a delegate to the Virginia Constitutional Convention before his death on June 28, 1836. He was the last surviving signer of the Constitution. Madison was honored on the United States $5,000 bill before it was taken out of circulation.

06 영어문제

In the context of the passage, the word "consider" means

(a) appraise
(b) value
(c) evaluate
(d) regard

문제 한글 해석

이 글의 문맥상, "consider"이 의미하는 것은?

(a) 평가하다
(b) 가치를 두다
(c) 평가하다
(d) 간주하다

문제해설

이 글의 문맥상 "consider"은 '~을/를 ~으로 생각하다, 고려하다, 간주하다'를 의미한다. 따라서 가장 가까운 의미의 (d) regard가 정답이 된다. 항상 기억해야 하는 사항은 이 어휘가 '문맥상, 지문 내에서' 어떻게 쓰였는가 이다.

07 영어문제

In the context of the passage, the word "elect" means

(a) appoint
(b) electric
(c) president
(d) element

문제 한글 해석

이 글의 문맥상, "elect"는 무엇을 의미하는가?

(a) 임명하다
(b) 전기의
(c) 대통령
(d) 요소

문제해설

이 글에서 "elect"는 '선출하다' '임명하다'의 의미로, (a) appoint '임명하다'와 가장 가까운 뜻을 가졌다.
(c) president는 '대통령'이란 의미의 관련어로 elect의 의미와 헷갈리게 하기 위한 함정이므로 유의해야한다.

MEMO

Part 2. Read the following magazine article and answer the questions.
The underlined words in the article are for vocabulary questions.

Child 'Vampire' Was Buried 1,550 Years Ago in Italy

Archaeologists have discovered the body of a 10-year-old child at an ancient Roman site in Italy which they believe was ritually buried to prevent it rising again from the dead. The skeletal remains were found by archaeologists from the University of Arizona (UA) and Stanford University, alongside Italians, with a stone placed purposefully in the child's mouth.

According to researchers, the stone was intentionally inserted as part of a funeral ritual designed to stopper diseases and the body from rising after being buried.

The unusual so-called "vampire burial" was described as "extremely eerie and weird" by archaeologist and professor David Soren, who has been excavating the site in Teverina since 1987.

"I've never seen anything like it," said Professor Soren, a Regents' Professor in the UA school of anthropology and department of religious studies and classics.

"Locally, they're calling it the 'Vampire of Lugnano'."

The find was unearthed at La Necropoli dei Bambini, or the Cemetery of Children, a burial site which dates back to a malaria outbreak in 400 AD which killed many vulnerable babies and small children in the area.

Archaeologists had previously believed the cemetery was exclusively for infants, toddlers and unborn fetuses - with the eldest body found of more than 50 burials being a three-year-old girl.

01

Why did the ancient Romans insert the stone purposefully in the child's mouth?

(a) Because they wanted to stop it digging out the graves
(b) Since they wanted to prevent the body from rising again
(c) The reason was that they were influenced by foreign cultures.
(d) Now that they wanted to punish the child

02

Which is true about the skeletal remains which archaeologists discovered?

(a) The buried child was less than 10 years old.
(b) The remains were placed at an ancient Roman site in Italy.
(c) Archaeologists found them in the University of Arizona and Stanford University.
(d) They were covered with several stones.

03

Which is NOT true about the vampire burial?

(a) It means a funeral ritual to insert the stone intentionally in the child's mouth.
(b) One of its reasons was to stop diseases.
(c) It is also called the 'Vampire of Lugnano.'
(d) Professor David Soren described it as a normal tradition.

04

What happened to many babies and small children in 400 AD?

(a) Countless children died of disease.
(b) They were expelled from the country.
(c) They didn't receive enough medical treatment.
(d) Many people offered them as a sacrifice to a god.

05

Which is NOT true about La Necropoli dei Bambini, or the Cemetery of Children?

(a) A lot of burials of young children were found there.
(b) The eldest body was a only ten-year-old child.
(c) It was for all people including the elderly.
(d) There were more than 50 burials of babies and small children.

06

In the context of the passage, the word "insert" means

(a) admit   (b) put
(c) enroll   (d) impound

07

In the context of the passage, the word "excavate" means

(a) dig   (b) yield
(c) produce   (d) sink

이탈리아에서 1550년 전에 매장된 '뱀파이어 아이'

고고학자들은 이탈리아의 고대 로마 유적지에서 그들이 믿기에 죽은 상태로부터 다시 살아나는 것을 막기 위해서 의식적으로 매장된 10살 아이의 시신을 발견했다. 유해는 Arizona 대학교와 Stanford 대학교의 고고학자들 및 이탈리아인들에 의해, 입 속에 의도적으로 돌이 놓인 채 발견되었다.

연구자들에 따르면, 매장된 후에 질병을 막고 그 시신이 다시 살아나지 못하도록 고안된 장례 의식의 일부로서 의도적으로 돌이 삽입되었다.

소위 뱀파이어 매장이라고 불리는 이 이상한 일은 1987년 이래로 Teverina에 있는 그 현장을 발굴해 온 고고학자이자 교수인 David Soren에 의해 "매우 괴상하고 이상하다"고 묘사되었다.

"이 같은 일은 결코 본 적이 없습니다,"라고 Arizona 대학교 인류학부 및 종교학과 고전학 전공의 석좌교수인 Soren 교수가 말했다.

"현지에서 그들은 그것을 Lugnano의 Vampire라고 부르고 있습니다."

그 발견물은 서기 400년에 많은 연약한 영아 및 유아들을 죽음에 이르게 했던 말라리아 발생 시점으로 거슬러 올라가 있었던 매장터인 La Necropoli dei Bambini, 또는 the Cemetery of Children라고 불리는 곳에서 발굴되었다.

이전에 고고학자들은 50개가 넘는 매장지 중에 가장 나이가 많은 시신이 3살짜리 여자아이였기 때문에 그 묘지가 오로지 영아, 유아, 그리고 태어나지 않은 태아를 위한 것이라고 믿었었다.

- archaeologist 고고학자
- prevent A from B A가 B를 못하게 막다
- alongside ~옆에, ~와 함께
- intentionally 의도적으로
- funeral ritual 장례 의식
- extremely 극단적으로
- weird 이상한
- anthropology 인류학
- outbreak 발생, 발발
- previously 이전에
- exclusively 오로지
- ritually 의식적으로
- skeletal 뼈대의, 해골의
- purposefully 의도적으로, 결단력 있게
- insert 삽입하다
- describe 묘사하다
- eerie 괴상한, 으스스한
- excavate 발굴하다
- unearth 파내다, 발굴하다
- vulnerable 취약한
- cemetery 묘지
- fetus 태아

정답 01. (b) 02. (b) 03. (d) 04. (a) 05. (c) 06. (b) 07. (a)

01

영어문제

Why did the ancient Romans insert the stone purposefully in the child's mouth?

(a) Because they wanted to stop it digging out the graves
(b) Since they wanted to prevent the body from rising again
(c) The reason was that they were influenced by foreign cultures.
(d) Now that they wanted to punish the child

문제 한글 해석

고대 로마 사람들이 의도적으로 아이의 입 속에 돌을 넣었던 이유는?

(a) 아이가 무덤을 파헤치는 것을 막기 위해서
(b) 그 시신이 다시 살아나는 것을 막기 위해서
(c) 외국 문화의 영향을 받아서
(d) 그 아이를 처벌하기 위해서

문제해설

이 글 첫 부분을 보면 당시 사람들이 죽은 시신이 다시 살아나는 것을 막기 위해서 의도적으로 돌을 삽입했다는 것을 알 수 있다.

> Archaeologists have discovered the body of a 10-year-old child at an ancient Roman site in Italy which they believe was ritually buried to prevent it rising again from the dead.
>
> The skeletal remains were found by archaeologists from the University of Arizona (UA) and Stanford University, alongside Italians, with a stone placed purposefully in the child's mouth.
>
> According to researchers, the stone was intentionally inserted as part of a funeral ritual designed to stopper diseases and the body from rising after being buried.

02

영어문제

Which is true about the skeletal remains which archaeologists discovered?

(a) The buried child was less than 10 years old.
(b) The remains were placed at an ancient Roman site in Italy.
(c) Archaeologists found them in the University of Arizona and Stanford University.
(d) They were covered with several stones.

문제 한글 해석

고고학자가 발견한 유해에 대한 설명으로 바른 것은?

(a) 매장된 아이는 10살 미만이었다.
(b) 그 유해는 이탈리아의 고대 로마 유적지에 위치해 있었다.
(c) 고고학자들이 그 유해를 Arizona 대학교와 Stanford 대학교에서 발견하였다.
(d) 그것들은 여러 개의 돌로 덮여있었다.

문제해설

이 글 첫 문단을 보면 유해는 이탈리아의 고대 로마 유적지에서 발견되었음을 알 수 있다.

> Archaeologists have discovered the body of a 10-year-old child at an ancient Roman site in Italy which they believe was ritually buried to prevent it rising again from the dead.

(a) 또한 매장된 아이는 10살 미만이 아니라, 10살임을 알 수 있으며, (c) 그 유해는 Arizona 대학교와 Stanford 대학교에서 발견된 것이 아니라, 그 대학교의 고고학자에 의해 발견된 것이다. 마지막으로 (d) 그 유해는 여러 개의 돌로 뒤덮여 있는 것이 아니라, 입에 돌이 삽입된 것이다.

> Archaeologists have discovered the body of (a) a 10-year-old child at an ancient Roman site in Italy which they believe was ritually buried to prevent it rising again from the dead.
> (c) The skeletal remains were found by archaeologists from the University of Arizona (UA) and Stanford University, alongside Italians, (d) with a stone placed purposefully in the child's mouth.

03

영어문제

Which is NOT true about the vampire burial?

(a) It means a funeral ritual to insert the stone intentionally in the child's mouth.
(b) One of its reasons was to stop diseases.
(c) It is also called the 'Vampire of Lugnano.'
(d) Professor David Soren described it as a normal tradition.

문제 한글 해석

뱀파이어 매장에 대한 설명으로 바르지 않은 것은?

(a) 아이의 입 속에 의도적으로 돌을 넣는 장례 의식을 의미한다.
(b) 이에 대한 이유 중 하나는 병을 막기 위함이었다.
(c) 이는 Lugnano의 Vampire라고 불리기도 한다.
(d) David Soren 교수는 이를 일반적인 전통으로 묘사했다.

문제해설

David Soren 교수는 "이것과 같은 것은 결코 한 번도 본적이 없습니다."라고 말하며, 이러한 장례 의식을 매우 괴상하고 이상하다고 묘사했다는 것을 알 수 있다.

> The unusual so-called "vampire burial" was described as "extremely eerie and weird" by archaeologist and professor David Soren, who has been excavating the site in Teverina since 1987.
> "I've never seen anything like it," said Professor Soren, a Regents' Professor in the UA school of anthropology and department of religious studies and classics.

04 영어문제 | 문제 한글 해석

What happened to many babies and small children in 400 AD?

(a) Countless children died of disease.
(b) They were expelled from the country.
(c) They didn't receive enough medical treatment.
(d) Many people offered them as a sacrifice to a god.

서기 400년에 많은 아기들과 어린 아이들에게 발생한 것은?

(a) 셀 수 없을 만큼 많은 아이들이 질병으로 죽었다.
(b) 그들은 나라로부터 추방을 당했다.
(c) 그들은 충분한 의학적 치료를 받지 못했다.
(d) 많은 사람들이 그들을 신에게 제물로 바쳤다.

문제해설

서기 400년에 말라리아 발생으로 이에 취약한 많은 아기들과 어린 아이들이 죽었다.

> The find was unearthed at La Necropoli dei Bambini, or the Cemetery of Children, a burial site which dates back to a malaria outbreak in 400 AD which killed many vulnerable babies and small children in the area.

05 영어문제 | 문제 한글 해석

Which is NOT true about La Necropoli dei Bambini, or the Cemetery of Children?

(a) A lot of burials of young children were found there.
(b) The eldest body was only a ten-year-old child.
(c) It was for all people including the elderly.
(d) There were more than 50 burials of babies and small children.

La Necropoli dei Bambini, 또는 the Cemetery of Children에 대한 설명으로 바르지 않은 것은?

(a) 많은 어린 아이들의 무덤들이 그곳에서 발견되었다.
(b) 가장 나이가 많은 시신이 고작 10살 아이였다.
(c) 노인을 포함하여 모든 사람을 위한 것이었다.
(d) 50개구 이상의 아기들과 아이들의 무덤들이 있었다.

문제해설

이 글 마지막 문단을 보면, 그 묘지는 오직 영아, 유아, 그리고 태어나지 않은 태아를 위한 것이라고 믿었다는 것을 알 수 있다.

> Archaeologists had previously believed the cemetery was exclusively for infants, toddlers and unborn fetuses - with the eldest body found of more than 50 burials being a three-year-old girl.

06 영어문제 | 문제 한글 해석

In the context of the passage, the word "insert" means
(a) admit
(b) put
(c) enroll
(d) impound

이 글의 문맥상 "insert"는 무엇을 의미하는가?
(a) 인정하다
(b) 넣다
(c) 기록하다
(d) 가두다

문제해설

이 글의 문맥상 "insert"는 '넣다, 삽입하다'를 의미한다. 따라서 가장 가까운 의미의 (b) put '넣다'가 정답이 된다. 나머지 단어들은 insert와 유의어들이지만 문맥상 의미인 '넣다'와는 거리가 있는 어휘들이다.

07 영어문제 | 문제 한글 해석

In the context of the passage, the word "excavate" means
(a) dig
(b) yield
(c) produce
(d) sink

이 글의 문맥상 "excavate"는 무엇을 의미하는가?
(a) 파다
(b) 생산하다, 양보하다
(c) 제작하다
(d) 가라앉다

문제해설

이 글에서 "excavate"는 '발굴하다'의 의미로, (a) dig '파다'와 가장 가까운 뜻을 가졌다. 그 외에 (b), (c), (d)는 '발굴하다'라는 의미와는 서로 다른 의미를 지닌 단어들이다.

PART 3. 독해 만렙 실전모의고사

Part 3. Read the following encyclopedia article and answer the questions. The underlined words in the article are for vocabulary questions.

The History of Pizza

The story of modern pizza as we know began in Naples, Italy, in the late 1800s.

Baker Raffaele Esposito is usually given credit for baking the first pizzas with tomato sauce, cheese, and toppings. According to legend, pizza was popularized when Esposito was asked to make a pizza for Italian King Umberto I and Queen Margherita when the royal pair visited Naples in 1889. Esposito allegedly baked three different pizzas. The Queen's favorite was the one in which Esposito had designed in honor of Italy's red, white, and green flag. It had basil, mozzarella cheese, and tomato sauce. Esposito named it Pizza Margherita in her honor.

Pizza, however, failed to immediately take hold in Italy. As Italian immigrants came to the United States, however, pizza came with them. In 1905, the first United States pizzeria was established in New York City. The pizzeria, called Lombardi's, still operates today. Soon, other pizzerias in New York City and beyond appeared. By World War II, pizza was one of America's most popular foods. In the 1950s, the Totino family, of Minnesota, was thought to have produced the first frozen pizzas.

In 1958, Frank and Dan Carney borrowed $600 from their parents and opened a pizzeria in Wichita, Kansas. They called their restaurant Pizza Hut because they didn't have space for additional letters on their first sign. Pizza Hut became very popular and soon the brothers opened new restaurants and hence, the first pizza franchise was born.

Today, there are more than 10,000 Pizza Hut restaurants. Similarly, Domino's was established by two brothers who borrowed $900 to purchase a pizzeria called Dominick's in Ypsilanti, Michigan. In 1984, John Schnatter founded Papa John's in Indiana. Today, Americans spend over 33 billion dollars each year on pizza.

In 2020, there are over 77,000 restaurants in America that serve pizza.

01

Which of the following is NOT true about the story of modern pizza according to the first paragraph?

(a) The first pizzas made by Esposito consisted of tomato sauce, cheese, and toppings.
(b) When Italian King Umberto I and Queen Margherita visited Naples in the late 1800s, Esposito was asked to make a pizza for them.
(c) Esposito offered one special kind of pizza to Italian King Umberto I and Queen Margherita.
(d) Esposito made one pizza with basil, mozzarella cheese, and tomato sauce for Italian King Umberto I and Queen Margherita.

02

Why was Pizza Margherita named so?

(a) The reason was that the pizza was the King's favorite.
(b) Because the Queen directly took part in making the pizza.
(c) Since the Queen was honored by Esposito with the pizza.
(d) It was because Esposito made the pizza only for the Queen.

03

Which of the following is true about the Pizza according to the second paragraph?

(a) As some Italians immigrated to the United States, they consumed a lot of pizza.
(b) New York City was the city where the first United States pizzeria opened.
(c) The first United States pizzeria, called Lombardi's, is no longer in business.
(d) After World War II, pizza started to become famous in the United States.

04

Which of the following is NOT true about Pizza Hut?

(a) Frank and Dan Carney opened the restaurant by getting a bank loan.
(b) It was named so because there was not enough space for additional letters on the first sign.
(c) It became a well-known restaurant.
(d) Frank and Dan Carney opened other restaurants, franchising it.

05

Which of the following did most recently happen according to the text?

(a) Frank and Dan Carney opened a pizzeria in Wichita, Kansas.
(b) The Totino family of Minnesota produced the first frozen pizzas.
(c) John Schnatter founded Papa John's in Indiana.
(d) Esposito baked the first pizzas with tomato sauce, cheese, and toppings.

06

In the context of the passage, the word "establish" means

(a) set   (b) shape
(c) determine   (d) organize

07

In the context of the passage, the word "appear" means

(a) attend   (b) present
(c) seem   (d) open

피자의 역사

우리가 아는 현대 피자의 이야기는 1800년대 후반에 Italy의 Naples에서 시작되었다.

제빵사 Raffaele Esposito는 토마토소스, 치즈, 그리고 토핑을 가지고 처음으로 피자를 구워낸 것으로 보통 인정받는다. 전설에 따르면, 피자는 1889년 이탈리아 왕 Umberto Ⅰ세와 Margherita 여왕, 왕족 부부가 Naples을 방문했을 때 Esposito가 그들을 위해 피자를 만들라고 요청받았을 때 유명해졌다. Esposito는 전해진 바에 따르면 3개의 다른 피자를 구웠다. 여왕이 가장 좋아했던 것은 Esposito가 이탈리아의 빨간색, 흰색, 그리고 초록색 국기를 기려서 고안한 것이었다. 그것은 바질, 모차렐라치즈, 그리고 토마토소스로 만들어졌다. Esposito는 그녀를 기려서 그것을 Margherita 피자라고 이름 붙였다.

그러나 피자는 이탈리아를 즉시 사로잡는 것에 실패했다. 그러나 이탈리아 이민자들이 미국으로 왔을 때, 피자가 그들과 함께 왔다. 1905년에, 첫 번째 미국 피자전문점이 뉴욕에 생겼다. Lombardi's라고 불리는 그 피자전문점은 오늘날 여전히 운영한다. 곧, 뉴욕과 그곳을 넘어서 다른 피자전문점들이 나타났다. 2차 세계대전 무렵에, 피자는 미국의 가장 인기 있는 음식들 중에 하나였다. 1950년대에, Minnesota의 Totino 가족이 최초의 냉동 피자를 생산했던 것으로 여겨진다.

1958년에, Frank와 Dan Carney는 그들의 부모님으로부터 600달러를 빌려서 Kansas주 Wichita에 피자전문점을 열었다. 그들은 그들의 첫 번째 간판에 글자를 더 추가할 공간이 없었기 때문에 그들의 레스토랑을 Pizza Hut이라고 이름 지었다. Pizza Hut은 매우 유명해졌고 곧 그 형제는 새로운 레스토랑들을 열었으며 이렇게 최초의 피자 프랜차이즈가 탄생했다.

오늘날, 10,000개가 넘는 Pizza Hut 레스토랑이 있다. 비슷하게, Domino's는 900달러를 빌려 Michigan주 Ypsilanti에 있는 Dominick's라고 불리는 피자전문점을 매입한 두 명의 형제에 의해 설립되었다. 1984년에, John Schnatter는 Indiana주에 Papa John's를 설립했다. 오늘날, 미국 사람들은 피자에 매년 330억 달러 이상을 소비한다.

2020년, 미국에는 피자를 제공하는 77,000개가 넘는 레스토랑이 있다.

- **credit** 신용, 칭찬, 인정
- **royal** 왕족의
- **flag** 국기, 깃발
- **immediately** 즉시
- **immigrant** 이민자
- **operate** 운영하다
- **borrow** 빌리다
- **similarly** 비슷하게
- **popularize** 대중화하다
- **allegedly** 이른바, 알려진 바에 의하면
- **name** 이름 붙이다
- **take hold** 장악하다, 사로 잡다
- **establish** 설립하다
- **pizzeria** 피자전문점
- **franchise** 체인점

정답 01. (c) 02. (c) 03. (b) 04. (a) 05. (c) 06. (a) 07. (d)

01 영어문제

Which of the following is NOT true about the story of modern pizza according to the first paragraph?

(a) The first pizzas made by Esposito consisted of tomato sauce, cheese, and toppings.
(b) When Italian King Umberto I and Queen Margherita visited Naples in the late 1800s, Esposito was asked to make a pizza for them.
(c) Esposito offered one special kind of pizza to Italian King Umberto I and Queen Margherita.
(d) Esposito made one pizza with basil, mozzarella cheese, and tomato sauce for Italian King Umberto I and Queen Margherita.

문제 한글 해석

첫 번째 문단에 따르면, 현대 피자의 이야기에 대한 내용으로 바르지 않은 것은?

(a) Esposito가 만든 첫 번째 피자는 토마토소스, 치즈, 그리고 토핑으로 구성되었다.
(b) 이탈리아 왕 Umberto I세와 Queen Margherita가 1800년대 말에 Naples을 방문했을 때, Esposito는 그들을 위해 피자를 만들어 줄 것을 요청 받았다.
(c) Esposito는 이탈리아 왕 Umberto I세와 Margherita 여왕에게 하나의 특별한 종류의 피자를 제공했다.
(d) Esposito는 이탈리아 왕 Umberto I세와 Margherita 여왕을 위해 바질, 모차렐라치즈, 그리고 토마토소스로 피자 하나를 만들었다.

문제해설

첫 번째 문단을 통해 Esposito가 이탈리아 왕 Umberto I세와 Margherita 여왕을 위해 세 가지 종류의 다른 피자를 만들었다는 사실을 알 수 있다.

> The story of modern pizza as we know began in Naples, Italy, in the late 1800s.
>
> (a) Baker Raffaele Esposito is usually given credit for baking the first pizzas with tomato sauce, cheese, and toppings. According to legend, pizza was popularized (b) when Esposito was asked to make a pizza for Italian King Umberto I and Queen Margherita when the royal pair visited Naples in 1889. (c) Esposito allegedly baked three different pizzas. The Queen's favorite was the one in which Esposito had designed in honor of Italy's red, white, and green flag. (d) It had basil, mozzarella cheese, and tomato sauce. Esposito named it Pizza Margherita in her honor.

02 영어문제

Why was Pizza Margherita named so?

(a) The reason was that the pizza was the King's favorite.
(b) Because the Queen directly took part in making the pizza
(c) Since the Queen was honored by Esposito with the pizza
(d) It was because Esposito made the pizza only for the Queen.

문제 한글 해석

Margherita 피자가 그렇게 이름이 붙여진 이유는?

(a) 그 이유는 왕이 그 피자를 가장 좋아했기 때문에
(b) 여왕이 그 피자를 만드는 데 직접 참여했기 때문에
(c) 여왕이 그 피자로 Esposito에 의해 기려졌기 때문에
(d) Esposito가 오직 여왕을 위해 그 피자를 만들었기 때문에

문제해설

첫 번째 문단의 마지막 문장을 통해, Esposito가 자신이 만든 피자에 여왕을 기려서 Margherita 피자라는 이름을 붙였다는 사실을 알 수 있다.

The story of modern pizza as we know began in Naples, Italy, in the late 1800s.

Baker Raffaele Esposito is usually given credit for baking the first pizzas with tomato sauce, cheese, and toppings. According to legend, pizza was popularized when Esposito was asked to make a pizza for Italian King Umberto I and Queen Margherita when the royal pair visited Naples in 1889. Esposito allegedly baked three different pizzas. The Queen's favorite was the one in which Esposito had designed in honor of Italy's red, white, and green flag. It had basil, mozzarella cheese, and tomato sauce. Esposito named it Pizza Margherita in her honor.

03 영어문제

Which of the following is true about the Pizza according to the second paragraph?

(a) As some Italians immigrated to the United States, they consumed a lot of pizza.
(b) New York City was the city where the first United States pizzeria opened.
(c) The first United States pizzeria, called Lombardi's, is no longer in business.
(d) After World War II, pizza started to become famous in the United States.

문제 한글 해석

2번째 문단에 따르면, 피자에 대한 내용으로 바른 것은?

(a) 몇몇 이탈리아인들이 미국으로 이민을 가면서, 많은 피자를 소비했다.
(b) 뉴욕은 첫 번째 미국의 피자전문점이 생긴 도시이다.
(c) Lombardi's라고 불리는 미국의 최초의 피자전문점은 더 이상 영업하지 않는다.
(d) 2차 세계대전이 끝난 후에, 피자는 미국에서 유명해지기 시작했다.

문제해설

2번째 문단을 통해, 1905년에 첫 번째 미국 피자 전문점이 뉴욕에 생겼다는 것과 이것이 Lombardi's라고 불린다는 사실을 알 수 있다.

> (a) Pizza, however, failed to immediately take hold in Italy. As Italian immigrants came to the United States, however, pizza came with them. In 1905, the first United States pizzeria was established in New York City. The pizzeria, called Lombardi's, (c) still operates today. Soon, other pizzerias in New York City and beyond appeared. (d) By World War II, pizza was one of America's most popular foods. In the 1950s, the Totino family, of Minnesota, was thought to have produced the first frozen pizzas.

(a) 몇몇 이탈리안들이 미국으로 이민을 가면서 그들이 피자를 많은 소비를 하기 시작한 것이 아니라, 피자가 그 이민자들과 함께 왔다는 사실을 알 수 있다.

(c) Lombardi's라는 미국의 첫 번째 피자 전문점은 현재까지도 여전히 영업을 한다는 사실을 알 수 있다.

(d) 2차 세계대전 무렵에 미국에서 피자가 유명해진 것이 아니라, 2차 세계대전에 피자가 미국의 가장 인기 있는 음식들 중에 하나였다는 사실을 알 수 있다.

04 영어문제 | 문제 한글 해석

Which of the following is NOT true about Pizza Hut?

(a) Frank and Dan Carney opened the restaurant by getting a bank loan.
(b) It was named so because there was not enough space for additional letters on the first sign.
(c) It became a well-known restaurant.
(d) Frank and Dan Carney opened other restaurants, franchising it.

Pizza Hut에 대한 내용으로 바르지 않은 것은?

(a) Frank와 Dan Carney는 은행 대출을 받아서 가게를 열었다.
(b) 그것은 최초의 간판에 글자를 추가할 충분한 공간이 없었기 때문에 그렇게 이름 지어졌다.
(c) 그것은 유명한 가게가 되었다.
(d) Frank와 Dan Carney는 다른 가게를 열어 그것을 프랜차이즈로 만들었다.

문제해설

세 번째 문단을 통해 Frank와 Dan Carney가 은행 대출이 아닌, 부모님으로부터 600달러를 빌려와서 피자전문점을 열었다는 사실을 알 수 있다.

In 1958, Frank and Dan Carney borrowed $600 from their parents and opened a pizzeria in Wichita, Kansas. (b) They called their restaurant Pizza Hut because they didn't have space for additional letters on their first sign. (c) Pizza Hut became very popular and soon (d) the brothers opened new restaurants and hence, the first pizza franchise was born.

05 영어문제

Which of the following did most recently happen according to the text?

(a) Frank and Dan Carney opened a pizzeria in Wichita, Kansas.
(b) The Totino family of Minnesota produced the first frozen pizzas.
(c) John Schnatter founded Papa John's in Indiana.
(d) Esposito baked the first pizzas with tomato sauce, cheese, and toppings.

문제 한글 해석

이 글에 따르면, 가장 최근에 발생한 것은?

(a) Frank와 Dan Carney는 Kansas주 Wichita에 피자 전문점을 열었다.
(b) Minnesota의 Totino 가족이 최초의 냉동 피자를 생산했다.
(c) John Schnatter는 Indiana 주에 Papa John's를 설립했다.
(d) Esposito는 토마토소스, 치즈, 토핑이 들어간 최초의 피자를 만들었다.

문제해설

(c) 가장 마지막 문단을 통해, 1984년에 John Schnatter는 Indiana 주에 Papa John's를 설립했다는 점을 알 수 있으며, 보기의 내용 중 가장 최근에 발생한 일이다.

> Today, there are more than 10,000 Pizza Hut restaurants. Similarly, Domino's was established by two brothers who borrowed $900 to purchase a pizzeria called Dominick's in Ypsilanti, Michigan. In 1984, John Schnatter founded Papa John's in Indiana. Today, Americans spend over 33 billion dollars each year on pizza. In 2020, there are over 77,000 restaurants in America that serve pizza.

(a) 세 번째 문단을 통해, Frank와 Dan Carney는 1958년에 피자 전문점을 열었다는 점을 알 수 있으며, 이를 통해 (b)와 비슷한 시기에 발생한 일이라는 것을 알 수 있다.

> In 1958, Frank and Dan Carney borrowed $600 from their parents and opened a pizzeria in Wichita, Kansas.

(b) 두 번째 문단의 마지막 문장을 통해, Totino 가족이 최초의 냉동 피자를 생산한 것으로 여겨지는 시기는 1950년 대라는 것을 알 수 있으며, 이를 통해 (a)와 비슷한 시기에 발생한 일이라는 것을 알 수 있다.

> In the 1950s, the Totino family, of Minnesota, was thought to have produced the first frozen pizzas.

(d) 첫 번째 문단을 통해, Esposito가 첫 번째 피자를 만든 이야기는 1800년대 말이므로, 보기의 내용 중 가장 처음에 발생한 일이라는 것을 알 수 있다.

> The story of modern pizza as we know began in Naples, Italy, in the late 1800s.
> Baker Raffaele Esposito is usually given credit for baking the first pizzas with tomato sauce, cheese, and toppings.

06 영어문제

In the context of the passage, the word "establish" means

(a) set
(b) shape
(c) determine
(d) organize

문제 한글 해석

이 글의 문맥상 "establish"는 무엇을 의미하는가?

(a) ~을/를 세우다
(b) 모양을 잡다
(c) 결심하다
(d) 조직하다

문제해설

이 글에서 "establish"는 '설립하다, 세우다'의 의미로, (a) set '~을/를 세우다'와 가장 가까운 뜻을 가졌다. 그 외의 보기들 (b) shape 모양을 잡다 (d) organize 조직하다는 '~을/를 세우다'와는 거리가 먼 단어들이다.

07 영어문제

In the context of the passage, the word "appear" means

(a) attend
(b) present
(c) seem
(d) open

문제 한글 해석

이 글의 문맥상 "appear"는 무엇을 의미하는가?

(a) 출석하다
(b) 보여주다
(c) ~처럼 보이다
(d) 열다

문제해설

이 글의 문맥상 "appear"은 '나타나다, 생겨나다'를 의미한다. 따라서 가장 가까운 의미의 (d) open '열다'가 정답이 된다. 나머지 단어들은 appear과 유의어들이지만 문맥에서 의미하는 바와는 거리가 먼 단어들이다.

MEMO

PART 4. 독해 만렙 실전모의고사

Part 4. Read the following business letter and answer the questions.
The underlined words in the article are for vocabulary questions.

The position of proofreader

486 Cedarbrook St.
Beaufort. SC 29916
Dec. 9th
Roy Cho
Human Resources Dept.
The Springfield Gazette

Dear. Roy Cho

Thank you for meeting with me last Wednesday, November 15, to discuss the position of proofreader at the Springfield Gazette. I was impressed with the company's ability to maintain such a high standard of journalism in such a competitive market. Its continued ability to cater to the specific needs of its readers was obvious.

I feel that through my past experiences I am capable of fulfilling the requirements you <u>outlined</u> for this position. While I was working as a section editor for the Daily Mississippian, I have become accustomed to the responsibilities <u>associated</u> with meeting deadlines and working under pressure. As I stated at our meeting, I enjoy the challenge of a competitive environment in which success is based on achievement.

Again, thank you for considering me for the position of proofreader.

I look forward to hearing from you again.

Sincerely,
Janet Kim
Royal Palace Road 82-10
617-809-6144
AwesomeJanet@gmail.com

01

What can be inferred about Janet Kim?

(a) She is seeking employees for the position of proofreader.
(b) She was selected as the proofreader.
(c) She discussed for the position of proofreader with Roy Cho.
(d) She wants to recommend a candidate for the position of proofreader.

02

Which of the following is NOT true about the Springfield Gazette?

(a) It maintains the ability to satisfy the specific needs of its readers.
(b) It has difficulty maintaining a high standard in a competitive market.
(c) It is considering hiring Janet Kim as the position of proofreader.
(d) It is aware of the readers' specific needs.

03

What did Janet Kim learn from working experience at the Daily Mississippian?

(a) Meeting various people and hanging out with them
(b) Handling and relieving a lot of stress
(c) Communicating well with a lot of people
(d) Doing the job well even under pressure

04

Which of the following is true about Roy Cho?

(a) He is working in the Human Resources Department at the Springfield Gazette.
(b) He has work experience at the Daily Mississippian.
(c) He is in charge of proofreading at the Springfield Gazette.
(d) He is a colleague of Janet Kim.

05

What is Janet Kim indeed hoping?

(a) to receive a reply from Roy Cho
(b) to be selected as the proofreader
(c) to be promoted to a higher position
(d) to hire Roy Cho as her employee

06

In the context of the passage, the word "outline" means

(a) portray
(b) summarize
(c) depict
(d) figure

07

In the context of the passage, the word "associate" means

(a) contact
(b) joint
(c) combine
(d) relate

해석

486 Cedarbrook St.

Beaufort. SC 29916

Dec. 9th
Roy Cho

Human Resources Dept.

The Springfield Gazette

친애하는 Roy Cho께

지난 수요일, 11월 15일에 The Springfield Gazette에서 교정자 직책에 대한 이야기를 나누기 위해서 저와 만나주셔서 감사합니다. 저는 경쟁이 치열한 시장에서 이렇게 높은 수준의 저널리즘 (언론, 기사)을 유지하는 회사의 능력에 감명 받았습니다. 독자의 특정한 요구를 충족시킬 회사의 지속적인 능력은 자명해 보였습니다.

저는 제 과거 경험을 통해 귀하가 이 직책에 대해 간략히 말씀하셨던 조건을 충족시킬 수 있다고 생각합니다. 제가 the Daily Mississippian의 부서 편집장으로서 일하는 동안, 마감 기한을 맞추고 압박 속에서 일하는 것에 관련된 책임감에 익숙해졌습니다. 미팅에서 언급했던 것처럼, 저는 실적이 성공의 기반이 되는 경쟁적인 환경에 대한 도전을 즐깁니다.

다시 한 번, 교정자 직책에 저를 고려해주셔서 감사합니다. 다시 귀하로부터 연락받기를 고대합니다.

Janet Kim 올림

Royal Palace Road 82-10

617-809-6144

AwesomeJanet@gmail.com

단어

- discuss 논의하다
- journalism 저널리즘, 기사 쓰는 일
- cater to ~의 구미에 맞추다
- be capable of ~을 가능하게 하다
- outline 윤곽; 윤곽을 잡다, 개요를 설명하다
- associated with ~와 연관된
- under pressure 압박을 느끼는
- look forward to ~ing ~하는 것을 기대하다, 고대하다
- proofreader 교정자
- competitive 경쟁력 있는
- obvious 분명한
- requirement 요구
- become accustomed to ~에 익숙해지다
- deadline 마감 기한
- consider 고려하다

정답 01. (c)　02. (b)　03. (d)　04. (a)　05. (b)　06. (b)　07. (d)

01 영어문제　　　　　　　　　　　　　　　　　문제 한글 해석

What can be inferred about Janet Kim?

(a) She is seeking employees for the position of proofreader.
(b) She was selected as the proofreader.
(c) She discussed for the position of proofreader with Roy Cho.
(d) She wants to recommend a candidate for the position of proofreader.

Janet Kim에 대하여 추론할 수 있는 것은?

(a) 그녀는 교정자 직책을 위한 직원을 찾고 있다.
(b) 그녀는 교정자로 선발되었다.
(c) 그녀는 Roy Cho와 교정자 직책에 대해 이야기를 나눴다.
(d) 그녀는 교정자 직책으로 후보자를 추천하기를 희망한다.

문제해설

첫 번째 문단을 통해, Janet Kim이 지난 수요일, 11월 15일에 메일 수신자인 Roy Cho와 교정자 직책에 대해 이야기 나눴음을 알 수 있다.

> Thank you for meeting with me last Wednesday, November 15, to discuss the position of proofreader at the Springfield Gazette. I was impressed with the company's ability to maintain such a high standard of journalism in such a competitive market.

02 영어문제

Which of the following is NOT true about the Springfield Gazette?

(a) It maintains the ability to satisfy the specific needs of its readers.
(b) It has difficulty maintaining a high standard in a competitive market.
(c) It is considering hiring Janet Kim as the position of proofreader.
(d) It is aware of the readers' specific needs.

문제 한글 해석

The Springfield Gazette에 대한 내용으로 바르지 않은 것은?

(a) 독자의 특정 요구를 충족시키는 능력을 유지한다.
(b) 경쟁이 치열한 시장에서 높은 수준을 유지하는 데 어려움을 겪고 있다.
(c) Janet Kim을 교정자 직책에 고용하는 것을 고려하고 있다.
(d) 독자의 특정 요구를 인식하고 있다.

문제해설

The Springfield Gazette는 경쟁이 치열한 시장에서 높은 수준의 저널리즘을 유지하는 회사의 능력을 갖추었다는 점을 알 수 있다.

> Thank you for meeting with me last Wednesday, November 15, to discuss the position of proofreader at The Springfield Gazette. I was impressed with the company's ability to maintain such a high standard of journalism in such a competitive market.

두 번째 문단을 통해 the Springfield Gazette는 독자의 특정 요구를 인식하고 있으며, 이를 충족시킬 수 있는 능력을 갖추었음을 알 수 있다. 또한 Janet Kim을 교정자 직책에 고용하는 것을 고려하고 있다는 점도 알 수 있다.

> (a), (d) Its continued ability to cater to the specific needs of its readers was obvious.
>
> I feel that through my past experiences I am capable of fulfilling the requirements you outlined for this position. While I was working as a section editor for the Daily Mississippian, I have become accustomed to the responsibilities associated with meeting deadlines and working under pressure. As I stated at our meeting, I enjoy the challenge of a competitive environment in which success is based on achievement.
>
> (c) Again, thank you for considering me for the position of proofreader.

03 영어문제 | 문제 한글 해석

What did Janet Kim learn from working experience at the Daily Mississippian?

(a) Meeting various people and hanging out with them
(b) Handling and relieving a lot of stress
(c) Communicating well with a lot of people
(d) Doing the job well even under pressure

Janet Kim이 the Daily Mississippian에서의 근무 경험을 통해 배운 것은?

(a) 많은 사람들과 만나고, 그들과 잘 어울리는 것
(b) 많은 스트레스를 다루고 해소하는 것
(c) 많은 사람들과 의사소통을 잘하는 것
(d) 압박 속에서도 일을 잘하는 것

문제해설

아래 문단의 내용을 통해, Janet Kim이 Daily Mississippian에서 부서 편집장으로 일하면서, 마감 기한을 맞추고 압박 속에서 일하는 것에 관련된 책임감에 익숙하게 되었다는 점을 알 수 있다.

> I feel that through my past experiences I am capable of fulfilling the requirements you outlined for this position. While I was working as a section editor for the Daily Mississippian, I have become accustomed to the responsibilities associated with meeting deadlines and working under pressure. As I stated at our meeting, I enjoy the challenge of a competitive environment in which success is based on achievement.

04 영어문제 | 문제 한글 해석

Which of the following is true about Roy Cho?

(a) He is working in the Human Resources Department at the Springfield Gazette.
(b) He has work experience at the Daily Mississippian.
(c) He is in charge of proofreading at the Springfield Gazette.
(d) He is a colleague of Janet Kim.

Roy Cho에 대한 내용으로 바른 것은?

(a) 그는 the Springfield Gazette의 인사팀에 근무하고 있다.
(b) 그는 the Daily Mississippian에서 일한 경험이 있다.
(c) 그는 the Springfield Gazette에서 교정 업무를 담당하고 있다.
(d) 그는 Janet Kim의 동료이다.

문제해설

메일 첫 부분의 내용을 보면, Roy Cho가 the Springfield Gazette의 인사팀에 근무하고 있다는 점을 알 수 있다.

> 486 Cedarbrook St.
> Beaufort. SC 29916
> Dec. 9th
> Roy Cho
> Human Resources Dept.
> The Springfield Gazette

05 영어문제 | 문제 한글 해석

What is Janet Kim indeed hoping?
(a) to receive a reply from Roy Cho
(b) to be selected as the proofreader
(c) to be promoted to a higher position
(d) to hire Roy Cho as her employee

Janet Kim이 진심으로 바라는 것은?
(a) Roy Cho로부터 회신을 받는 것
(b) 교정자로 선발되는 것
(c) 더 높은 직책으로 승진하는 것
(d) Roy Cho를 자신의 직원으로 고용하는 것

문제해설

이 글의 마지막 부분을 볼 때, Janet Kim은 자신을 교정자 직책에 고려했다는 점을 감사하다고 하고 있으며, 다시 한 번 연락받기를 고대한다고 말하고 있다. 이를 통해 Janet Kim이 교정자 직책에 선발되기를 희망한다는 것을 알 수 있다.

> Again, thank you for considering me for the position of proofreader.
> I look forward to hearing from you again.

06 영어문제 | 문제 한글 해석

In the context of the passage, the word "outline" means
(a) portray
(b) summarize
(c) depict
(d) figure

이 글의 문맥상 "outline"는 무엇을 의미하는가?
(a) 묘사하다
(b) 요약하다, 개요를 설명하다
(c) 묘사하다
(d) 생각하다

문제해설

이 글의 문맥상 "outline"은 '윤곽을 잡다, 개요를 설명하다'를 의미한다. 따라서 가장 가까운 의미의 (b) summarize '요약하다, 개요를 설명하다'가 정답이 된다. 나머지 단어들은 outline과 유의어들이긴 하나 문맥상 쓰인 뜻과는 거리가 있는 어휘들이다.

07 영어문제

In the context of the passage, the word "associate" means
(a) contact
(b) joint
(c) combine
(d) relate

문제 한글 해석

이 글의 문맥상 "associate"는 무엇을 의미하는가?
(a) 연락하다
(b) 결합시키다
(c) 합치다
(d) 연관되다

문제해설

이 글에서 "associate"는 '관련시키다'의 의미로, 문맥상에서는 associated '~과 관련된, 연관된'이란 의미로 쓰였다. 그러므로 (d) relate '연관되다'와 가장 가까운 뜻을 가졌다. 그 외에 단어들은 유의어이기는 하나 문맥상 쓰인 의미와는 서로 다른 의미를 지닌 단어들이다.

필수 단어, 표현, 숙어 암기노트

단어, 표현, 숙어	의미

필수 단어, 표현, 숙어 암기노트

단어, 표현, 숙어	의미

독해 만렙을 위한
실전모의고사

4S G-TELP

SIGNATURE

PART 1. 독해 만렙 실전모의고사

Part 1. Read the following biographical article and answer the questions. The underlined words in the article are for vocabulary questions.

Alexander Graham Bell

Alexander Graham Bell was born in Edinburgh, Scotland on March 3, 1847.

When he was only eleven years old, he invented a machine that could clean wheat. Graham studied anatomy and physiology at the University of London, but moved with his family to Quebec, Canada in 1870.

Bell soon moved to Boston, Massachusetts. In 1871, he began working with deaf people and published the system of Visible Hearing that was developed by his father. Visible Hearing illustrated how the tongue, lips, and throat are used to produce vocal sounds. In 1872, Bell founded a school for the deaf which soon became part of Boston University.

Alexander Graham Bell is best known for his invention of the telephone. While trying to discover the secret of transmitting multiple messages on a single wire, Bell heard the sound of a plucked string along some of the electrical wire. One of Bell's assistants, Thomas A. Watson, was trying to reactivate a telephone transmitter. After hearing the sound, Bell believed he could send the sound of a human voice over the wire. After receiving a patent on March 7, 1876 for transmitting sound along a single wire, he successfully transmitted human speech on March 10th. Bell's telephone patent was one of the most valuable patents ever issued. He started the Bell Telephone Company in 1877.

Bell went on to invent a precursor to the modern day air conditioner, and a device called a "photophone" that enabled sound to be transmitted on a beam of light. Today's fiber optic and laser communication systems are based on Bell's photophone research. Bell also helped found Science Magazine, one of the most respected research journals in the world.

Alexander Graham Bell died August 2, 1922. On the day of his burial, in honor of Bell, all telephone services in the United States were stopped for one minute.

01

How was Alexander Graham Bell's childhood?

(a) Alexander Graham Bell made it possible to clean wheat by invention.
(b) He wasn't satisfied with studying in anatomy and physiology.
(c) He tried to help deaf people and worked with them.
(d) For his study, he moved to another city several times.

02

What was the function of Visible Hearing which Alexander Graham Bell's father developed?

(a) It made deaf people understand precisely what they heard.
(b) Visible Hearing was used to produce vocal sounds.
(c) Its main function was to illustrate how deaf people produced vocal sounds.
(d) It demonstrated the principle of making vocal sounds.

03

Which of the following is true about Alexander Graham Bell?

(a) He was inspired by a sound of a plucked string, and transmitted human speech over the wire.
(b) He tried to interpret the several transmitted messages on a single wire.
(c) He invented the first telephone transmitter.
(d) He applied for a patent of his invention, air conditioner.

04

Which of the following is NOT true about a "photophone?"

(a) Photophone is Bell's invention, along with telephone.
(b) It transmitted sound on a beam of light.
(c) His invention, photophone was introduced through Science Magazine.
(d) The ground of fiber optic and laser communication systems are on the photophone.

05

In honor of Bell, what happened in the United States?

(a) The United States built a monument to his memory.
(b) The United States had all telephone services not work for a certain time.
(c) Bell's bereaved families received appreciation plagues.
(d) The government offered a testimonial to Bell's bereaved families.

06

In the context of the passage, the word "found" means

(a) discover
(b) establish
(c) reveal
(d) mold

07

In the context of the passage, the word "transmit" means

(a) send
(b) broadcast
(c) spread
(d) donate

Alexander Graham Bell은 1847년 3월 3일 스코틀랜드 에든버러에서 태어났다.

그가 고작 11살이었을 때 밀을 깨끗하게 하는 기계를 발명했다. Graham은 런던 대학교에서 해부학과 생리학을 공부했지만, 1870년에 가족과 함께 캐나다 퀘벡으로 이사했다.

Bell은 곧 매사추세츠 주 보스턴으로 이사했다. 1871년에 그는 청각 장애인과 함께 일하기 시작했고 아버지가 개발한 Visible Hearing 시스템을 공개했다. Visible Hearing은 어떻게 혀, 입술 및 목이 음성의 소리를 생성하는 데 사용되는지 보여준다. 1872년에 Bell은 청각 장애인을 위한 학교를 설립하였는데, 그것은 곧 보스턴 대학의 소속이 되었다.

Alexander Graham Bell은 전화기 발명으로 가장 잘 알려져 있다. 단일 회선으로 복합적인 메시지를 전송하는 비밀을 알아내기 위해 노력하고 있을 때, Bell은 일부 전기 회선을 따라 줄이 튕겨지는 소리를 들었다. Bell의 조수들 중 한 명인 Thomas A. Watson은 전화 전송기를 재가동하기 위해 애쓰고 있었다. 그 소리를 들은 후에, Bell은 사람의 목소리를 회선 너머로 보낼 수 있다고 믿었다. 1876년 3월 7일에 단일 회선을 따라 소리를 전송한 것에 대한 특허를 받은 후에, 3월 10일에 그는 사람의 말을 성공적으로 전송했다. Bell의 전화기 특허는 여태껏 출원된 것 중 가장 가치 있는 특허들 가운데 하나이다. 그는 1877년에 Bell Telephone Company를 운영하기 시작했다.

계속해서 Bell은 현대식 에어컨의 전신이 되는 것과 더불어 소리가 광선 위로 전송되게 하는 "광선전화"를 발명했다. 오늘날의 광섬유와 레이저 통신 체계는 Bell의 광선 전화에 대한 연구를 기초로 한다. Bell은 또한 세계에서 가장 높이 평가받는 연구 학술지 중 하나인 Science Magazine을 설립하는 것을 도왔다.

Alexander Graham bell은 1922년 8월 2일에 사망했다. 그의 장례식 날, 그를 기리기 위해, 미국의 모든 전화 서비스가 1분 동안 멈췄다.

- anatomy 해부학
- deaf 청각 장애가 있는
- transmit 전송하다
- pluck 뽑다, 뜯다
- reactivate 재가동하다
- issue 발행하다, 교부하다
- fiber optic 광섬유의
- burial 묘지, 매장
- physiology 생리학
- be known for ~로 알려져 있다
- multiple 복합적인
- electrical 전기의
- patent 특허권
- precursor 선구자, 전신
- be based on ~에 근거하다, 기초하다
- in honor of ~에게 경의를 표하여, ~을 기념하여

정답 01. (a) 02. (d) 03. (a) 04. (c) 05. (b) 06. (b) 07. (a)

01

영어문제

How was Alexander Graham Bell's childhood?
(a) Alexander Graham Bell made it possible to clean wheat by invention.
(b) He wasn't satisfied with studying in anatomy and physiology.
(c) He tried to help deaf people and worked with them.
(d) For his study, he moved to another city several times.

문제 한글 해석

Alexander Graham Bell의 어린 시절은 어떠했는가?
(a) Alexander Graham Bell은 발명품으로 밀을 깨끗하게 하는 것을 가능하게 만들었다.
(b) 그는 해부학 및 생리학을 공부하는 것이 만족스럽지 않았다.
(c) 그는 청각 장애인들을 돕기 위해 노력했으며 그들과 함께 일했다.
(d) 공부를 위해, 그는 여러 번 다른 도시로 이사했다.

문제해설

첫 번째 문단을 통해, Alexander Graham Bell은 11살이었을 때, 밀을 깨끗하게 세척하는 기계를 발명했다는 사실을 알 수 있다.

> Alexander Graham Bell was born in Edinburgh, Scotland on March 3, 1847. When he was only eleven years old, he invented a machine that could clean wheat. Graham studied anatomy and physiology at the University of London, but moved with his family to Quebec, Canada in 1870.

02

영어문제

What was the function of Visible Hearing which Alexander Graham Bell's father developed?
(a) It made deaf people understand precisely what they heard.
(b) Visible Hearing was used to produce vocal sounds.
(c) Its main function was to illustrate how deaf people produced vocal sounds.
(d) It demonstrated the principle of making vocal sounds.

문제 한글 해석

Alexander Graham Bell의 아버지가 개발한 Visible Hearing의 기능은 무엇이었는가?
(a) 청각장애인들이 그들이 들은 것을 정확히 이해할 수 있도록 만들었다.
(b) Visible Hearing은 음성의 소리를 만들어내는 데 사용되었다.
(c) 그것의 주요 기능은 어떻게 청각 장애인들이 음성의 소리를 만들어내는지 보여주는 것이었다.
(d) 그것은 음성의 소리를 만드는 원리를 보여주었다.

문제해설

1871년에 Bell은 청각 장애인들과 일하기 시작했고, Visible Hearing을 개발했는데, 이는 어떻게 혀, 입술 그리고 목구멍이 음성의 소리를 만드는 데 사용되었는지, 즉 음성의 소리를 만드는 원리를 보여주는 것이라는 사실을 알 수 있다.

> Bell soon moved to Boston, Massachusetts. In 1871, he began working with deaf people and published the system of Visible Hearing that was developed by his father. Visible Hearing illustrated how the tongue, lips, and throat are used to produce vocal sounds. In 1872, Bell founded a school for the deaf which soon became part of Boston University.

03 영어문제 | 문제 한글 해석

Which of the following is true about Alexander Graham Bell?

(a) He was inspired by a sound of a plucked string, and transmitted human speech over the wire.
(b) He tried to interpret the several transmitted messages on a single wire.
(c) He invented the first telephone transmitter.
(d) He applied for a patent of his invention, air conditioner.

Alexander Graham Bell에 대한 내용 중 사실인 것은?

(a) 그는 줄이 튕겨지는 소리에서 영감을 받았고, 사람의 말을 전선을 통해 전송했다.
(b) 그는 단일 전선으로 전송된 여러 가지 메시지를 해석하기 위해 노력했다.
(c) 그는 최초의 전화 송화기를 발명했다.
(d) 그는 그의 발명품, 에어컨에 대한 특허를 신청했다.

문제해설

Bell은 전선을 따라서 줄이 튕겨지는 소리를 들은 후에, 전선을 통해 사람의 말을 전송할 수 있다고 믿었고, 전화를 발명했다.

Alexander Graham Bell is best known for his invention of the telephone. While trying to discover the secret of transmitting multiple messages on a single wire, Bell heard the sound of a plucked string along some of the electrical wire. One of Bell's assistants, Thomas A. Watson, was trying to reactivate a telephone transmitter. After hearing the sound, Bell believed he could send the sound of a human voice over the wire. After receiving a patent on March 7, 1876 for transmitting sound along a single wire, he successfully transmitted human speech on March 10th. Bell's telephone patent was one of the most valuable patents ever issued. He started the Bell Telephone Company in 1877.

04 영어문제 | 문제 한글 해석

Which of the following is NOT true about a "photophone?"

(a) Photophone is Bell's invention, along with telephone.
(b) It transmitted sound on a beam of light.
(c) His invention, photophone was introduced through Science Magazine.
(d) The ground of fiber optic and laser communication systems are on the photophone.

'광선전화'에 대한 사실로 올바르지 않은 것은?

(a) 광선전화는 전화와 더불어 Bell의 발명품이다.
(b) 그것은 광선을 통해 소리를 전송했다.
(c) 그의 발명품인 광선전화는 Science Magazine을 통해 소개되었다.
(d) 광섬유 및 레이저 통신 체계의 근거는 광선전화에 있다.

문제해설

Bell이 세계에서 가장 높이 평가받는 연구 학술지 중 하나인 Science Magazine을 설립하는 것을 도운 것은 사실이나, 광선 전화가 그 잡지에 소개되었다는 사실은 확인할 수 없다.

(a) Bell went on to invent a precursor to the modern day air conditioner, and a device called a "photophone" (b) that enabled sound to be transmitted on a beam of light. (d) Today's fiber optic and laser communication systems are based on Bell's photophone research. Bell also helped found Science Magazine, one of the most respected research journals in the world.

05

영어문제

In honor of Bell, what happened in the United States?

(a) The United States built a monument to his memory.
(b) The United States had all telephone services not work for a certain time.
(c) Bell's bereaved families received appreciation plagues.
(d) The government offered a testimonial to Bell's bereaved families.

문제 한글 해석

Bell을 기리기 위하여, 미국에서 어떤 일이 발생했는가?

(a) 미국은 그를 기리며 기념비를 세웠다.
(b) 미국은 특정 시간 동안 모든 전화 서비스를 작동하지 않도록 했다.
(c) Bell의 유가족은 감사패를 받았다.
(d) 정부는 Bell의 유가족에게 감사장을 전달했다.

문제해설

Bell이 죽은 후 그를 묻은 날, 그를 기리기 위해 미국에서 모든 전화 서비스가 1분 동안 멈춰졌다는 사실을 알 수 있다.

> Alexander Graham Bell died August 2, 1922. On the day of his burial, in honor of Bell, all telephone services in the United States were stopped for one minute.

06

영어문제

In the context of the passage, the word "found" means

(a) discover
(b) establish
(c) reveal
(d) mold

문제 한글 해석

이 글의 문맥상 "found"는 무엇을 의미하는가?

(a) 발견하다
(b) 설립하다
(c) 밝히다, 드러내다
(d) 주조하다

문제해설

이 글의 문맥상 "found"는 '설립하다'를 의미한다. 따라서 가장 가까운 의미의 (b) establish '설립하다'가 정답이 된다. 여기서 found를 find '찾다'의 과거형으로 착각하지 말아야 한다.

07

영어문제

In the context of the passage, the word "transmit" means

(a) send
(b) broadcast
(c) spread
(d) donate

문제 한글 해석

이 글의 문맥상 "transmit"은 무엇을 의미하는가?

(a) 보내다
(b) 방송하다
(c) 퍼트리다
(d) 기부하다

문제해설

이 글에서 "transmit"은 문맥상에서 '~을/를 보내다, 전송하다'의 의미로, (a) send '보내다'와 가장 가까운 뜻을 가졌다. 그 외에 단어들은 유의어이기는 하나 문맥상 쓰인 의미와는 서로 다른 의미를 지닌 단어들이다.

PART 2. 독해 만렙 실전모의고사

Part 2. Read the following magazine article and answer the questions.
The underlined words in the article are for vocabulary questions.

First Alien Moon Detected Outside Our Solar System

Over the last couple of decades, astronomers have <u>identifi</u>ed thousands of planets outside our solar system. However, they have been unable to find confirmation of a moon revolving around any of the distant worlds, mainly because the generally smaller satellites are harder to spot. Now, some researchers from Columbia University believe they have found evidence of an alien moon orbiting a gaseous exoplanet, which lies almost 8,000 light years away.

For their study, astronomers Alex Teachey and David Kipping, who have been searching for alien moons for nearly a decade, focused on the 284 exoplanets discovered by the planet-hunting Kepler spacecraft. The distant worlds were considered the best candidates for potential exomoons due to their relatively wide orbits that span more than 30 days.

Specifically, the scientists were searching for two dips in light – one caused by the exoplanet as it passed in front of its star and the second by another, most likely smaller, celestial body. After sifting through the data collected by Kepler, the researchers were able to identify one exoplanet, Kepler-1625b, that looked promising. "We saw little deviations and wobbles in the light curve that caught our attention," Kipping said.

To <u>confirm</u> their suspicions, the team used the Hubble telescope to monitor the planet before and during its 19-hour-long transit across the face of its star. Sure enough, about 3.5 hours after the Kepler-1625b had passed, Hubble detected a second, much smaller decrease in the star's brightness, which Kipping said was consistent with "a moon trailing the planet like a dog following its owner on a leash."

Their exomoon hypothesis was further confirmed when the planet began its transit 1.25 hours earlier than predicted. This happens only when an orbiting moon pulls at the planet and causes it to wobble, as is the case with our own moon. "An extraterrestrial civilization watching the Earth and Moon transit the Sun would note similar anomalies in the timing of Earth's transit," Kipping explained.

01

For the last couple of decades, what were astronomers unable to do?

(a) The astronomers were not able to identify thousands of planets outside our solar system.
(b) They could not spot a moon rotating around the distant worlds.
(c) The astronomers were unable to find any gaseous exoplanet revolving around the distant worlds.
(d) They had no ability to take the first confirmed picture of a certain planet.

02

Why were the distant worlds regarded as the best candidates for potential exomoons?

(a) The reason was that the distant worlds orbited a gaseous exoplanet.
(b) It was because they were identified by astronomers.
(c) Because of their wide orbits which span more than 30 days
(d) Now that they couldn't find any other possible candidates except the distant worlds

03

How different are two dips in light which the scientists were searching for?

(a) They were different because each of two dips was made by different methods.
(b) They had no difference because both were made by a celestial body.
(c) They were different only in terms of size.
(d) One generated the exoplanet while the other made another planet.

04

Through using the Hubble telescope, what did the team find out?

(a) The telescope could not solve the team's suspicions about the Kepler-1625b.
(b) They monitored how to transit the planet across the face of its star.
(c) The team figured out the fact that the Kepler-1625b did not make any difference in the star's brightness.
(d) They could confirm that there was a much smaller decrease in the star's brightness, after the Kepler-1625b had passed.

05

According to the last paragraph, when did the planet's transit 1.25 hours earlier than predicted happen?

(a) It happened in a case where it caused the moon to wobble.
(b) At the time when the exomoon hypothesis was further researched
(c) It happened when the Earth's transit was discovered.
(d) It only happened when an orbiting moon pulled at the planet.

06

In the context of the passage, the word "identify" means

(a) associate   (b) recognize
(c) discover   (d) observe

07

In the context of the passage, the word "confirm" means

(a) prove   (b) accept
(c) approve   (d) ensure

태양계 밖에서 최초로 탐지된 외계 위성

지난 수 십 년 동안, 천문학자들은 우리 태양계 밖에서 수천 개의 행성을 발견해왔다. 그러나 그들은 일반적으로 더 작은 위성을 찾기가 더 어렵기 때문에 먼 외계를 따라 회전하는 하나의 위성의 확인(증거)도 찾지 못했다. 오늘날, Columbia 대학교의 일부 연구원들은 그들이 거의 8,000 광년 떨어진 기체로 된 외계행성을 맴도는 한 외계 위성에 대한 증거를 찾았다고 믿는다.

연구를 위해, 거의 10년 동안 외계 위성들을 찾고 있었던 천문학자 Alex Teachey와 David Kipping은 행성을 탐사하는 Kepler 우주선에 의해 발견된 284번 외계행성에 주목했다.

주기가 30일이 넘는 상대적으로 넓은 궤도 때문에 그 외계는 외계 위성이 존재할 수도 있는 잠재력이 높은 것으로 알려졌다.

구체적으로, 과학자들은 빛이 휘어지는 두 가지 경우를 찾고 있었는데, 첫 번째 것은 외계행성이 그것의 위성 앞을 지나갈 때 만들어졌고, 두 번째 것은 또 다른, 아마도 더 작은, 천체에 의해 만들어졌다. Kepler에 의해 수집된 데이터를 면밀히 조사한 후에, 연구원들은 가능성 있어 보이는 한 외계행성인 Kepler-1625b를 확인할 수 있었다. "우리는 우리의 주의를 사로잡은 빛 곡선에서 약간의 편차와 흔들림을 봤어요."라고 Kipping이 말했다.

그들의 추측을 확인하기 위해, 그 팀은 총 19시간에 이르는, 위성의 표면을 횡단하기 전과 횡단하는 동안의 행성의 움직임을 관찰하기 위해 Hubble 망원경을 사용했다. 확실히, Kepler-1625b가 지나가고 약 3.5시간 후에, Hubble은 두 번째 위성 밝기에서 훨씬 더 적은 감소를 발견했는데, Kipping은 "위성이 행성을 뒤쫓는 것이 개가 줄에 매인 채 주인을 따라가는 것"과 동일하다고 말했다.

그들의 외계 위성에 대한 가설은 그 행성이 예측보다 1.25 시간 더 빨리 횡단을 시작했을 때 더욱 확실해졌다. 이것은 궤도를 따라 도는 위성이 행성을 끌어당길 때에만 발생하고, 달의 경우와 마찬가지로 행성이 흔들리게 만든다. "지구와 달이 태양을 횡단하는 것을 보는 외계문명은 지구가 통과하는 시기에서의 비슷한 변칙을 알아차릴 것이다"라고 Kipping은 설명했다.

- astronomer 천문학자
- satellite 인공위성
- span 기간; (기간에) 걸치다, 기간
- potential 잠재적인
- sift through 면밀히 조사하다
- deviation 일탈, 편차
- suspicion (막연한) 느낌, 의심, 의혹
- transit 횡단; 횡단하다
- trail 뒤쫓다
- extraterrestrial 외계의
- revolve 회전하다
- orbit 궤도; 궤도를 돌다
- candidate 후보
- celestial body 천체
- promise 가망이 있다
- wobble 흔들리다; 흔들림
- telescope 망원경
- be consistent with ~와 일치하다
- hypothesis 가설
- anomaly 변칙, 이례

| 정답 | 01. (b) | 02. (c) | 03. (a) | 04. (d) | 05. (d) | 06. (c) | 07. (a) |

01

영어문제

For the last couple of decades, what were astronomers unable to do?

(a) The astronomers were not able to identify thousands of planets outside our solar system.
(b) They could not spot a moon rotating around the distant worlds.
(c) The astronomers were unable to find any gaseous exoplanet revolving around the distant worlds.
(d) They had no ability to take the first confirmed picture of a certain planet.

문제 한글 해석

지난 수 십 년 동안 천문학자들은 무엇을 할 수 없었는가?

(a) 천문학자들은 우리 태양계 밖의 수천 개의 행성의 신원을 확인할 수 없었다.
(b) 그들은 외계 주변을 따라 회전하는 하나의 위성도 발견할 수가 없었다.
(c) 천문학자들은 외계 주변을 맴도는 그 어떠한 기체로 이루어진 외계행성도 찾을 수가 없었다.
(d) 그들은 특정 행성의 최초로 공인된 사진을 찍을 수 있는 능력을 가지지 못했다.

문제해설

첫 번째 문단을 통해, 지난 수 십 년 동안, 천문학자들은 우리 태양계 밖에 있는 수천 개의 행성을 발견해왔지만, 외계를 따라 회전하고 있는 하나의 위성도 확인할 수가 없었다는 사실을 알 수 있다.

> Over the last couple of decades, astronomers have identified thousands of planets outside our solar system. However, they have been unable to find confirmation of a moon revolving around any of the distant worlds, mainly because the generally smaller satellites are harder to spot. Now, some researchers from Columbia University believe they have found evidence of an alien moon orbiting a gaseous exoplanet which, lies almost 8,000 light years away.

02 영어문제

Why were the distant worlds regarded as the best candidates for potential exomoons?

(a) The reason was that the distant worlds orbited a gaseous exoplanet.
(b) It was because they were identified by astronomers.
(c) Because of their wide orbits which span more than 30 days
(d) Now that they couldn't find any other possible candidates except the distant worlds

문제 한글 해석

그 외계가 외계 위성들이 존재할 가능성이 있는 가장 좋은 후보로 여겨진 이유는 무엇인가?

(a) 그 이유는 그 외계가 기체로 된 한 외계행성을 돌기 때문이었다.
(b) 왜냐하면 그들이 천문학자들에 의해 확인되었기 때문이었다.
(c) 주기가 30일 이상을 넘는 넓은 궤도 때문에
(d) 천문학자들이 외계를 제외한 다른 가능한 후보를 찾을 수가 없었기 때문에

문제해설

두 번째 문단을 통해, 그 외계는 주기가 30일이 넘는 비교적 넓은 궤도 때문에 외계 위성이 잠재적으로 존재한다고 여겨지는 사실을 알 수 있다.

> For their study, astronomers Alex Teachey and David Kipping, who have been searching for alien moons for nearly a decade, focused on the 284 exoplanets discovered by the planet-hunting Kepler spacecraft. The distant worlds were considered the best candidates for potential exomoons due to their relatively wide orbits that span more than 30 days.

03 영어문제

How different are two dips in light which the scientists were searching for?

(a) They were different because each of two dips was made by different methods.
(b) They had no difference because both were made by a celestial body.
(c) They were different only in terms of size.
(d) One generated the exoplanet while the other made another planet.

문제 한글 해석

과학자들이 찾고 있었던 빛이 휘어지는 두 가지 경우는 서로 어떻게 다른가?

(a) 두 가지 빛의 휘어짐은 각각 다른 방법으로 만들어졌기 때문에 달랐다.
(b) 두 가지 다 모두 천체에 의해 만들어졌기 때문에 차이점이 없었다.
(c) 그들은 오직 크기 면에서 달랐다.
(d) 하나는 외계행성을 생성하고, 다른 하나는 다른 행성을 생성했다.

문제해설

세 번째 문단을 통해, 과학자들은 빛이 휘어지는 두 가지 경우를 찾고 있었는데, 첫 번째 것은 외계행성이 그것의 위성 앞을 지나갈 때 만들어졌고, 두 번째 것은 또 다른, 아마도 더 작은, 천체에 의해 만들어졌다는 사실을 알 수 있다. 즉, 각각의 다른 방법으로 만들어졌기 때문에 다르다는 설명의 (a)가 옳은 보기이다.

> Specifically, the scientists were searching for two dips in light – one caused by the exoplanet as it passed in front of its star and the second by another, most likely smaller, celestial body. After sifting through the data collected by Kepler, the researchers were able to identify one exoplanet, Kepler-1625b, that looked promising. "We saw little deviations and wobbles in the light curve that caught our attention," Kipping said.

04 영어문제 | 문제 한글 해석

Through using the Hubble telescope, what did the team find out?

(a) The telescope could not solve the team's suspicions about the Kepler-1625b.
(b) They monitored how to transit the planet across the face of its star.
(c) The team figured out the fact that the Kepler-1625b did not make any difference in the star's brightness.
(d) They could confirm that there was a much smaller decrease in the star's brightness, after the Kepler-1625b had passed.

Hubble 망원경의 사용을 통해, 그 팀은 어떤 것을 발견해냈는가?

(a) 그 망원경은 Kepler-1625b에 대한 그 팀의 의구심을 해결할 수 없었다.
(b) 그들은 어떻게 행성이 그 위성의 표면을 횡단할 수 있는지를 관찰했다.
(c) 그 팀은 Kepler-1625b가 위성의 밝기에 어떠한 차이도 만들지 않는다는 사실을 알아냈다.
(d) 그들은 Kepler-1625b가 지나간 후, 그 위성의 밝기에서 훨씬 더 적은 감소가 있다는 것을 확인할 수 있었다.

문제해설

네 번째 문단을 통해, 그 팀은 Hubble 망원경을 사용함으로써, Kepler-1625b가 지나가고 약 3.5시간 후에, Hubble은 위성의 밝기가 훨씬 더 적게 감소했다는 사실을 알아냈다는 내용을 확인할 수 있다.

To confirm their suspicions, the team used the Hubble telescope to monitor the planet before and during its 19-hour-long transit across the face of its star. Sure enough, about 3.5 hours after the Kepler-1625b had passed, Hubble detected a second, much smaller decrease in the star's brightness, which Kipping said was consistent with "a moon trailing the planet like a dog following its owner on a leash."

05 영어문제 | 문제 한글 해석

According to the last paragraph, when did the planet's transit 1.25 hours earlier than predicted happen?

(a) It happened in a case where it caused the moon to wobble.
(b) At the time when the exomoon hypothesis was further researched
(c) It happened when the Earth's transit was discovered.
(d) It only happened when an orbiting moon pulled at the planet.

마지막 문단에 따르면, 예측보다 1.25 시간 더 이른 행성의 횡단은 언제 발생했는가?

(a) 그것이 달을 흔들리게 하는 경우에 발생했다.
(b) 외계 위성 가설에 대한 연구가 더 진척되었을 때에
(c) 그것은 지구가 횡단하는 것이 발견될 때 발생했다.
(d) 그것은 궤도를 따라 도는 위성이 행성을 끌어당겼을 때에만 발생했다.

문제해설

마지막 문단을 통해, 그들의 외계 위성에 대한 가설은 그 행성이 예측보다 1.25시간 더 빠르게 통과하기 시작했을 때 더욱 확실해지는데, 이것은 궤도를 따라 도는 위성이 행성을 끌어당길 때에만 발생한다는 사실을 알 수 있다.

Their exomoon hypothesis was further confirmed when the planet began its transit 1.25 hours earlier than predicted. This happens only when an orbiting moon pulls at the planet and causes it to wobble, as is the case with our own moon. "An extraterrestrial civilization watching the Earth and Moon transit the Sun would note similar anomalies in the timing of Earth's transit," Kipping explained.

06 영어문제 | 문제 한글 해석

In the context of the passage, the word "identify" means

(a) convince
(b) attempt
(c) discover
(d) observe

이 글의 문맥상 "identify"는 무엇을 의미하는가?

(a) 설득시키다
(b) 시도하다
(c) 발견하다
(d) 관찰하다

문제해설

이 글의 문맥상 "identify"는 '확인하다, 발견하다'를 의미한다. 따라서 가장 가까운 의미의 (c) discover '발견하다'가 정답이 된다.

07 영어문제

In the context of the passage, the word "confirm" means
(a) prove
(b) accept
(c) approve
(d) ensure

문제 한글 해석

이 글의 문맥상 "confirm"은 무엇을 의미하는가?
(a) 증명하다
(b) 받아들이다
(c) 승인하다
(d) 보장하다

문제해설

이 글에서 "confirm"은 '확인하다, 확정하다'의 의미로, 문맥상에서 '의혹을 증명, 확인하기 위하여'로 나오므로 (a) prove '증명하다, 확인하다'와 가장 가까운 뜻을 가졌다.

PART 3. 독해 만렙 실전모의고사

Part 3. Read the following encyclopedia article and answer the questions. The underlined words in the article are for vocabulary questions.

Friday the 13th

Friday the 13th is considered a day in which bad things occur. It is a superstition.

A superstition is a belief of something ominous without actual reason. The origin of this superstition is unclear. Both Friday and the number 13 have been considered unlucky for hundreds of years. Bad luck associated with the number 13 may have biblical roots. Some believe Eve bit the apple from the Tree of Knowledge on the 13th day. Others point to the idea that there were 13 people present for Jesus's Last Supper, the day before Good Friday. The number 13 was considered so unlucky that many hotels and buildings were built without a 13th floor! It wasn't until the 20th century, however, that Friday and "13" were paired together in bad luck. In 1907, author Thomas Lawson wrote Friday, the Thirteenth. The book was about a stock broker who purposely caused the stock market to crash on that day.

The Friday the 13th superstition, however, gained serious traction with the Friday the 13th horror film series. Originally released in 1980, the story centers around the "ghost" of Jason Voorhees. In the movie, Jason, with his iconic hockey mask, hunts the hapless characters who come to vacation at Crystal Lake – the lake he drowned in as a child. Twelve movies later, the Friday the 13th series remains one of the most successful horror film franchises in history.

Is Friday the 13th actually unlucky compared to other days? Not really. There is no actual evidence to suggest that events that have occurred on Friday the 13th throughout history are worse than events that have occurred on other days. Some studies have shown that Friday the 13th is actually safer than other days, because people are more anxious and attentive. People may actually find Friday the 13th to be lucky. It is thought that air travel is cheaper and booking a wedding is much cheaper on Friday the 13th than other days. It is clear, however, that Friday the 13th will be around for a long time. Over the next 4,800 months, the 13th will occur on Friday more than any other day!

01

Which of the following is NOT true about the possible origin of Friday the 13th?

(a) Such misfortune may be related to biblical roots.
(b) Not a few accommodations were made without a 13th floor.
(c) There were 13 presents for Jesus's Last Supper, the day before Good Friday.
(d) On the 13th day, Eve ate the apple from the Tree of Knowledge.

02

How did author Thomas Lawson handle Friday the 13th in his book?

(a) The author described Friday the 13th as bad luck through a story about one stockbroker.
(b) Regardless of the superstition about Friday the 13th, he did not indicate it as unfortunate.
(c) In his book, one stockbroker was featured as a person who tried to solve the stock market problem.
(d) His book was mainly focused on how the superstition of Friday the 13th came out.

03

What can be inferred about Friday the 13th horror film series?

(a) Such movies overturned the superstition that the Friday the 13th meant bad luck.
(b) In one of the Friday the 13th horror film series, Jason hunted the hapless characters every Friday.
(c) Thirteen movies later, these series became the highest-grossing movie franchises at that time.
(d) These movies further strengthened the superstition of Friday the 13th.

04

According to the last paragraph, how is Friday the 13th related to bad luck?

(a) Actual evidence shows that Friday the 13th is actually unlucky.
(b) Friday of the 13th is regarded safer than other days by some research.
(c) Historical evidence supports the idea that Friday the 13th means bad luck.
(d) Some studies consider Friday the 13th safer on the grounds that people are more comfortable every Friday.

05

What can be inferred about the basic idea of this passage?

(a) It is certain that Friday the 13th is actually unlucky.
(b) The superstition of the Friday the 13th would disappear because it is an old notion.
(c) Even though there is the superstition of Friday the 13th and it would last, there is no actual evidence about it.
(d) People may require more actual evidence about the superstition of Friday the 13th.

06

In the context of the passage, the word "hapless" means

(a) felicitous
(b) flourishing
(c) prosperous
(d) unfortunate

07

In the context of the passage, the word "attentive" means

(a) cautious
(b) fascinated
(c) conscientious
(d) absorbed

13일의 금요일

13일의 금요일은 나쁜 일이 일어나는 날이라고 여겨진다. 이것은 미신이다.

미신은 실제 이유 없이 무언가가 불길하다고 믿는 것을 가리킨다. 이 미신의 기원은 불분명하다. 금요일과 숫자 13은 수백 년 동안 불행한 것으로 여겨져 왔다. 숫자 13과 관련된 불운은 성경적인 기원을 가지고 있을 수도 있다. 일부 사람들은 Eve가 Tree of Knowledge(선악과나무)의 열매를 13일에 먹었다고 믿는다. 다른 사람들은 Jesus의 Last Supper(최후의 만찬)에 13명이 참석했는데 그날이 Good Friday(성 금요일) 전날이라고 주장한다. 숫자 13은 매우 불길한 숫자로 여겨져서, 많은 호텔과 건물들이 13층 없이 지어졌다! 그러나 금요일과 "13"이 불운의 의미로 조합이 된 것은 20세기에 이르러서였다. 1907년에, 작가 Thomas Lawson은 "Friday, the Thirteenth"를 썼다. 그 책은 그 날 (13일의 금요일) 주식 시장을 고의로 붕괴시킨 한 증권 중개사에 대한 내용이다.

그러나 13일의 금요일 미신은 13일의 금요일 공포 영화 시리즈로 인해 상당한 이목을 끌었다. 처음 1980년에 출시되었는데, 줄거리는 Jason Voorhees의 "유령"에 중점을 둔다. 그 영화에서 Jason은 그의 상징인 하키 복면을 쓰고 Crystal 호수에 휴가를 즐기러 온 불운한 등장인물들을 사냥하는데 그 호수는 그가 어릴 때 익사한 곳이다. 12편의 작품을 낸 13일의 금요일 시리즈는 역사상 가장 성공적인 공포 영화 시리즈로 남았다.

13일의 금요일은 정말로 다른 날들에 비해 운이 없을까? 실제로 그렇지는 않다. 역사 전체에 걸쳐 13일의 금요일에 발생한 사건들이 다른 날들에 발생한 사건들보다 더 안 좋다는 점을 제시하는 실제 증거는 없다. 어떤 연구는 13일의 금요일이 사실은 다른 날들보다 더 안전하다는 것을 보여주는데, 그 이유는 사람들이 더 불안해하고 신경을 쓰기 때문이다. 사실 사람들은 13일의 금요일에 운이 좋다고 생각하게 될 수도 있다. 다른 날보다 13일의 금요일이 항공권이 더 저렴하고, 결혼식 예약도 훨씬 저렴하다고 생각되어지기 때문이다. 하지만, 분명한 것은 13일의 금요일(에 대한 미신)은 오랜 시간 지속될 것이다. 앞으로 4800달 동안, 13일은 다른 모든 요일보다 금요일이 더 많을 것이다!

- superstition 미신
- biblical 성경의
- pair 짝을 짓다
- purposely 고의로
- traction 견인력
- center around ~에 중점을 두다
- hapless 불행한
- franchise 체인점, 프랜차이즈
- attentive 신경을 쓰는
- ominous 불길한
- present 출석하다, 참석하다
- stock broker 증권 중개사
- crash 폭락, 붕괴; 폭락시키다, 붕괴시키다
- originally 원래, 본래
- iconic ~의 상징이 되는
- drown 익사하다
- anxious 불안해하는

정답
01. (c) 02. (a) 03. (d) 04. (b) 05. (c) 06. (d) 07. (a)

01 영어문제

Which of the following is NOT true about the possible origin of Friday the 13th?

(a) Such misfortune may be related to biblical roots.
(b) Not a few accommodations were made without a 13th floor.
(c) There were 13 presents for Jesus's Last Supper, the day before Good Friday.
(d) On the 13th day, Eve ate the apple from the Tree of Knowledge.

문제 한글 해석

13일의 금요일의 기원으로 가능한 것에 대한 설명으로 바르지 않은 것은?

(a) 그러한 불행은 성경적인 기원과 관련이 있을 수도 있다.
(b) 꽤 많은 숙박업소들이 13층 없이 만들어졌다.
(c) Good Friday(성 금요일) 전날에 Jesus의 Last Supper(최후의 만찬)에서 13개의 선물들이 있었다.
(d) 13일에, Eve가 Tree of Knowledge(선악과 나무)에서 열매를 먹었다.

문제해설

아래 문단을 통해, Jesus의 Last Supper(최후의 만찬)에 13개의 선물들이 아니라, 13명의 사람들이 참석했으며, 그 날이 Good Friday(성 금요일) 전날이라는 사실을 알 수 있다.

A superstition is a belief of something ominous without actual reason. The origin of this superstition is unclear. Both Friday and the number 13 have been considered unlucky for hundreds of years. (a) Bad luck associated with the number 13 may have biblical roots. (d) Some believe Eve bit the apple from the Tree of Knowledge on the 13th day. (c) Others point to the idea that there were 13 people present for Jesus's Last Supper, the day before Good Friday. (b) The number 13 was considered so unlucky that many hotels and buildings were built without a 13th floor! It wasn't until the 20th century, however, that Friday and "13" were paired together in bad luck. In 1907, author Thomas Lawson wrote Friday, the Thirteenth. The book was about a stock broker who purposely caused the stock market to crash on that day.

02 영어문제

How did author Thomas Lawson handle Friday the 13th in his book?

(a) The author described Friday the 13th as bad luck through a story about one stockbroker.
(b) Regardless of the superstition about Friday the 13th, he did not indicate it as unfortunate.
(c) In his book, one stockbroker was featured as a person who tried to solve the stock market problem.
(d) His book was mainly focused on how the superstition of Friday the 13th came out.

문제 한글 해석

저자 Thomas Lawson은 그의 책에서 13일의 금요일을 어떻게 다루었는가?

(a) 그 저자는 한 증권 중개사에 대한 이야기를 통해 13일의 금요일을 불운으로 묘사했다.
(b) 13일의 금요일에 대한 미신과 상관없이, 그는 그것을 불운으로 묘사하지 않았다.
(c) 그의 책에서, 한 증권 중개사는 주식 시장 문제를 해결하려고 노력한 사람으로 묘사되었다.
(d) 그의 책은 주로 13일의 금요일에 대한 미신이 어떻게 생겨났는지에 대해 집중하고 있다.

문제해설

1907년에, 작가 Thomas Lawson은 "Friday, the Thirteenth"를 썼다. 그 책은 그 날(13일의 금요일)에 주식 시장을 고의로 붕괴시킨 한 증권 중개사에 대한 내용이다. 따라서 작가 Thomas Lawson은 13일의 금요일을, 불행한 일이 일어난 날로 묘사하고 있다는 내용의 (a)가 옳은 보기이다.

A superstition is a belief of something ominous without actual reason. The origin of this superstition is unclear. Both Friday and the number 13 have been considered unlucky for hundreds of years. Bad luck associated with the number 13 may have biblical roots. Some believe Eve bit the apple from the Tree of Knowledge on the 13th day. Others point to the idea that there were 13 people present for Jesus's Last Supper, the day before Good Friday. The number 13 was considered so unlucky that many hotels and buildings were built without a 13th floor! It wasn't until the 20th century, however, that Friday and "13" were paired together in bad luck. In 1907, author Thomas Lawson wrote Friday, the Thirteenth. The book was about a stockbroker who purposely caused the stock market to crash on that day.

03 영어문제

What can be inferred about Friday the 13th horror film series?

(a) Such movies overturned the superstition that the Friday the 13th meant bad luck.
(b) In one of the Friday the 13th horror film series, Jason hunted the hapless characters every Friday.
(c) Thirteen movies later, these series became the highest-grossing movie franchises at that time.
(d) These movies further strengthened the superstition of Friday the 13th.

문제 한글 해석

13일의 금요일 공포 영화 시리즈에 대해 유추할 수 있는 것은?

(a) 그러한 영화는 13일의 금요일이 불행을 의미했다는 미신을 뒤집었다.
(b) 13일의 금요일 공포 영화 시리즈 중 하나에서는, Jason이 매주 금요일마다 불운한 등장인물들을 사냥했다.
(c) 13편의 작품이 나오고, 이 시리즈는 그 당시 가장 돈을 많이 번 영화 시리즈가 되었다.
(d) 이러한 영화는 13일의 금요일 미신을 더욱 강화시켰다.

문제해설

13일의 금요일 미신은 13일의 금요일 공포 영화 시리즈로 인해 상당한 이목을 끌었다는 내용을 통해 그 미신이 더욱 견고해졌다는 사실을 알 수 있다.

The Friday the 13th superstition, however, gained serious traction with the Friday the 13th horror film series. Originally released in 1980, the story centers around the "ghost" of Jason Voorhees. In the movie, Jason, with his iconic hockey mask, hunts the hapless characters who come to vacation at Crystal Lake – the lake he drowned in as a child. Twelve movies later, the Friday the 13th series remains one of the most successful horror film franchises in history.

04 영어문제

According to the last paragraph, how is Friday the 13th related to bad luck?

(a) Actual evidence shows that Friday the 13th is actually unlucky.
(b) Friday of the 13th is regarded safer than other days by some research.
(c) Historical evidence supports the idea that Friday the 13th means bad luck.
(d) Some studies consider Friday the 13th safer on the grounds that people are more comfortable every Friday.

문제 한글 해석

마지막 문단에 따르면, 13일의 금요일은 불운과 어떻게 관련이 있는가?

(a) 실제 증거가 13일의 금요일이 실제로 불행하다는 것을 보여준다.
(b) 13일의 금요일은 일부 연구에 따르면 다른 날보다 더 안전한 것으로 여겨진다.
(c) 역사적인 증거가 13일의 금요일이 불운을 의미한다는 생각을 지지한다.
(d) 사람들이 매주 금요일에 편안함을 느끼는 것을 근거로, 일부 연구는 13일의 금요일을 더 안전하게 여긴다.

문제해설

마지막 문단에 따르면, 13일의 금요일은 정말로 다른 날들에 비해 운이 없다는 증거가 없으며, 어떤 연구는 13일의 금요일이 사실은 다른 날들보다 더 안전하다는 것을 보여준다는 내용을 알 수 있으므로 정답은 (b)이다. 단, 그렇게 안전하게 여겨지는 이유는 사람들이 더 불안해하고 신경을 쓰기 때문이므로, 편안함을 느끼기 위함이라고 설명한 (d)는 틀린 보기이다.

Is Friday the 13th actually unlucky compared to other days? Not really. There is no actual evidence to suggest that events that have occurred on Friday the 13th throughout history are worse than events that have occurred on other days. Some studies have shown that Friday the 13th is actually safer than other days, because people are more anxious and attentive. People may actually find Friday the 13th to be lucky. It is thought that air travel is cheaper and booking a wedding is much cheaper on Friday the 13th than other days. It is clear, however, that Friday the 13th will be around for a long time. Over the next 4,800 months, the 13th will occur on Friday more than any other day!

05 영어문제 | 문제 한글 해석

What can be inferred about the basic idea of this passage?

(a) It is certain that Friday the 13th is actually unlucky.
(b) The superstition of the Friday the 13th would disappear because it is an old notion.
(c) Even though there is the superstition of Friday the 13th and it would last, there is no actual evidence about it.
(d) People may require more actual evidence about the superstition of Friday the 13th.

이 글의 기본적인 생각은 어떻게 추론할 수 있는가?

(a) 13일의 금요일은 실제로 불행한 것이 확실하다.
(b) 13일의 금요일 미신은 오래된 개념이기 때문에, 그 미신은 사라질 것이다.
(c) 13일의 금요일의 미신이 있고, 그것이 지속될 것이지만, 그것에 대한 실제의 증거는 없다.
(d) 사람들은 13일의 금요일 미신에 대해 더 많은 실제적 증거를 요구할 수도 있다.

문제해설

마지막 문단을 통해, 13일의 금요일이 오랜 시간 지속될 것이지만, 역사 전체에 걸쳐 13일의 금요일에 발생한 사건들이 다른 날들에 발생한 사건들보다 더 안 좋다는 점을 제시하는 증거는 없다는 사실을 알 수 있다.

Is Friday the 13th actually unlucky compared to other days? Not really. There is no actual evidence to suggest that events that have occurred on Friday the 13th throughout history are worse than events that have occurred on other days. Some studies have shown that Friday the 13th is actually safer than other days, because people are more anxious and attentive. People may actually find Friday the 13th to be lucky. It is thought that air travel is cheaper and booking a wedding is much cheaper on Friday the 13th than other days. It is clear, however, that Friday the 13th will be around for a long time. Over the next 4,800 months, the 13th will occur on Friday more than any other day!

06 영어문제

In the context of the passage, the word "hapless" means

(a) felicitous
(b) flourishing
(c) prosperous
(d) unfortunate

문제 한글 해석

이 글의 문맥상 "hapless"는 무엇을 의미하는가?
(a) 경사스러운
(b) 번영하는
(c) 번영하는
(d) 불행한

문제해설

이 글의 문맥상 "hapless"는 '불행한'을 의미한다. 따라서 가장 가까운 의미의 (d) unfortunate '불운한, 불행한'이 정답이 된다. 나머지 단어들은 hapless의 반의어들이다.

07 영어문제

In the context of the passage, the word "attentive" means

(a) cautious
(b) fascinated
(c) conscientious
(d) absorbed

문제 한글 해석

이 글의 문맥상 "attentive"는 무엇을 의미하는가?
(a) 조심스러운
(b) 매료된
(c) 양심적인
(d) 열중한

문제해설

이 글에서 "attentive"는 '조심스러운'의 의미로, (a) cautious '조심스러운, 신중한'과 가장 가까운 뜻을 가졌다. 그 외에 단어들은 유의어이기는 하나 문맥상 쓰인 의미와는 서로 다른 의미를 지닌 단어들이다.

MEMO

PART 4. 독해 만렙 실전모의고사

Part 4. Read the following business letter and answer the questions.
The underlined words in the article are for vocabulary questions.

Employee Absence Warning Letter

Dear Ms. Brown:

Re: Written Warning

On September 30th, you failed to report for your scheduled shift at 9 a.m. You did not <u>notify</u> your manager of your absence in advance. Furthermore, upon your return to work on October 1st, you failed to provide a justifiable excuse for your absence or your failure to notify your manager in advance. This conduct is unacceptable and will not be tolerated by AceTop Inc.

A review of your record <u>indicates</u> that you have failed to report to work without notice or justifiable excuse on several occasions in the past. In the past 12 months alone, you were absent in this manner on two other occasions. These absences were on July 7th and August 15th. On both of those occasions, you were given verbal warnings and directed to notify your manager in advance of every absence.

In light of the foregoing, we have no choice but to issue this written warning. We trust that this discipline will ensure that you correct your behaviour in the future.

However, please note that if you engage in further misconduct of any kind, you may be subject to more severe discipline, up to and including suspensions and dismissal.

AceTop Inc.

Union representative, Halan Edward

01
What is the purpose of this e-mail?

(a) The purpose is to notify Ms. Brown of the company policy related to employee absence.
(b) To ask Ms. Brown to fill out written warning related to absence
(c) Halan Edward wrote this e-mail to refuse an excuse for Ms. Brown's absence.
(d) In order to warn on the grounds that Ms. Brown was absent without notice to her manager in advance

02
According to the first paragraph, when Ms. Brown failed to notify her manager of her absence in advance, what was Ms. Brown supposed to do?

(a) Ms. Brown had to report for her scheduled shift.
(b) She should have given a justifiable excuse for her absence or her failure to notify her manager in advance.
(c) Ms. Brown had an obligation to notify her colleague of her absence in advance.
(d) She had to contact her manager first as soon as she came back.

03
Which of the following is true about her record related to her absence?

(a) She has failed to report to work several times before.
(b) It is her first time to fail to report to work without notice.
(c) She reported her absence with correct notice in July and August.
(d) Ms. Brown had never received any warning with regard to absence verbally or in writing.

04
What does "we have no choice but to issue this written warning" mean?

(a) We had a lot of alternative options, but we chose to issue this written warning.
(b) Finally, we decided not to issue this warning.
(c) We had only one option not to issue this warning.
(d) We could not help issuing this written warning.

05
What if Ms. Brown keeps engaging in misconduct of any kind?

(a) She would be subject to face-to-face warning.
(b) In spite of more severe discipline, she may not be subject to dismissal.
(c) Ms. Brown may be fired on the grounds of stronger discipline.
(d) She will have to submit a letter of apology to her representative.

06
In the context of the passage, the word "notify" means

(a) spread   (b) publish
(c) declare   (d) inform

07
In the context of the passage, the word "indicate" means

(a) convey   (b) designate
(c) symbolize   (d) denote

해석

직원 부재 경고문

Brown씨께:

회신: 서면 경고

9월 30일, 당신은 오전 9시에 예정된 교대 근무에 대한 보고를 하지 않았습니다. 당신은 미리 당신의 상사에게 결근을 알리지 않았습니다. 게다가, 10월 1일에 회사에 복귀했을 때, 당신은 결근이나 상사에게 (결근에 대해) 알리지 않은 것에 대해 타당한 이유를 제시하지 못했습니다. 이 행동은 용납할 수 없고 AceTop 사에서 허용될 수 없습니다.

기록을 검토해보면 당신이 과거에 여러 번 통지나 타당한 사유 없이 출근하지 않았다는 것을 알 수 있습니다. 지난 12개월만 해도, 당신은 이러한 방식으로 두 번의 다른 경우로 결근했습니다. 이러한 결근은 7월 7일과 8월 15일에 있었습니다. 그 두 가지 경우 모두, 당신은 구두 경고를 받았고 모든 결근에 대해 당신의 상사에게 미리 알리라는 지시를 받았습니다. 앞서 말한 내용을 고려하여, 우리는 이 서면 경고장을 발부할 수밖에 없습니다. 우리는 이 징계로 인해 당신이 미래에 당신의 행동을 반드시 고칠 것이라 믿습니다.

하지만, 만약 당신이 미래에 어떠한 종류든 잘못된 행동을 지속한다면, 정직이나 해고를 포함한 더 엄격한 징계의 대상이 될 수도 있다는 것을 알아두시기 바랍니다.

AceTop 사

노조 대표 Halan Edward

- **shift** 교대 근무
- **absence** 부재, 결근
- **conduct** 행동
- **indicate** 나타내다
- **direct** 지시하다
- **foregoing** 앞서 말한 내용
- **discipline** 규율, 훈육
- **engage** 종사하다, (일에) 관계하다
- **suspension** 정학, 정직
- **notify** 알리다, 통지하다
- **justifiable** 타당한
- **tolerate** 용인하다
- **manner** (일하는) 방식
- **in light of** ~에 비추어, ~을 고려하여
- **issue** 발부하다
- **ensure** 반드시 ~하게 하다
- **be subject to** ~의 대상이다
- **dismissal** 해고

정답 01. (d)   02. (b)   03. (a)   04. (d)   05. (c)   06. (d)   07. (a)

01 영어문제 | 문제 한글 해석

What is the purpose of this e-mail?

(a) The purpose is to notify Ms. Brown of the company policy related to employee absence.
(b) To ask Ms. Brown to fill out written warning related to absence
(c) Halan Edward wrote this e-mail to refuse an excuse for Ms. Brown's absence.
(d) In order to warn on the grounds that Ms. Brown was absent without notice to her manager in advance

이 이메일의 목적은 무엇인가?

(a) 그 목적은 Brown 씨에게 결근과 관련한 회사 정책을 알려주기 위함이다.
(b) Brown 씨에게 결근과 관련한 서면 경고를 작성하는 것을 요청하기 위하여
(c) Halan Edward는 Brown 씨의 결근에 대한 해명을 거절하기 위하여 이 이메일을 썼다.
(d) Brown 씨는 사전에 그녀의 상사에게 통지하지 않고 결근한 것을 근거로 경고하기 위하여

문제해설

첫 문단을 통해, Brown 씨가 그녀의 상사에게 미리 결근을 알리지 않았고, 이에 대해 타당한 이유를 제시하지 않았다고 설명하고 있다. 또한 이 행동은 용납할 수 없고 AceTop 사에서 허용될 수 없다고 설명하고 있다. 따라서 Brown 씨의 무단결근과 관련하여 경고를 하고 있다는 내용의 (d)가 옳은 보기이다.

> On September 30th, you failed to report for your scheduled shift at 9 a.m. You did not notify your manager of your absence in advance. Furthermore, upon your return to work on October 1st, you failed to provide a justifiable excuse for your absence or your failure to notify your manager in advance. This conduct is unacceptable and will not be tolerated by AceTop Inc.

02 영어문제

According to the first paragraph, when Ms. Brown failed to notify her manager of her absence in advance, what was Ms. Brown supposed to do?

(a) Ms. Brown had to report for her scheduled shift.
(b) She should have given a justifiable excuse for her absence or her failure to notify her manager in advance.
(c) Ms. Brown had an obligation to notify her colleague of her absence in advance.
(d) She had to contact her manager first as soon as she came back.

문제 한글 해석

첫 번째 문단에 따르면, Brown 씨가 그녀의 상사에게 결근에 대해 미리 알리지 못했을 때, Ms. Brown은 무엇을 했어야 했는가?

(a) Brown 씨는 그녀의 예정된 교대 근무를 보고해야만 했다.
(b) 그녀는 그녀의 결근이나 그녀의 상사에게 미리 알리지 못한 것에 대해 타당한 이유를 제시했어야 했다.
(c) Brown 씨는 그녀의 동료에게 미리 그녀의 결근에 대해 알려야할 의무가 있었다.
(d) 그녀는 돌아오자마자 상사에게 가장 먼저 연락해야 했다.

문제해설

첫 번째 문단을 통해, Brown 씨가 그녀의 상사에게 미리 결근을 알리지 않았고, 나아가 그녀가 일하기 위해 돌아왔을 때, 미리 상사에게 결근에 대해 알리지 않은 것에 대해 타당한 이유를 제시하지 못했다고 설명하고 있다. 즉, 미리 Brown는 그녀의 결근에 대해 상사에게 알리지 못한 경우, 그녀는 그녀의 결근에 대해 또는 그녀의 매니저에게 미리 통지하지 못한 것에 대해 타당한 이유를 제공했어야 했다는 것을 알 수 있다.

> On September 30th, you failed to report for your scheduled shift at 9 a.m. You did not notify your manager of your absence in advance. Furthermore, upon your return to work on October 1st, you failed to provide a justifiable excuse for your absence or your failure to notify your manager in advance. This conduct is unacceptable and will not be tolerated by AceTop Inc.

03 영어문제 | 문제 한글 해석

Which of the following is true about her record related to her absence?

(a) She has failed to report to work several times before.
(b) It is her first time to fail to report to work without notice.
(c) She reported her absence with correct notice in July and August.
(d) Ms. Brown had never received any warning with regard to absence verbally or in writing.

그녀의 결근과 관련된 기록에 대해 사실인 것은?

(a) 그녀는 이전에도 출근을 여러 번 하지 않았다.
(b) 그녀가 통지 없이 일에 대한 보고를 하지 않은 것은 이번이 처음이다.
(c) 그녀는 7월과 8월에는 올바른 통지로 그녀의 결근에 대해 보고했다.
(d) Brown 씨는 그녀의 결근과 관련하여 구두나 서면으로 어떠한 경고를 받은 적이 없다.

문제해설

Ms. Brown의 기록에 대한 보고서에 따르면, 그녀가 과거에 여러 번 통지나 타당한 사유 없이 출근하지 않았다는 것을 나타낸다는 사실을 알 수 있다.

A review of your record indicates that you have failed to report to work without notice or justifiable excuse on several occasions in the past. In the past 12 months alone, you were absent in this manner on two other occasions. These absences were on July 7th and August 15th. On both of those occasions, you were given verbal warnings and directed to notify your manager in advance of every absence.

04 영어문제 | 문제 한글 해석

What does "we have no choice but to issue this written warning" mean?

(a) We had a lot of alternative options, but we chose to issue this written warning.
(b) Finally, we decided not to issue this warning.
(c) We had only one option not to issue this warning.
(d) We could not help issuing this written warning.

"우리는 서면 경고장을 발부할 수밖에 없습니다"가 의미하는 것은?

(a) 우리는 많은 다른 선택지가 있었지만, 서면 경고장을 발부하기로 선택했다.
(b) 결국, 우리는 서면 경고장을 발부하지 않기로 결정했다.
(c) 우리는 서면 경고장을 발부하지 않는 유일한 선택권을 가지고 있었다.
(d) 우리는 서면 경고장을 발부할 수밖에 없었다.

문제해설

아래 문장은 "앞서 말한 내용을 고려하여, 우리는 이 서면 경고장을 발부할 수밖에 없습니다"는 내용이므로, (d)가 옳은 내용의 보기이다.

In light of the foregoing, we have no choice but to issue this written warning. We trust that this discipline will ensure that you correct your behaviour in the future.

05 영어문제 | 문제 한글 해석

What if Ms. Brown keeps engaging in misconduct of any kind?

(a) She would be subject to face-to-face warning.
(b) In spite of more severe discipline, she may not be subject to dismissal.
(c) Ms. Brown may be fired on the grounds of stronger discipline.
(d) She will have to submit a letter of apology to her representative.

만약 Brown 씨가 어떠한 잘못된 행위를 지속한다면 어떻게 되는가?

(a) 그녀는 대면 경고의 대상이 될 것이다.
(b) 더 강력한 징계에도 불구하고, 그녀는 해고의 대상은 되지 않을 수 있다.
(c) Brown 씨는 더 강력한 징계로 해고될 수 있다.
(d) 그녀의 대표에게 사과문을 제출해야 할 것이다.

문제해설

마지막 문단을 통해, 하지만, 만약 Brown 씨가 미래에 어떠한 종류든 잘못된 행동을 지속한다면, 정직이나 해고를 포함한 더 엄벌을 받을 수도 있다는 사실을 알 수 있다.

> However, please note that if you engage in further misconduct of any kind, you may be subject to more severe discipline, up to and including suspensions and dismissal.

06 영어문제 | 문제 한글 해석

In the context of the passage, the word "notify" means

(a) spread
(b) publish
(c) declare
(d) inform

이 글의 문맥상 "notify"는 무엇을 의미하는가?

(a) 퍼트리다
(b) 출판하다
(c) 선언하다
(d) 알리다

문제해설

이 글의 문맥상 "notify"는 '통보하다, 알리다'를 의미한다. 따라서 가장 가까운 의미의 (d) inform '통보하다, 알리다'가 정답이 된다. 나머지 단어들은 notify와 유의어들이긴 하나 문맥상 쓰인 뜻과는 거리가 있는 어휘들이다.

07 영어문제

In the context of the passage, the word "indicate" means

(a) convey
(b) designate
(c) symbolize
(d) denote

문제 한글 해석

이 글의 문맥상 "indicate"는 무엇을 의미하는가?

(a) 나타내다, 암시하다
(b) 지명하다
(c) 상징하다
(d) 표시하다

문제해설

이 글에서 "indicate"는 문맥상에서 '나타내다'의 의미로, (a)convey '나타내다, 의미하다'와 가장 가까운 뜻을 가졌다. 그 외에 단어들은 유의어이기는 하나 문맥상 쓰인 의미와는 서로 다른 의미를 지닌 단어들이다.

필수 단어, 표현, 숙어 암기노트

단어, 표현, 숙어	의미

필수 단어, 표현, 숙어 암기노트

단어, 표현, 숙어	의미